MINDS WIDE SHUT

Minds Wide Shut

HOW THE NEW
FUNDAMENTALISMS DIVIDE US

GARY SAUL MORSON

MORTON SCHAPIRO

With a new preface by the authors

PRINCETON UNIVERSITY PRESS
PRINCETON *&* OXFORD

Published by Princeton University Press
41 William Street, Princeton, New Jersey 08540
99 Banbury Road, Oxford OX2 6JX

press.princeton.edu

All Rights Reserved

First paperback edition, with a new preface by the authors, 2023
Paperback ISBN 978-0-691-21492-4
Cloth ISBN 978-0-691-21491-7
E-book ISBN 978-0-691-24257-6
Library of Congress Control Number 2020032355

British Library Cataloging-in-Publication Data is available

Editorial: Peter Dougherty and Alena Chekanov
Production Editorial: Sara Lerner
Jacket/Cover Design: Karl Spurzem
Production: Erin Suydam
Publicity: James Schneider and Kathryn Stevens

This book has been composed in Arno

To our families, our friends, and our students;
To those who agree and those who disagree;
We hope to keep the conversation going.

For high hopes and noble causes, for faith without fanaticism, for understanding of views not shared. . . .

—*MISHKAN T'FILAH,* ADOPTED FROM
O. EUGENE PICKETT'S "FOR THE EXPANDING
GRANDEUR OF CREATION"

CONTENTS

Acknowledgments   xiii

Preface to the Paperback Edition   xv

Preface: Toward Dialogue   xxiii

1 Fundamentalism Writ Large   1

The End of Days?   1

Fundamentalism Abounds   4

2 Fundamentalism and Its Alternatives:
   From Fanaticism to Dialogue   12

Part 1: The Fundamentalist Style of Thought   12

   Conception and Evolution   12

   Fundamentalist Criterion #1: Certainty   22

   Negative Fundamentalism   35

   Fundamentalist Criterion #2: The Perspicuity
   of Truth   39

   Fundamentalist Criterion #3: Foundational
   Text or Revelation   47

Part 2: Alternatives   51

   Assertion and Dialogue   51

   Alternatives: Just in Case   57

Avoiding Extremisms   64

Alternatives: The Wisdom of the Novel   65

Acquiring Wisdom   67

Alternatives: Dialogue and Truth   70

3   Divided We Stand: The Politics of Hate   75

Joined Together by Hatred of the "Other"   75

Tables Turned   78

Fundamentalism and Democracy in Tension   84

Pseudoscience   90

Criticism and the Experience of Others   100

Criticism and Certainty   103

Novels and Utopias   110

Satire and Systems   116

The Silo   121

United by Hatred or Hope?   124

4   Price and Prejudice: Economics and the Quest for Truth   129

Another Kind of Fundamentalism   129

The Economics of Hate?   140

Learning from Objective Analyses   142

Let Justice Be Done, Though the World Perish: Dealing with Climate Change   145

Not Just Climate Change   156

Prejudice and Price   165

A Way Forward Based on Facts?   176

Back to Adam Smith   177

5 Searching for Eternal Truths: Religion and Its Discontents   181

A Rabbi's Parable   181

The Clock and the Dictionary   182

When Standards Become Mere Prejudice   186

Challenging Stories   189

The Relevance of the Timeless   194

Compassion and Holiness   200

Equivalents   206

How Scripture Reads   212

The Difference That Science Makes   215

How Old Is the World?   219

Propositions and Prayer   226

The Great Dialogue   232

Adjusting the Clock   236

6 Literature: How to Ruin It and Why You Shouldn't   239

Alibis for Reading   239

Literature Lost   247

The Need for Stories   257

World Literature   263

Equivalent Centers of Self   265

7 A Path Forward   273

   How the New Fundamentalisms Are Connected   275

   Return to Dialogue   279

   Chekhov with the Final Word   283

                        Index   291

ACKNOWLEDGMENTS

WELCOME TO our quarantine book.

On March 10, 2020, we cotaught the final session of our winter quarter class on what economics can learn from the humanities. As we celebrated with our usual coffee and tea, we lamented the fact that if we only had a month or so in which we could devote more attention to our manuscript, we could get it done sooner rather than later. After working on the book for almost a year, we needed a final push.

Careful what you wish for. Days later the coronavirus struck in full force.

It has been alleged that, nine months after the great New York City blackout of July 1977, maternity wards were packed. If that baby boomlet really happened, that says something about what most people do when they are forced to stay at home. But we all know what academics do when sheltering in place—we write! So it wouldn't surprise us if there were a book boom right about now.

We received a great deal of advice and support through multiple drafts of this book. We never could have completed it without Rob Asghar's extraordinary assistance. We have benefited from his countless reference suggestions, edits, and other comments, large and small.

We were most out of our comfort zones in writing the chapter on religion. Fortunately, we were encouraged by Rabbi Nate

Crane from Beth Hillel B'nai Emunah in Wilmette, Illinois; Rabbi Steve Lowenstein of Am Shalom in Glencoe, Illinois; and Rabbi Annie Tucker of Temple Israel Center in White Plains, New York. It was Rabbi Tucker's memorable sermon that introduced us to the story of the clock tower, which ended up serving as a unifying theme for chapter 5. Biblical scholar Diana Lipton was also instrumental in helping us with that chapter, as were philosophy professor Sandy Goldberg and professor of religious studies Christine Helmer. Mistakes, of course, are our own.

Many others read drafts of the book and provided helpful comments. These include Bertie Buffett, Stacy Cochran, Paula Peterson, Katie Porter, Alissa Schapiro, and Mimi Schapiro. The three Princeton University Press readers were generous with their suggestions, which improved the book immeasurably. Lastly, what a great pleasure it is to work with editor Peter Dougherty. Without his unwavering support and guidance throughout the entire process, neither this book, nor our previous one, would have ever seen the light of day.

12/19/23

PREFACE TO THE
PAPERBACK EDITION

The bold font used on the front page of the Sunday Review section of the *New York Times* proclaimed: "America Has a Free Speech Problem."[1] The subtitle stated, "A new Times Opinion poll finds that many Americans believe they are losing one of their fundamental rights as citizens of a free country: the right to speak their minds."

Nothing in that article surprises us. Fundamentalism has been flourishing well beyond its theological roots, impeding free speech and creating a serious challenge for democratic societies. It exists on the ideological left, the right, and even the center, and has taken root in contemporary social thought generally, not just in politics. It leads to a radical simplification of complex questions and an unwillingness to learn from experience or opposing views. There is little hope of compromise. It gives rise to dueling monologues of abuse between those who are certain that they can't be wrong, that truth and justice are exclusively on their side, and that their opponents must be either evil or delusional. The rise of the new fundamentalisms has fueled "cancel culture" and stifled the type of informed discussion that underpins democracy.

1. Editorial Board, "America Has a Free Speech Problem," Sunday Review, *New York Times*, March 20, 2022.

The data from that *New York Times* survey are sobering: 84 percent said that it is either a somewhat or very serious problem that some Americans do not exercise their freedom of speech in everyday situations out of fear of retaliation or harsh criticism. In an all-too-rare example of political agreement, that sentiment varies little by political allegiance. An earlier piece in the same paper provides some justification for why we wrote *Minds Wide Shut*. It was titled "Growing Threat to American Democracy: Us vs. Them."[2] The subtitle, "Sectarian camps that don't just disagree—they see one another as the enemy," is a theme throughout this book. Its chapters, which consider diverse fields extending from economics and politics to religion and the humanities, analyze where we are and how we got here. This 2021 *Times* article cites some disturbing statistics: more than half of Republicans and more than 40 percent of Democrats tend to think of the other party not as "political opponents" but as "enemies," while a majority of Americans said that the greatest threat to America was other Americans. One-third believe that violence could be justified to achieve political objectives. One-fifth of Democrats and one-third of Republicans say they would support secession. Secession! Who would have thought that there would be serious support for breaking up the United States?

Not surprisingly, college students are at the forefront of these concerns. In another recent survey, 60 percent said they were reluctant to speak out on politics, religion, race, sexual orientation, or gender.[3] What's left? While Asian and white students

2. Nate Cohn, "Growing Threat to American Democracy: Us vs. Them," *New York Times*, April 22, 2021.

3. S. Zhou, M. Stiksma, and S. C. Zhou, "Understanding the Campus Expression Climate: Fall 2021," Heterodox Academy, 2022, https://heterodoxacademy.org/wp-content/uploads/2021/03/CES-Report-2020.pdf.

were especially hesitant to discuss controversial topics, that was true for all ethnic and racial groups. Overall, 63 percent of students said that campus climate prevents people from saying what they believe. If adults fear being canceled, one can only imagine what it must be like to face the opprobrium of those in your classes and in your dorms.[4]

In chapter 3, "Divided We Stand: The Politics of Hate," we tell the story of a friend, a fanatic Auburn University football fan, who said that as much as he loved watching his Tigers win, he got even more joy out of watching the Alabama Crimson Tide lose. The hatred he had for his rival overpowered even the love he had for his alma mater. That attitude now rules far from the sports arenas. The authors of a particularly insightful article in *Science* trace forty years of survey results tracking the strength of positive feelings toward one's own political party and the strength of negative feelings toward the opposing party.[5] Between 1975 and around 2010, in-party love was a stronger force than out-party hate. But respect for the other party has plummeted over time, and it is now the case that hatred of the opposing party is considerably stronger than affection for one's own. America can surely survive scorn for your athletic rival, but can it survive this?

Do Americans loathe their political opponents because of what their opponents actually believe or because of what they

---

4. A different survey found even more troubling numbers, with more than 80 percent of college students saying that they self-censor at least some of the time on campus, with racial inequality being an especially difficult topic to discuss. Almost one in four students said it was acceptable to use violence to stop a campus speech, while at elite colleges it was one of three. See Maria Carrasco, "Survey: Most Students Self-Censor on Campus and Online," *Inside Higher Ed*, September 23, 2021.

5. Eli Finkel et al., "Political Sectarianism in America," *Science* 370, no. 6516 (October 30, 2020): 533–36.

think they believe? A recent article unpacks this question effectively. People systematically overestimate the ideological extremity of their rivals.[6] They imagine most people on the other side hold views that only a few (on whom one's own side's press focuses) truly do. Have real differences in views on key policies diverged over time? Yes. But nowhere as much as is commonly thought, and nowhere near as much as hatred of the other side has increased.[7] What explains the increase in "false issue polarization"?

We argue that many of us live in echo chambers, hearing our words and the words of those like us played back, reinforcing our own opinions rather than challenging them. Whenever one is in a group of like-minded people, opinion drifts to more extreme positions because they are never challenged, and one does not have to convince anyone. By contrast, when we speak and listen to those with whom we differ, the opposite dynamic takes place. Echo chambers incubate fundamentalisms; mixed communities foster tolerance.

We didn't always live this way. Remember the days when we got our news from network television, newspapers, and magazines? Whether we favored Dan Rather on CBS, Tom Brokaw on NBC, or Peter Jennings on ABC, there was little discernable political slant. While *Newsweek*, *Time*, and *U.S. News and World Report* might have had more pronounced political agendas, compare that with MSNBC versus Fox News, with the *New York Times* versus the *Washington Times*, with Don Lemon versus Tucker Carlson. People became aware of the arguments on the

---

6. James N. Druckman et al., "(Mis)estimating Affective Polarization," *Journal of Politics* 84, no. 2 (April 2022): 1106–17.

7. We discuss the surprising level of agreement among economists in Gary Saul Morson and Morton Owen Schapiro, "American Democracy Is Ailing: Thinking like an Economist Can Help," *Washington Post*, April 10, 2019.

other side, and to refute them, they had to first understand them. In an echo chamber, one's own side might not report inconvenient facts, but if one hears from both sides, one becomes aware that not everything supports a preferred narrative.

In one of our op-eds drawing on the themes in this book, "Extremism Imperils Us All," we cited a poll of likely New Hampshire Democratic voters on the eve of their primary leading up to the 2020 presidential election.[8] When asked which of the following they would prefer: "Donald Trump wins reelection" or "a giant meteor strikes the Earth, extinguishing all human life," 62 percent picked the meteor. Even if they didn't actually mean it—it is hard to believe they did—it is still terrifying that they were willing to (or felt obliged to?) say it.

So what can be done? First of all, it is important to identify the fundamentalism in each of us—that there are certain areas where we unequivocally know that we are right, and it is therefore impossible to convince us otherwise.[9] For Schapiro, an observant Jew, there is nothing that can cause him to question the existence of a benevolent G-d, or as an economist, that there is any realistic hope of developing an alternative to markets as a way to allocate scarce resources. For Morson, the idea that great literature really exists and has important things to teach us seems almost axiomatic, as does the related idea that open-ended dialogue is valuable not just for its results but for its own sake as well. As one of the prepublication reviewers of this book put it, "We want to keep our minds wide open, but not so wide open that our brains fall out."

8. Gary Saul Morson and Morton Schapiro, "Extremism Imperils Us All," *Los Angeles Times*, March 9, 2020.

9. See Gary Saul Morson and Morton Schapiro, "We Have Met the Fundamentalists and They Are Us," *The Hill*, April 18, 2021.

Yet, when we look in the mirror and discover that the majority—or even a significant minority—of our views are not open to refutation, we must face the fact that we may be part of the problem. Perhaps liberals can learn something from watching Fox News and taking seriously articles, books, and op-eds written by thoughtful conservatives in *Commentary*, *National Review*, and *First Things*; conservatives can do similarly with CNN, the *New York Times*, *The Nation*, the *New York Review of Books*, and the like. And of course, anyone familiar with our work will understand that we suggest engaging with literature that can inspire and inform us, moving beyond fundamentalism into true understanding.[10] Realist fiction, in particular, offers a master class in empathy, both emotional and intellectual, with those unlike ourselves.[11]

We attempt to model real dialogue in our classrooms.[12] We find today's students not only remarkably confident in their views on nearly everything, but desperately scared of being ostracized. Getting students to consider that they might just be wrong, to be comfortable articulating not only their opinions but also willing to entertain the best arguments of those on the other side, is in our view the greatest challenge facing campuses today. If students don't learn to do that, then, whatever they have learned, they haven't learned to learn.

10. That was a central theme of our previous book, Gary Saul Morson and Morton Schapiro, *Cents and Sensibility: What Economics Can Learn from the Humanities* (Princeton, NJ: Princeton University Press, 2017).

11. It can also help us understand current events, as we argued in Gary Saul Morson and Morton Schapiro, "What's on Vladimir Putin's Reading List?" *Wall Street Journal*, April 2–3, 2022.

12. For more detail, see Gary Saul Morson and Morton Schapiro, "Break the Silence: How to Create a Safe Space for Real Debate in the Classroom," *Persuasion*, September 22, 2021.

In a course we have been team-teaching over the past dozen years, we focus on facilitating civil and constructive conversation. For one thing, we openly disagree about key issues. For another, we ask our students to write a series of papers with a common directive: to defend their own views, not those of (either one of) the professors. Still more important: in making their case for their own position, they must argue against the *strongest* position of the other side. As one of our colleagues explains, a prize fighter gets no credit for knocking out a kindergartener, and a thinker gets no credit for arguing against a fool. Each week we remind them of John Stuart Mill's famous dictum: "He who knows only his own side of the case knows little of that."

The influence of many professors extends far beyond the classroom.[13] Through their publications and media appearances, they play an outsize role in influencing cultural norms. With that influence comes responsibility. Those who acquiesce to violence and intimidation in the name of "justice" in fact invite massive injustices. Once the intelligentsia condones such excesses, actions inconceivable in one year become fringe the next and, before long, mainstream. Eventually, history suggests, the cancelers are themselves canceled. (Think of Robespierre and Trotsky.)

So where do we go from here? Almost all of our interviews about this book conclude by asking us whether we are optimistic about the future. One of us, Schapiro, cites the Biden election in support of his view that we are on a pendulum, swinging back toward mutual respect and meaningful engagement. Morson, as a specialist in Russia's lugubrious experience, sees matters

13. See Gary Saul Morson and Morton Schapiro, "Beliefs Aren't Facts," *Persuasion*, May 21, 2021.

differently. Instead of a pendulum, he prefers the metaphor of a snowball of intolerance, gaining size and momentum. When conditions are worse than they have been before, they are not guaranteed to swing back but may, as in the French and Russian revolutions, lead to still greater intolerance.

It might seem strange to have an optimistic economist foreseeing a fairer and more caring world, while the pessimistic humanist shops for winter clothes in anticipation of the gulag. But we agree on one thing—what is at stake is nothing less than the future of democracy.

Toward Dialogue

Come now, and let us reason together.

—ISAIAH 1:18

"Facebook Shut Efforts to Become Less Polarizing" reads a headline on the front page of the *Wall Street Journal*.[1] "A Facebook Inc. team had a blunt message for senior executives," the article begins. "The company's algorithms weren't bringing people together. They were driving people apart."

The team wrote, "Our algorithms exploit the human brain's attraction to divisiveness." If left unchecked, Facebook would be feeding its users "more and more divisive content in an effort to gain user attraction & increase time on the platform." The article points out that Facebook CEO Mark Zuckerberg had expressed concern about "sensationalization and polarization," but, in the end, it reports, "Facebook's interest was fleeting."

When people are polarized and "tribalized," honest disagreement becomes impossible. Anyone who disagrees is either

---

1. Jeff Horwitz and Deepa Seetharman, "Facebook Shut Efforts to Become Less Polarizing," *Wall Street Journal*, Wednesday, May 27, 2020, A1.

willfully stupid or deliberately malicious. In a democracy, politics involves compromise, give-and-take, and seeing the other side's point of view; in a polarized world, everything becomes a zero-sum game. He who is not with us is against us. And those on one's own side who are lukewarm, and who may counsel compromise, are in effect working for the enemy and must be shamed into silence.

Democracy cannot long survive under these conditions. If right is all on one side—if one is absolutely certain that there is nothing to learn from those with whom we disagree—then there is no reason not to have a one-party state. Elections that one loses become inherently illegitimate, and so people feel strong pressure to make sure the other side cannot gain power through the ballot box, or any other way. Once power is secured, the same process continues within the victorious party as it roots out disagreement within its own ranks.

Could this be where we are headed?

People with minds that work this way are dangerous. Their characteristic way of thinking—which we call "fundamentalist," in a special sense of that word—assures them that they simply cannot be wrong.[2] The title of Anthony Trollope's novel *He Knew He Was Right* captures this mindset; another entitled *The Way We Live Now* might be updated to "The Way We Think Now." Fundamentalism, as we understand it, is not confined to politics; it can be positive, with an answer to all questions, or negative, denying the possibility of answers. Everywhere it springs up, it leads to radical simplification of complex questions and the inability to learn either from experience or from

---

2. Given how promiscuously the term "fundamentalism" has been used since it was coined a century ago to refer to a set of basic Christian beliefs, we go to considerable lengths in chapter 2 to describe exactly how we are using it.

opposing views. And the habits developed in one field transfer easily to other areas. Each fundamentalism feeds the others.

What are those mental habits? How do they vary over time and discipline? Can we learn to recognize them in ourselves? And what alternatives are there? This last question is especially important. Once the fundamentalist way of thinking takes hold, it seems that the only alternative to one fundamentalism is another; the essence of fundamentalism is to deny the existence of a principled middle ground. For the Soviets, agnostics were people without the courage of their convictions, and liberals were weak-kneed compromisers more distasteful than outright opponents.

But there are principled alternatives. In the pages that follow, we first discuss the fundamentalist mindset in general, and then how it manifests itself in politics, economics, religion, and literary studies, while explaining what real and robust alternatives exist. If we cultivate those alternatives, we argue, we might live in a world where democracy can thrive, better opinions can be arrived at in different fields, and serious dialogue is possible.

In our world, at this moment, dialogue is dying, and righteous indignation abounds. People shout over each other, screaming louder and louder, but it isn't clear that anybody is listening. While some say that crises bring out the best in people, they also bring out the worst. Wherever we turn, we face a barrage of accusations of fake news, fake science, and fake concern for others. The volume may be turned up, but our dueling monologues speak only to ourselves and to our allies.

What we need most is to understand and revitalize the dialogic spirit. We offer the present book as a contribution to that effort.

If anything, the twin crises of the past year—the pandemic and the aftermath of the killing of George Floyd—demonstrate that the dialogic spirit is more critical, if more elusive, than ever. COVID-19 made it extraordinarily clear that viruses, like many other ills, care nothing for national borders, and that having blind faith in everything masquerading as "science" is as foolish as having no faith. With the long-overdue recognition of how many kinds of racism and inequality, especially in regard to Blackness, contribute to differential health outcomes and overall opportunities, perplexing questions are raised about how to bring about real, long-lasting change for the better.

We recall two relevant talks. Chicago mayor Lori Lightfoot spoke at Northwestern's virtual 2020 commencement ceremony. As she traced "our nation's long and still incomplete journey toward full equality and justice," she went on to say that "being engaged doesn't mean screaming the loudest. It doesn't mean issuing a set of demands and then villainizing anyone who doesn't immediately pledge allegiance to your favorite manifesto." She added: "The public square should be about robust debate, working to muster the facts and arguments to persuade. Building coalitions, finding common ground and of course leaning into what you believe—yes, that's all part of what makes this continuing, evolving American experiment with democracy great and enduring. . . . Democracy will fail, it will utterly fail, if we do not see the humanity in each other."[3]

The more important an issue is, the more important it is to arrive at the best policies to address it, and that means appreciating arguments and unintended consequences we had not

---

3. See Gregory Pratt and Sophie Sherry, "Chicago Mayor Lori Lightfoot Delivers Commencement Speech at Northwestern, Says Democracy Will Fail 'If We Do Not See The Humanity in Each Other,'" *Chicago Tribune*, June 19, 2020, https://www .chicagotribune.com/coronavirus/ct-northwestern-university-graduation-chicago -lori-lightfoot-20200619-lkk3qpyi75byjalmjj05p3kamm-story.html.

considered. Overcoming the legacy of racial inequality is not easy, or it would have disappeared long ago. We need to listen, reflect, and question even those in our own camp. People of goodwill can legitimately disagree, and if in our moral fervor we surrender the possibility of dialogue we may never be able to get it back. Then, when still worse evils arise, we will not be able to address or, indeed, even learn about them. The twentieth century offers too many examples of how moral certainty, even as a response to crying injustice, creates previously unimaginable tyranny. We need to cultivate the skills of self-questioning, recognizing our own limitations, and attentive listening to those who differ—all of which are necessary for respectful, productive dialogue.

A few years earlier, civil rights legend Diane Nash was the main speaker at Northwestern's annual celebration of Martin Luther King Jr. She, too, spoke about effective activism and pointed out that advocates for social and institutional change have a choice to make. Being consumed by moral outrage, she argued, doesn't necessarily lead to progress. Treat your opponents with a modicum of respect, resisting the temptation to vilify them. First of all, it is a lot easier to convince people that you are correct if you treat them in a civil manner, and, even if you fail, treating people as humans rather than as symbols embodying all you hate is the right thing to do. She echoed the words of Dr. King: "You have very little morally persuasive power with people who can feel your underlying contempt."

Amen.

MINDS WIDE SHUT

1

Fundamentalism Writ Large

The End of Days?

Perhaps the world balances on a precipice. Could it be that if
we make the slightest mistake, life as we know it would end? Or
does that way of thinking reflect what sociologist Barry Glassner has aptly called "the culture of fear"?[1]

Our predispositions can mislead either way: complacency
can be comforting, but looming disaster makes us feel important. Movements that warn of an imminent apocalypse usually
foresee special treatment for a favored few, a "saving remnant."
Or they at least flatter those who can discern the signs others
miss.

Climate change is upon us, political differences have become
toxic, authoritarian governments are on the rise, and younger
generations are losing confidence that market economies and
democratic processes can lead to equitable outcomes. It seems
that the latest industrial revolution is destroying jobs every day.
The notion of free speech for all—an axiom until recently—has

---

1. See Barry Glassner, *The Culture of Fear: Why Americans Are Afraid of the Wrong Things*, 10th anniversary ed. (New York: Hachette, 2018).

grown almost quaint. And when people are not allowed to criticize orthodoxies, societies get locked into destructive thought patterns and policies.

Doom, it seems, is everywhere. If anything, the global pandemic has made things even worse.

But when haven't predictions of impending disaster been the norm? It seems that what all generations share is the conviction that they live at the most important, and often most perilous, period in human history.[2] And they think so sincerely, because the criteria of importance belong to the present, while what earlier epochs regarded as important seems much less so as time goes on. How, we wonder today, could people have fought wars about the nature of divine grace, or what exactly goes on during the Eucharist?

The trademark irony that marks Edward Gibbon's masterpiece *The Decline and Fall of the Roman Empire* depends on the difference between what his age and what antiquity regarded as of supreme significance. What the early Christians were willing to die for now seems almost impossible to explain, let alone take seriously. In his ironic catalog of theological squabbles that, in the opinion of the early Christians, would determine the salvation of humanity, he mentions one about the exact wording of the Trisagon, the chant of "Holy, holy, holy is the Lord God of Hosts" that the angels sing to God: "In the fever of the times, the sense, or rather the sound, of a syllable was sufficient to disturb the peace of an empire.... The Trisagon ... was chanted in the cathedral by two adverse choirs, and when

---

2. Perhaps they feel that way because, as Marcel Proust put it, we "imagine ourselves always to be going through an experience which is without precedents in the past." Proust, *In Search of Lost Time*, vol. 1., trans. C. Scott Moncrieff and Stephen Hudson, loc. 23336 of 51336, Kindle.

their lungs were exhausted, they had recourse to the more solid arguments of sticks and stones."[3] We laugh today at the absurd fears and controversies of our predecessors, but we, too, succumb to a "fever of the times."

All the same, to understand an earlier period is to grasp what people then feared or expected. What Bertrand de Jouvenel called "futuribles"—the sense of possible futures—are an inescapable part of each present moment, which those living through it almost inevitably regard as singled out by destiny. There is an egoism of time, and part of this sense of unparalleled importance is that unprecedented dangers await just around the corner.

We take some comfort in the fact that this type of thinking almost always proves incorrect. Are today's challenges really as threatening as, for example, the destruction wrought by Genghis Khan, or the twentieth century's two world wars? Is there anyone now who poses as great a danger as Adolf Hitler or Joseph Stalin? We both remember the daily terror of nuclear annihilation that, in our school years, had children crouching next to their lockers or under their desks, coats covering our heads, as we waited to see how the Cuban Missile Crisis turned out.[4] By that standard, even in the wake of COVID-19, these days don't seem quite so scary.

And yet, as amateur golfers know when they hit a six iron and end up a foot from the hole, unlikely things do happen. Some predictions of disaster are, alas, realized; catastrophes do occur, and they make skeptics look foolish. The outbreak of the

---

3. Edward Gibbon, *The Decline and Fall of the Roman Empire*, ed. J. B. Bury (New York: Heritage, 1846), 1557.

4. While we did what we were told, we never quite understood how our coats would protect us from a nuclear attack.

coronavirus may remind us that the Black Death, which wiped out a substantial part of the world's population, could be repeated, if not by this pandemic, then by another. Those who successfully predict catastrophes—the way Dostoevsky predicted what we now call "totalitarianism"—are in their time regarded as, at best, highly eccentric. They become prophets only in retrospect.

Perhaps this time the world really *is* on a precipice, with democracy, freedom, and other cherished principles at risk should it teeter in the wrong direction. While we do not see the present as the most dangerous of times, we do discern some serious threats with common features that need to be addressed. And the sooner, the better.

Fundamentalism Abounds

So urgent . . . is the necessity of believing, that the fall of any system of mythology, will most probably be succeeded by the introduction of some other mode of superstition.

—EDWARD GIBBON, *DECLINE AND FALL OF THE ROMAN EMPIRE*[5]

We sense a danger in what we call a new "fundamentalism," a term we use in a special sense elaborated at length in chapter 2. That fundamentalism has infected not only politics, but also many other areas of thought. Not so long ago, it seemed as if belief in "grand narratives," or "metanarratives," as Jean-François Lyotard observed, was over.[6] No longer would people rush to

---

5. In *English Poetry and Prose, 1660–1880: A Selection*, ed. Frank Brady and Martin Price (New York: Holt, Rinehart & Winston, 1961), 397.

6. Jean-François Lyotard, *The Postmodern Condition: A Report on Knowledge*, trans. Geoff Bennington and Brian Massumi (Minneapolis: University of Minnesota Press, 1984), xxiv.

adopt theories that purport to explain everything (or, at least, everything pertaining to a whole domain of human experience). Also not so long ago, it was an unchallenged commonplace that cultures are undergoing a far-reaching secularization that, in spite of occasional resistance, is unstoppable. The rise of militant Islam, and what some have termed "fundamentalist Hinduism," have called the "secularization thesis" into question. Where are the inevitabilities of yesteryear?

We often flatter ourselves that, when ideas or policies lead to terrible consequences, people eventually admit their error and change course. But, in matters touching their very sense of self, or a movement's very reason for being, the opposite often happens; disconfirmation turns into confirmation. Failure, it is argued, was due to lack of sufficient rigor in executing the policy. That is the logic that led Stalin to proclaim the "intensification of the class struggle" after the Revolution, when no opposition was visible. Greater vigilance is demanded, and a bigger dose of the dubious medicine is administered. The more extreme the theory, the less is disconfirmation possible.

When people adopt extreme theories, they discover dangers that justify extreme actions. That is because such theories teach a way of viewing the world that (as we shall see) reveals only confirming evidence. When extreme and still more extreme action is taken, the result may indeed be horrific. What was meant to solve a serious problem creates a still more serious one. Call it "the self-fulfilling catastrophe."

In the United States and Europe, discussions of political polarization are everywhere. The rise both of the far left and the far right poses a threat different in both degree and kind from that entailed by a bad policy decision, which might be corrected. Some of these movements may fall prey to forms of fundamentalist thinking that make correction impossible. Matters grow still worse when one fundamentalism confronts another.

Clinging to opposite poles, they accuse each other of all sins, including polarization.

Beyond the political arena, we see analogous conflicts among fundamentalisms. What might be called "market fundamentalism" (as opposed to a general inclination to market solutions) insists categorically, and on a priori grounds, on deploying market solutions everywhere economically possible. And not only there: it also applies market models to disciplines and areas of life remote from economics. These models are offered not as a contribution to another discipline, but as its replacement. Just as some sociobiologists have never met a human behavior they could not explain, so some economists have never encountered problems that could not best be solved by the tools of economics.

This market fundamentalism encounters an opposite one, a revival of the sort of thinking that the failure of the "socialist bloc" had seemingly consigned to what Leon Trotsky called "the dustbin of history."[7] In this view, capitalism cannot be compassionate any more than the plague can be healthy. Some have described these opposites in terms of a generation gap—which, if true, seems as wide as the Grand Canyon.

We are speaking here not of arguments between those who favor either a market or a government solution to this or that problem, but to those who think categorically, so that the answer to any question is known as soon as the question is posed. The answer is always privatization or nationalization, drastically

---

7. When the Mensheviks walked out of the 1917 Congress of Soviets, Trotsky (as tradition has it) told them: "Go to the place where you belong from now on—the dustbin of history!" See William Safire, "On Language; Dust Heaps of History," *New York Times*, October 16, 1983, https://www.nytimes.com/1983/10/16/magazine/on-language-dust-heaps-of-history.html.

cutting or increasing regulations, radically lowering or raising taxes.   *what?*

Categorical thinking admits no compromise and allows no correction in light of results. On the contrary, as we have noted, it makes the failure of a policy the reason for more of it. It is this kind of thinking, not just the bad solutions to which it might lead, that we find especially dangerous. While dangerous in it-self, it is still more so because it prevents learning from experience. Alchemy failed to transmute base metals into gold, but *?* this intellectual alchemy successfully converts reasons against a course of action into reasons for still more of it.

Some fundamentalisms cause more havoc than others. The political is usually the most dangerous, with the economic close behind. But when a given way of thinking becomes routine, it affects areas less vital but still significant. It is worth examining these areas to see how the fundamentalist way of thinking manifests itself. The more examples, the clearer it becomes. And, by the same token, if one can show what the alternative looks like in area after area, one might more successfully arrest the harmful tendency.

In our classes, we have seen students who adopt fundamentalist ways of thinking almost by default: not as a choice, but because they imagine that is just what thinking *is*. These students seem genuinely surprised that there are situations where one cannot find a uniquely correct answer, where one needs to make choices under uncertainty, and where those who recommend a different course of action might turn out to be right. By showing what other ways of thinking there might be, we have at least encouraged some of them, even if they remain fundamentalists, to be so more reflectively, precisely because what had been automatic has become a choice. As Mikhail Bakhtin liked to say, the old way of regarding things has become "contested, contestable, and contesting."[8] As we discuss in chapter 2, when that happens, people have moved from a "Ptolemaic universe," which they regard as the unchallenged center of things, to a "Galilean" one, where theirs is but one of many planets—or as sociologists like to say, their world has lost its "taken-for-grantedness."[9]

Some students take the next step and recognize that the more circumspect alternatives we offer may be better. Each time students recognize them, they become more thoughtful. In a course we teach together, we treat a variety of disciplines, including economics, city planning, history, and philosophy. In the present volume, we turn our attention to two others: religion and literary study. The fate of the world does not depend, as English professors sometimes seem ready to maintain, on the nature of the canon or of interpretation, but the issues are still significant. They happen to display one or another version of fundamentalism, different from but recognizably resembling those we have seen in politics and economics.

We wonder about the persistence of an old conflict in religion, which has been with us for a century or more, but may now be reviving and intensifying. Like the early twentieth-century Christian fundamentalists, who invented this sobriquet, there are those who see no alternative to an unchangeable idea of the sacred and what it demands, other than a radical relativism that makes Scripture and faith mean whatever seems most in accord with present beliefs. By the same token, those

8. Mikhail Bakhtin, "Discourse in the Novel," in *The Dialogic Imagination: Four Essays*, ed. Michael Holquist, trans. Caryl Emerson and Michael Holquist (Austin: University of Texas Press, 1981), 332.

9. See Peter Berger and Anton Zijderveld, *In Praise of Doubt: How to Have Convictions Without Becoming a Fanatic* (New York: HarperCollins, 2009), 13–17, 71.

who think that Scripture means whatever current thought needs it to mean see no alternative to their view but rigid adherence to ideas that at best make no sense and, at worst, are morally repellent. The idea of a principled middle ground seems like cowardice or intellectual inconsistency. In a pattern we shall see repeated, a positive fundamentalism encounters a negative fundamentalism, and ne'er the twain shall meet.

In the study of the humanities, a similar dynamic repeats itself in various issues. This is hardly surprising for disciplines that abandoned structuralism, with its aspiration to be a theory of everything, for deconstruction and other theories of nothing. Almost overnight, a purported hard science of culture was replaced by a radical skepticism denying the possibility of knowledge. One would have made even Plato smile, the other even Hume blush. One might suppose that a radical skeptic would, like Hume, be anything but militant, but, when we are dealing with fundamentalisms, the very reverse is the case. There is such a thing as missionary nihilism, and in the humanities we have seen it.

The questions surrounding "the canon" pertain not just to what works should be included in it, or what qualities make literary works great, but to the very notion of great literature. In literary studies there seem to be no positive fundamentalists left, or, at least, none that admit to being so. Negative fundamentalism reigns supreme. Few would defend, at least publically, the proposition that the determinate meaning of a text is to be found either in the author's intention or in the text itself. The very notion of determinate meaning, like that of objective value, is suspect. It is not that nonsubjective meaning and value are difficult to ascertain, and that evidence can point in different directions; rather, they are, like God for Nietzsche—dead. Issues remote from these, which are not really literary at all, have consequently taken their place. Literary scholars, who for decades have been denouncing, deconstructing, and decolonizing the canon, and who have established the orthodoxy that literary value is a myth, wonder why enrollments in literature courses have declined. Somewhere there must be atheist pastors baffled by their empty pews.

In our view, great literature, which surely exists, teaches a lesson the very opposite of fundamentalisms, positive or negative. That is especially true of the great realist novels, which often take fundamentalist styles of thinking as their topic ("the novel of ideas"). As we shall see, all literary genres have presuppositions—you don't write a saint's life if you don't believe in holiness, or an epic if you scorn heroism—and the realist novel presumes the irreducible complexity of individual psychology, culture, society, and ethical questions. The finest novelists (Leo Tolstoy, Fyodor Dostoevsky, Joseph Conrad, Henry James, George Eliot, and Jane Austen) offer readers marvelous experiences in nonfundamentalist thinking. Their works contain a deep wisdom, a real alternative to fundamentalisms, and we shall therefore be returning to them frequently. If we allow them to teach us to think more complexly, we can address many other questions more wisely.

We suspect that these new fundamentalisms, in politics, economics, religion and literature, demand a common response. It is time to be sure at least that fundamentalism is not adopted by default.

Talking with colleagues and students, we sometimes have the impression that they have no clear idea as to what an alternative way of thinking might be. They seem to suppose either that the only alternative to a positive fundamentalism is a negative one, or that anything else is at best makeshift accommodation. But it is not true that anything short of a totalizing theory is somehow flawed, at best a stopgap until such a theory is found. Aristotle was right to maintain that "it is the mark of an educated person to look for precision in each class of things just so far as the nature of the subject admits."[10] It is therefore important to clarify what alternatives are available, and why they are superior to totalisms in explaining human affairs, understanding specific people and cultures, formulating policies, and judging moral actions. To be effective, policies must respond to reality and therefore may go badly wrong when they are based on premises that look neat, appear symmetrical, and sound magnificent, but are untrue. *wow*

The Bolsheviks thought that human nature was infinitely malleable and perfectible to those with the right theory, who could be, in Stalin's famous phrase, "engineers of human souls" (inzhinery chelovecheskikh dush).[11] Immanuel Kant maintained the opposite view: "From the crooked timber of humanity no straight thing was ever made."[12] When we build with such material, we must not assume all logs are straight and must look for the intransigent knots. We hope that this book will be a lesson in the carpentry appropriate for crooked timber.

image

10. Aristotle, "Nichomachean Ethics," in *The Basic Works of Aristotle*, ed. Richard McKeon (New York: Random House, 1941), 936.

11. From Stalin's speech in Maxim Gorky's apartment, October 26, 1932, as cited in David Joravsky, "The Construction of the Stalinist Psyche," in *Cultural Revolution in Russia, 1928–1931*, ed. Sheila Fitzpatrick (Bloomington: Indiana University Press, 1984), 127. For the Russian text, see https://citaty.su/inzhenery-chelovecheskix -dush.

12. Immanuel Kant, *Idea for a Universal History from a Cosmopolitan Point of View*, proposition 6, in *On History*, ed. Lewis White Beck (Indianapolis: Bobbs-Merrill, 1977), 17–18, where the line is given as: "From such crooked wood as man is made of, nothing perfectly straight can be built." To render the German (Aus so krummem Holze, als woraus der Mensch gemacht ist, kann nichts ganz Gerades gezimmert werden), we prefer Isaiah Berlin's version. See Berlin, *The Crooked Timber of Humanity: Chapters in the History of Ideas* (New York: Knopf, 1991), xi.

2

Fundamentalism and
Its Alternatives

FROM FANATICISM TO DIALOGUE

Part 1: The Fundamentalist Style of Thought

Conception and Evolution

The term "fundamentalism" has been used so promiscuously, by so many authors, to refer to such a variety of things, that it pays to indicate just what we mean and do not mean when we use it. We wish to stress at the outset that we are *not* offering a new definition of this term, designed to replace previous ones. Moreover, we do not recommend our usage as a singular "correct" one. For that matter, this book is not a study of fundamentalist religious movements and their place in the United States or anywhere else. Rather, since we are adapting this term for special purposes, we simply wish to specify what we have in mind when we refer to a style of thinking as "fundamentalist." Readers can judge whether we use this term consistently instead of—as happens all too often—adjusting its meaning to fit whatever argument we happen to be making at a given moment.

As commentators routinely explain, the term "fundamental-ism" can be traced to American pamphlets, published between 1910 and 1915, in a series called "The Fundamentals." The series was financed by two brothers, Lyman and Milton Stewart, who had made their money in the oil business, and was intended, as George Marsden's classic study has observed, as "a great 'Testimony to the Truth' and even something of a scholarly *tour de force*."[1] Stewart hired as his first editor A. C. Dixon, a well-known author and pastor of the Moody Church in Chicago. Dixon and his two successors enlisted an impressive group of American and British scholars, along with popular authors to provide the content. Some three million pamphlets were delivered free of charge to "every pastor, missionary, theological professor, Sunday school superintendent, and religious editor in the English-speaking world."[2]

Despite wide distribution, the series at first had little impact. It represented the movement in a moderate stage. The most controversial belief of many adherents, a form of millenarian-ism called "dispensational premillennialism," was almost entirely absent. The authors defended what they took to be the most basic Christian beliefs, including the inerrancy of Scripture. Such a defense had become urgent because of what was called "the higher criticism," the work of a school of German scholars who, through textual analysis tracing the authorship of particular passages, had demonstrated that biblical books had multiple authors. Rather than integral wholes, these books were, in effect, patchworks assembled at different times, with

1. George M. Marsden, *Fundamentalism and American Culture: The Shaping of Twentieth-Century Evangelicalism, 1870–1925* (Oxford: Oxford University Press, 1980), 118.

2. Marsden, *Fundamentalism and American Culture*, 119.

resulting errors and contradictions. These contradictions were real, not merely apparent, because they were the consequence of how the books were written or, rather, assembled. As we discuss in chapter 5, as this critical tradition developed—right up to the present day—it came to threaten not only biblical inerrancy but even, if pushed far enough, biblical meaningfulness. If the Bible is just an inconsistent patchwork, or rather an anthology of patchworks, how could one even speak of what "the Bible" says?

The threat posed by biblical criticism, therefore, was to prove significant not just for fundamentalists but also for other believers, including Orthodox Jews and many other Christians. But fundamentalists, with their belief in absolute inerrancy, felt the threat strongly early on. Especially because Protestantism originated and defined itself in terms of the principle *sola scriptura* (scripture alone, not church tradition as the highest authority), many Protestants regarded the higher criticism as posing an existential challenge.

The fundamentalist movement entered a more combative phase in response to World War I and its aftermath. Liberal theologians from the University of Chicago Divinity School questioned their conservative opponents' patriotism. Professor Shirley Jackson Case, author of *The Millennial Hope: A Phase of War Time Thinking* (1918), detected a conspiracy in which the conservatives aided the Germans and probably received secret payments. He suggested that the government investigate them. The idea that we must rely on God for any dramatic improvement, he reasoned, could only hamper the effort to make the world safe for democracy.[3] Indeed, it stood in the way of all progress. In response, some conservative thinkers pointed out

3. Marsden, 146–47.

that the higher criticism was itself German, and that its weakening of Christian belief had contributed to the moral collapse of German civilization and its consequent aggression; so had the Darwinian belief in violent struggle, abetted by Nietzscheanism. As we would say today, each side detected in the other a German asset.

In 1920, Curtis Lee Laws, editor of the Baptist paper the *Watchman Examiner*, coined the word "fundamentalist." He defined "fundamentalists" as those who "do battle for the Fundamentals" of the faith. In fact, there was no well-defined group called fundamentalists. The movement was, in Marsden's words, "a mosaic of divergent and sometimes contradictory tendencies that could never be totally integrated."[4] They included people of different denominations, premillenialists and nonpremillenialists, intellectuals and know-nothings. Since it is unfair to characterize any movement by its most disreputable members, and, as the theologian William Hordern observes, "no system can be judged by what fanatics do in its name,"[5] we shall instead—using what philosophers have called "the principle of charitable interpretation"—refer to the ideas of its most rational thinkers.[6]

After the disastrous performance of William Jennings Bryan at the Scopes Trial in 1925, the term "fundamentalist" became, and has remained, a term primarily of abuse. It is now "a theological swear-word," as J. I. Packer observes, "and the important

4. Marsden, 43.

5. As cited in Marsden, 200.

6. On the "principle of charity," see Simon Blackburn, *The Oxford Dictionary of Philosophy* (Oxford: Oxford University Press, 1994), 62. "In various versions [the principle of charity] constrains the interpreter to maximize the truth or rationality in the subject's sayings." The principle has been traced to Rabbi Meir Bal HaNes, a Tannaim (a sage whose views appear in the Mishnah).

thing about a swear-word, of course, is not what it means but the emotion it expresses."[7] Words used this way are applied ever more loosely until they lose all value as a meaningful description, a process Packer calls "the unchanging law of the vocabulary of insult."[8]

Understandably enough, the term came to be applied to other extreme religious movements, and that is how scholars, as well as many lay people, now use the term. Gabriel A. Almond, R. Scott Appleby, and Emmanuel Sivan begin their authoritative study *Strong Religion: The Rise of Fundamentalism around the World* by observing that movements that might be called fundamentalist have taken power in five countries: Iran in 1979, Sudan in 1993, Turkey and Afghanistan in 1996, and India in 1996 and again in 1998 and 1999. In addition, fundamentalist movements include Hamas, Al Qaeda, "elements of the Jewish underground," the Algerian Armed Islamic Group, Islamic revolutionaries in Chechnya and Dagestan, and Christian radicals in the United States.[9] Christianity, Judaism, Islam, Buddhism, Sikhism, and Hinduism have all generated fundamentalist groups.

Critics have argued that it is misleading to lump these very different groups together. As Karen Armstrong observes, "Each 'fundamentalism' is a law unto itself and has its own dynamic."[10] It is also problematic to call them "fundamentalist"; the term misleads in suggesting that those called "fundamentalists" are

7. J. I. Packer, *"Fundamentalism" and the Word of God: Some Evangelical Principles* (Grand Rapids, MI: Eerdmans, 1966), 30.

8. Packer, *Fundamentalism*, 30.

9. Gabriel A. Almond, R. Scott Appleby, and Emmanuel Sivan, *Strong Religion: The Rise of Fundamentalisms around the World* (Chicago: University of Chicago Press, 2003), 1.

10. Karen Armstrong, *The Battle for God* (New York: Ballantine, 2001), xii.

intensely conservative, whereas, in Armstrong's view, they are typically "essentially modern and highly innovative."[11] What is more, as many have pointed out, all observant Muslims believe in the inerrancy of the Koran, so the term can hardly be used to single out an extreme Islamic movement. Similarly, Talmudic sages presumed the inerrancy of the Torah. Given how different these groups are, countless other objections have been raised to the term and the very concept.

The scholars who collaborated on the five-volume Fundamentalist Project of the American Academy of Arts and Sciences resorted to Ludwig Wittgenstein's notion of "family resemblances."[12] So have other, less rigorous commentators.[13] Indeed, scholars in many disciplines often invoke "family resemblances" as a way to avoid clarifying just what they mean. Instead of specifying what one means by "literature," for instance, a literary theorist dismisses the issue with a reference to "family resemblances," which licenses whatever meaning might be convenient at the moment.

Rarely has so much sloppy thinking been generated by so brilliant an idea. In his *Philosophical Investigations*, Ludwig Wittgenstein constantly returns to the way in which words can bedevil thought. He asks us to consider "games"; a moment's reflection suggests that we apply the term to a vast variety of activities. We might imagine that, since "games" is one word, all games must share a defining quality, but that turns out not to be the case. Using a favorite phrase, Wittgenstein advises,

11. Armstrong, *Battle for God*, xii.

12. The volumes were published by the University of Chicago Press between 1991 and 1995.

13. See, for instance, Malise Ruthven, *Fundamentalism: A Very Short Introduction* (Oxford: Oxford University Press, 2007). Ruthven's first chapter is entitled "Family Resemblances."

"Don't think, but look!"[14] If you do, you will see "a complicated network of similarities overlapping and criss-crossing: sometimes overall similarities, sometimes similarities of detail. I can think of no better expression to describe these similarities than 'family resemblances'; for the various resemblances between members of a family . . . overlap and criss-cross in the same way. And I shall say, 'games' form a family."[15]

Wittgenstein's brilliant observation is right on the mark, but its careless use can be irritating. In practice, it often justifies using a key term to mean quite different things as an argument proceeds. One can "play fast and loose" (the term "fast" here means "close" or "tight") by employing a narrow characterization when one wants to make a specific claim but, when challenged, resort to a broad, even tautological, one easier to defend.

Sometimes the group that thinkers identify is less like "games" than like "weeds." Their similarity, and the reason for grouping them together, lies not in their overlapping features but in the thinker's attitude. Fundamentalists, like weeds, are those one does not like. In the hands of someone with an animus against religion—like Stuart Sim, who repeatedly says he lacks the "religion gene"—the term "fundamentalism," especially if extended or contracted at will, sometimes seems like a mere grunt signifying disapproval.[16]

Of course, the term can also be applied to nonreligious movements one does not like. Sim's popular book, *Fundamentalist*

14. Ludwig Wittgenstein, *Philosophical Investigations*, trans. G. E. M. Anscombe (New York: Macmillan, 1968), paragraph 66, 31e.

15. Wittgenstein, *Philosophical Investigations*, paragraphs 66–67, 32e.

16. Stuart Sim, *Fundamentalist World: The New Dark Age of Dogma* (Crows Nest, NSW, AU: Allen & Unwin, 2005), 4.

World: The New Dark Age of Dogma shifts meanings with abandon. Having evoked the reader's horror at the actions of terror-
ists or the pronouncements of obscurantists of all sorts, he calls
very different groups "fundamentalist" in the same indignant
tone. The term soon broadens to include all monotheistic religions, since, "by definition, monotheistic religions can't coun-
tenance competition."[17] Catholicism qualifies since it "continues to regard itself" as "the only true religion (universal theory
comes no more universal)."[18] Of course, to believe in any religion almost always entails the belief that it is truer than others.
What else could belief in a religion mean? Sim deems the Mos-
lem statement of faith—"There is no God but God, and Muhammed is the messenger of God"—fundamentalist because
"it admits no counter-argument."[19] Switching grounds again, he
calls the Crusades "fundamentalist" not because no counterar-
gument was possible, but because the Crusades were a violent
attempt to recover Christian holy sites.[20]

The same sloppiness characterizes Sim's ventures outside
religion. As will soon be clear, we have no problem with using
the term to include some nonreligious movements, and we, like
Sim, speak of "market fundamentalism." But Sim uses it to refer
to any policy grounded in market economics, each search for
market solutions, and all privatizations. Much as all monotheism (or all religion) turns out to be fundamentalist, so this
"theological swear-word" soon characterizes all thinking informed by mainstream economics. By the same token, "British-
ness," with its distrust of the European Union, is an example of

17. Sim, *Fundamentalist World*, 8.
18. Sim, 39.
19. Sim, 12.
20. Sim, 31, 36.

"Western democratic political fundamentalism," and Sim also gives qualified approval to Tariq Ali's thesis that American imperialism is "the mother of all fundamentalisms."[21] Ambrose Bierce's definition of obstinate—"inaccessible to the truth as it is manifest in the splendor and stress of our advocacy"—would fit Sim's and Ali's uses of fundamentalism.[22] For that matter, Sim (and others) use the terms "dogmatism" and "denial" to describe anyone who does not think his evidence for a political opinion is sufficient. We wish we could say that this promiscuous use of otherwise serviceable terms is exceptional.

Wittgenstein's approach to language and his concept of family resemblances suggest that it is possible to draw boundaries variously. The term "literature" in one usage could include all significant writing (as the Chinese term usually translated as "literature" once did), or it could refer only to belles lettres, or to works that are fictional.[23] It can be evaluative, so that, if a work is bad, it is not literature at all, or descriptive; the lines can be drawn to include folklore (oral literature) or, as the etymology of the word suggests, only written texts. It can be identified by its formal features, by how it is read, or by its social functions. The term "novels" has also been identified quite variously.

In our view, it is legitimate to apply such terms in different ways on different occasions, so long as one specifies how one is

21. Sim, 136. See Tariq Ali, *The Clash of Fundamentalisms: Crusades, Jihads, and Modernity* (London: Verso, 2002), 281.

22. Ambrose Bierce, *The Devil's Dictionary* (Garden City, NY: Doubleday, n.d.), 147.

23. In the twentieth century, Lu Hsun redrew the boundaries to include fiction previously dismissed as mere "chit-chat" (Hsiao-shuo). See the opening chapter of Lu Hsun, *A Brief History of Chinese Fiction*, trans. Yang Hsien-Yi and Gladys Yang (Beijing: Foreign Languages Press, 2014).

going to use it in a particular study and then applies that usage consistently. If one focuses on one set of features pertaining to the original Christian fundamentalists, one might properly wind up including only religious movements, as Armstrong and the authors of *Strong Religion* do. But it is also possible, by picking different features, to include some nonreligious movements or philosophies. It is no accident that Marxism-Leninism has often been described as a religion.[24]

In Armstrong's careful usage, it makes no sense to use the term to refer to movements before the twentieth century—her fundamentalism is "an essentially twentieth-century movement"[25]— let alone to the Reformation, because she means to describe certain movements rejecting the modern world.[26] And she succeeds: her powerful argument yields conclusions that illuminate more than the movements she discusses.

Although we focus on the present, we do not limit the term in this way, nor do we set as a criterion, as some have understandably done, the propensity to violence. Violence is an all too present temptation for many fundamentalists, but there are fundamentalists—like those we call "market fundamentalists"— who are pacific folk. For that matter, the authors of "The Fundamentals," and the theologians who sided with them, neither

24. For a treatment of Soviet Marxism as a fundamentalism, see Ernest Gellner, "Fundamentalism as a Comprehensive System: Soviet Marxism and Islamic Fundamentalism Compared," in *The Fundamentalism Project, Fundamentalisms Comprehended*, vol. 5, ed. Martin E. Marty and R. Scott Appleby (Chicago: University of Chicago Press, 1995), 277–87.

25. Armstrong, *Battle for God*, xii.

26. Berger and Zijderveld concur, since they (like other scholars) regard fundamentalism as a reaction to modernity. See Peter Berger and Anton Zijderveld, *In Praise of Doubt: How to Have Convictions Without Becoming a Fanatic* (New York: HarperCollins, 2009), 69–71.

practiced nor advocated violence. How, then, are we using the term in the present volume?

Fundamentalist Criterion #1: Certainty

"Fundamentalists," as we use the term, share some or all of several characteristics. For one, they profess a doctrine that provides complete certainty. Isaiah Berlin famously distinguished between two types of thinkers: hedgehogs, who have one big truth to explain the world, and foxes, for whom there are many competing truths:

> For there exists a great chasm between those, on one side, who relate everything to a single central vision, one system . . . in terms of which they understand, think, and feel—a single, universal organizing principle in terms of which alone all that they are and say has significance—and, on the other side, those who pursue many ends, often unrelated and even contradictory, connected, if at all, only in some *de facto* way . . . these last lead lives, perform acts, and entertain ideas that are centrifugal rather than centripetal, their thought is scattered or diffused . . . seizing upon the essence of a vast variety of experiences and objects for what they are in themselves, without, consciously or unconsciously, seeking to fit them into . . . any one unchanging, all- embracing . . . at times fanatical, unitary inner vision.[27]

Plato, Lucretius, and Hegel are archetypal hedgehogs; Shakespeare, Montaigne, and Erasmus are foxes. Hedgehogs offer comprehensive answers while foxes raise skeptical questions.

---

27. Isaiah Berlin, "The Hedgehog and the Fox," in *Russian Thinkers*, ed. Henry Hardy and Aileen Kelly (Harmondsworth, UK: Penguin, 1986), 22. The essay was first published as a book in 1953.

For hedgehogs, what we need is certainty, and they claim to provide it; for foxes, we need good judgment, which can never be formalized.

Fundamentalists are hedgehogs. Their certainty may pertain either to knowledge, to moral evaluation, or, often enough, to both. If it pertains to knowledge, all other ways of looking at things are ignorant; if it pertains to moral evaluation, they are evil. The source of certainty can be a divine revelation, which is infallible because it comes from God, or a philosophical system, which, over the past three centuries, is infallible because it is "science." The hedgehog's system is as certain as physics or astronomy. Ever since Isaac Newton explained the bafflingly complex movements of the planets in terms of four simple laws—three laws of motion and the law of universal gravitation—social thinkers have aspired to do the same for the world of human beings. Since people are part of nature, it was reasoned, they must be explicable by some social form of natural science.

In practice, it is a short step from believing that a hard social science is possible, to claiming that one has at last established one. Time and again, "moral Newtonians," as Élie Halévy famously called them, have offered systems purporting to be sciences.[28] We shall encounter a few of these, but here one can say that the purported science may have different starting points. Some, like Jeremy Bentham and Sigmund Freud, begin with individual psychology. Others start with society as it functions at a given moment. Bronislaw Malinowski, the founder of anthropology as a discipline, regarded his "scientific theory of culture" as one that could achieve "prediction of the future," and before Auguste Comte coined the term "sociology," he

---

28. Élie Halévy, *The Growth of Philosophic Radicalism*, trans. Mary Morris (Boston: Beacon, 1955), 6.

meant to call his new discipline "social physics."[29] Even more ambitiously, some aspiring scientists explained history—that is, everything that happens—as did several nineteenth-century thinkers, not just Karl Marx and Friedrich Engels. In our time, Jared Diamond discovered principles allowing him "to provide a short history of everybody for the last 13,000 years."[30]

Whatever their starting point, these hedgehogs often venture beyond it. Bentham offered to explain morals and proposed scientific principles for reconstructing society; Freud examined culture as a whole, which he analyzed in terms derived from his work on individual psychology. B. F. Skinner was sure his behavioristic approach to the psyche offered a path to utopia and wrote a popular utopian novel, *Walden Two* (1948).

In short, there is no need for so many distinct disciplines! Simplify, simplify! Economist Gary Becker won a Nobel Prize for showing how "the economic approach to human behavior" can illuminate such apparently noneconomic social phenomena as marriage and crime. "The economic approach," he concludes, "provides a united framework for understanding behavior that has long been sought by and eluded Bentham, Comte, Marx, and others."[31] Certainty, it seems, tends to be imperialistic.

Edward O. Wilson, the world's authority on ant societies and the inventor of sociobiology, argues that, in the final analysis, the multiplicity of disciplines could be reduced to singularity, a

29. Bronislaw Malinowski, *A Scientific Theory of Culture and Other Essays* (Chapel Hill: University of North Carolina Press, 1994), 8.

30. Jared Diamond, *Guns, Germs, and Steel: The Fates of Human Societies* (New York: Norton, 1997), 9.

31. Gary S. Becker, *The Economic Approach to Human Behavior* (Chicago: University of Chicago Press, 1976), 14.

process he called "consilience."[32] As he explains, he succumbed to what historian of science Gerald Holton called "the Ionian enchantment": the belief, traceable to the pre-Socratic Ionian philosopher Thales of Miletus, "in the unity of the sciences— a conviction, far deeper than a mere working proposition, that the world can be explained by a small number of natural laws."[33] Wilson is unusual in acknowledging that his belief in a unitary scientific model of the natural and social world derives not from science but from something "far deeper," a kind of "enchantment."

For a hedgehog, explanation must not only be comprehensive and capable of unifying all disciplines, but it must do so with only a few laws. God and nature are parsimonious. This is Newtonianism with a vengeance. Wilson quotes with approval the observation of the Marquis de Condorcet: "The sole foundation for belief in the natural sciences is that the general laws directing the phenomena of the universe, known or unknown, are necessary and constant. Why should this principle be any less true for the development of the intellectual and moral faculties of man than for other operations of nature?"[34] Before turning to science, Wilson explains, he had adhered to "fundamentalist religion. I had been raised a Southern Baptist, laid backward under the water in the sturdy arm of a pastor, been born again. I knew the healing power of redemption." He did not so much abandon faith, as change faiths. "Perhaps science is a continuation [of Holy Writ] on new and better-tested

32. See Edward O. Wilson, *Sociobiology: The New Synthesis* (Cambridge, MA: Harvard University Press, [1975] 2000).

33. Edward O. Wilson, *Consilience: The Unity of Knowledge* (New York: Knopf, 1998), 4.

34. Cited in Wilson, *Consilience*, 20.

ground to attain the same end," he reasons. "If so, then science is religion liberated and writ large."[35]

And vice versa. As Wilson's science was a "continuation" of his religious fundamentalism, so the original Christian fundamentalists thought of themselves as proponents of science. (Again, we are speaking of their serious thinkers.) As Marsden, Armstrong, and others have explained, and as the fundamentalist Packer affirms, fundamentalist thinkers revered Newton and Francis Bacon, whom they interpreted in light of Scottish Common Sense philosophy. Authentic Christianity, Packer explains, desires not to eliminate scientific study of the Bible, but to make it "genuinely scientific—that is to say, fully biblical in its method."[36] We should recall that Newton, usually described as the model of rationalism, devoted far more energy to his commentaries on the Bible, including a treatise on the Apocalypse, than to the achievements in physics and mathematics that ensured his fame. The fundamentalist thinkers were convinced that nature and the Bible, both creations of God, could not contradict each other.

Armstrong astutely observes that, in an age when the prestige of science is at its height, what she calls "mythos"—the part of religion that expresses not specific facts but eternal truths and timeless realities—may be reinterpreted as logos, or pragmatic thought concerned with facts. The fundamentalists, she believes, did exactly that: "The old myths were now seen as factual *logoi*, the only form of truth people could recognize."[37] If the Bible was not scientifically correct, they reasoned, then it was not correct at all. Thus Dixon, the first editor of "The Fun-

35. Wilson, 6.

36. Packer, *Fundamentalism*, 20.

37. Armstrong, *Battle for God*, 138.

damentals," insisted in a 1920 speech, "I am a Christian because I am a thinker . . . a rationalist . . . a scientist."[38] Those who argue that science is one thing and religion another are mistaken, insisted J. Gresham Machen, professor of New Testament at Princeton Seminary. "The question of the resurrection of our Lord," he contends, "in accordance with the common-sense definition of 'resurrection' . . . does concern 'matter,' it concerns the emergence or non-emergence of the body from the tomb." The question is "whether the events really took place"; to pretend otherwise is to surrender to "modern anti-intellectualism."[39]

The fundamentalists did not regard their rejection of Darwinism as antiscientific, but as a properly Baconian suspicion of any theory that goes well beyond the facts. The synthesis of genetics with evolution as described by Charles Darwin, after all, lay two decades in the future. The fundamentalist perspective is more understandable if we recall that those who argued for Darwinism and attacked fundamentalism often regarded what we now call "social Darwinism" as an intrinsic part of it.

Progressives favored eugenics, which was advocated by a progressive bible, Edward Bellamy's utopian novel *Looking Backward, 2000–1887*.[40] Part of what the fundamentalist William B. Riley called "this pseudo-science" really *was* pseudoscience. And it was morally repellent. The idea maintained by some social Darwinists that the strong had the moral right—indeed, obligation—to oppress the weak ran directly counter

38. Cited in Marsden, *Fundamentalism and American Culture*, 217.

39. Cited in Marsden, 216–17.

40. See Robert C. Bannister, *Social Darwinism: Science and Myth in Anglo-American Social Thought* (Philadelphia: Temple University Press, 1979), 171–75.

to Christian doctrine, which, of course, held that the meek, not "the fittest," would inherit the earth.

Perhaps the best way to understand Christian fundamentalism is to classify it with the other great pseudosciences of the early twentieth-century, including Marxism, social Darwinism, and Freudianism. If a pseudoscience is a doctrine that professes to be scientific when it is not, then fundamentalism qualifies as well as psychoanalysis and dialectical materialism. The reason this conclusion may seem surprising is, of course, that fundamentalism maintained the existence of supernatural causes. One might reply that so did its pseudoscientific competitors, with the sole difference being that they pretended that these causes were natural. The idea that we are inevitably destined for a utopian future, as maintained by Marxism and some other systems, can be derived only by disguising the concept of Providence as a law of nature. In place of God we have a God substitute, which, without God, does what a beneficent God would do.

When Morson spent a year at Oxford studying the history of "dialectical materialism," he was struck by the very term.[41] How can materialism be "dialectic," when "dialectic" refers to the forms of human argumentation? It is as odd to speak of dialectical materialism as it would be to speak of aesthetic materialism, juridical materialism, or, for that matter, theological materialism. Dialectical materialism smuggles the nonmaterial into materialism by making thought an aspect of matter itself. The dialectic comes from Hegel, but, as Engels explains, these "laws of thought" are now discovered to be laws of matter. Instead of

41. On the development of dialectical materialism from Marx and (especially) Engels to its formulation in Soviet thought, see the classic study by Gustav A. Wetter, *Dialectical Materialism: A Historical and Systematic Survey of Philosophy in the Soviet Union*, trans. Peter Heath (New York: Praeger, 1963).

foisting these laws of thought on nature, Hegel should have derived them from nature. Matter itself is dialectically constructed,
"nature works dialectically,"[42] and "there could be no question
of building the laws of dialectics into Nature, but of discovering
them in it."[43]

In short, "dialectical laws are really laws of the development
of nature," and therefore these laws of thought are "valid also
for theoretical natural science."[44] Lenin concurred that contradiction, which had been taken as a phenomenon of thought and
category of logic, is to be found "in the very essence of objects."[45]
Soviet physicists were expected to confirm these laws or, at
least, to make no discoveries that would call them into doubt.
By the same token, much of the appeal of the Freudian system
lay in its ability to transform myths into scientific facts. The
fable of Oedipus became a fact of human history in the stage of
the primal horde. In this way, science ceased to be one thing and
meaning another: mythos became logos. Materialists and atheists now had access to the comforts provided by religion and
myth.[46]

The pattern is a common one. Some essentially moral idea
is attributed to nature itself so that science, which deals with
facts rather than values, can discover the desired values as facts.

42. Friedrich Engels, "Socialism: Utopian and Scientific," in Karl Marx and Friedrich Engels, *Basic Writings on Politics and Philosophy*, ed. Lewis S. Feuer (Garden City,
NY: Doubleday, 1959), 85.

43. As cited in Neil Harding, *Leninism* (Durham, NC: Duke University Press,
1996), 229.

44. Frederick Engels, *Dialectics of Nature* (N.p.: Leopard, n.d.), 57–58.

45. As cited in Harding, *Leninism*, 231.

46. We paraphrase the argument of Ernest Gellner, *The Psychoanalytic Movement:
The Cunning of Unreason* (Evanston, IL: Northwestern University Press, 1996). See
also Frederick Crews, *Freud: The Making of an Illusion* (New York: Henry Holt, 2017).

Secular pseudosciences represent the supernatural as a part of nature; religious fundamentalists who claim to be scientific are open in classifying the supernatural as scientific fact. In an age when science enjoys unique prestige, every cockamamie theory will claim to be a science, and genuine scientists who venture outside their discipline to make social or moral pronouncements will represent those pronouncements as part of the science itself. Both will dismiss those who contest these claims as antiscientific ignoramuses. If genuine scientists want to maintain respect for genuinely scientific disciplines, they need to contest the claims of those who purport mistakenly to speak in the name of science. If they do not, they are responsible for public skepticism of scientific claims. How is the average person to distinguish a scientific from a pseudoscientific argument if scientists do not? (We return to this point in chapter 3, when we consider how the global pandemic has raised doubts about the efficacy of scientific claims.)

The claim of certainty leads to some notable characteristics of the fundamentalist mindset. One is a special tone of disdain for the unenlightened fools who have not yet come around. "The typical historian and many anthropologists," Malinowski condescends to explain, "spend most of their theoretical energy and epistemological leisure hours in refuting the concept of scientific law in cultural processes, in erecting watertight compartments for humanism as against science, and in claiming that the historian or anthropologist can conjure up the past by some specific insight or revelation, in short, that he can rely on the grace of God instead of on a methodical system of conscientious work."[47] Historians or anthropologists, of course, would not describe their work using terms like "watertight compart-

47. Malinowski, *Scientific Theory of Culture*, 8.

ments," "conjure up," or "revelation," nor would they profess to "rely on the grace of God": this is the language with which the enlightened speaks about the muddle-headed, who could not possibly have an intelligent objection to enlightened theory. Wilson speaks in much the same tone, and Becker, in one of his final published works that advocated a "market for [human] organs," anticipated the day when reason would triumph and no one would doubt the worthiness of his proposal: "Eventually, the advantages of allowing payment for organs would become obvious. At that point, people will wonder why it took so long to adopt such an obvious and sensible solution to the shortage of organs for transplant."[48] The repetition of the word "obvious" reflects the unshakeable confidence that there could be no rational alternative. The light shineth in the darkness, but the darkness comprehendeth it not (John 1:5).

As it happens, Christian fundamentalists also regard their viewpoint as so obviously true that no reasonable person could reject it. Arthur T. Pierson, author of *Many Infallible Truths*, insists that if Scripture is approached "in a truly impartial and scientific spirit," it cannot be doubted. "If there is one candid doubter living who has faithfully studied the Bible and the evidences of Christianity, he has not yet been found," he maintains. The only reason that the Bible has not convinced Muslims and Catholics, in Pierson's view, is that they are forbidden to read it.[49]

When the claim is that, at long last, after ages of groping in the dark, a hard science has been found, history is divided into

48. Gary S. Becker and Julio J. Elias, "Cash for Kidneys: The Case for a Market for Organs," *Wall Street Journal*, January 18, 2014, https://www.wsj.com/articles/cash-for-kidneys-the-case-for-a-market-for-organs-1389992925.

49. Marsden, *Fundamentalism and American Culture*, 57.

two, just as for religious believers it is split between before and after, BC and AD. For the Soviets, it was before Marx and after (a form of dating Aldous Huxley parodied in *Brave New World* where events begin in 632 AF—that is, After Ford).[50] Night becomes day. "Just as Darwin discovered the law of development of organic nature," Engels explains, "so Marx discovered the law of development of human history: the simple fact hitherto concealed by an overgrowth of ideology."[51] "Hitherto concealed": the truth became visible at a single moment and everything changed.

The propositions of any true science are open to disconfirmation, but fundamentalist systems, even when they claim to be sciences, are not. As Karl Popper famously remarked, they preclude "falsification." The possibility of counterevidence is ruled out in principle. Whether a predicted event happens or does not happen, the system claims confirmation. For a Marxist-Leninist, the very fact that an objection differs from Marxism-Leninism proves it is wrong, inasmuch as Marxism-Leninism is itself the standard of truthfulness. Observations deceive, but dialectical materialism does not. If genetics, or the chemical theory of resonance (a molecule can resonate between two configurations), contradict Lenin, then they are wrong.[52] Both Marxism-Leninism and Freudianism can always explain objections as coming from a tainted source, whether a bourgeois with a stake in the capitalist system, or someone who does not want to admit the painful truth.

50. Aldous Huxley, *Brave New World* (New York: Harper & Row, 1946), 2.

51. As cited in *The Macmillan Book of Social Science Quotations*, ed. David L. Sills and Robert K. Merton (New York: Macmillan, 1991), 59.

52. See Gustav A. Wetter, *Dialectical Materialism: A Historical and Systematic Survey of Philosophy in the Soviet Union*, trans. Peter Heath (New York: Praeger, 1963). On genetics, see 455–69; on resonance and chemistry, see 432–36.

Far from escaping the notice of adherents, this aspect of the system appeals to them as one of its greatest strengths. Since nothing can prove it false, it must be true. In his classic account of his years as a member of the Communist Party, Arthur Koestler remarks that his acceptance of Communism did not resemble the acceptance of any other fact or theory he had ever experienced. "To say that one had 'seen the light' is a poor description of the mental rapture which only the convert knows (regardless of what faith he has been converted to)," he explains. "The new light seems to pour from all directions across the skull; the whole universe falls into pattern like the stray pieces of a jigsaw puzzle assembled by magic at one strike."[53] Above all, doubt becomes a thing of the past. The world is divided into those who have accepted the truth and those benighted souls, on whom one looks down with pity or contempt, living "in dismal ignorance in the tasteless, colorless world of those who *don't know.*"[54]

Koestler is most illuminating when describing how precisely he learned to handle counterevidence or contradiction. When, as a novice, he pointed out that the Party newspaper, for which he worked, had published complete falsehoods against the Social Democrats (then called "Social Fascists"), the editor, with "a tolerant" smile, replied that Koestler still had "the mechanistic outlook" and must learn to think "dialectically," a process that revealed what was really going on behind merely observable facts.[55] In Party terms, he had to learn to discover what was "objectively" happening.[56]

53. "Arthur Koestler," in *The God That Failed*, ed. Richard Crossman (New York: Harper & Row, 1949), 23.

54. "Arthur Koestler," 23.

55. "Arthur Koestler," 34.

56. This use of the term "objectively" puzzles the noninitiate, who, as a first step, might translate it as "subjectively."

Gradually, Koestler learned to distrust his "mechanistic pre-occupation with facts" and instead regard the world "in the light of dialectical interpretation. It was a satisfactory and indeed a blissful state. Once you had assimilated the technique you were no longer disturbed by facts; they automatically . . . fell into their proper place."[57] Harder than handling inconvenient facts was dealing with situations when the infallible Party abruptly reversed itself and declared what had just been false to be true. In such cases, Koestler recalls, we groped in our memory for traces of former thoughts "which would prove to ourselves that we had always held the required opinion."[58] Koestler memorably concludes that, as one gained experience at adapting to changes in the Party line, it all became "rather like the game of the Queen of Hearts [in *Alice in Wonderland*], in which the hoops moved about the field and the balls were live hedgehogs. With this difference, that when . . . the Queen shouted 'Off with his head,' the order was executed in earnest."[59]

At times, the appeal of certainty is primarily moral: those who do not accept the revelation are not so much ignorant as evil. There are the saved and the lost, the pure and the tainted. In such cases, there may or may not be a comprehensive interpretive system. By the same token, there are fundamentalisms, like market fundamentalism, that do not offer a moral sorting. In the case of Bolshevism, which professed both kinds of certainty, good was *defined* as what the Party wanted—there was no "objective" standard of good and evil outside of class interest—and so anyone who deviated from the Party line was automatically evil for that reason alone. In Plato's *Euthyphro*, Socrates asks whether the gods love piety because it is pious or

57. "Arthur Koestler," 34.
58. "Arthur Koestler," 50.
59. "Arthur Koestler," 48.

whether something is pious simply because the gods love it—
so that if the gods loved murder that would automatically make
murder pious. The Bolsheviks chose the latter view: something
is moral simply because the Party, as the agent of history, wants
to do it.

Religious and secular fundamentalisms that combine both
certainties often add an element of urgency as well. In religious
terms, they tend to apocalypticism; in secular, to what prerevolutionary Russians called "revolutionism." In the last days, or
when the Revolution has triumphed, all will be made clear:
"Now we see as through a glass darkly, but then face to face"
(1 Cor. 13:12)—and there will be a last judgment separating the
saved and the damned, the proletariat and the bourgeoisie, the
oppressors and the oppressed. There are no agnostics at Armageddon or waverers at the revolution. The closer one draws to
the end, the less middle ground remains.

Negative Fundamentalism

"Hm . . . what you've just said is a 'commonplace in reverse.'"
   "What? What do you mean by that?"
   "I'll tell you: to say that education is beneficial, for
instance, that's a commonplace; but to say that education is
injurious, that's a commonplace in reverse. There's more style
about it, so to say, but in reality it's one and the same."

   —IVAN TURGENEV, FATHERS AND CHILDREN[60]

Fundamentalism sometimes appears in reverse. "Negative fundamentalists," as we might call them, share with their positive
counterparts the assumption that knowledge, to be real, must

---

60. Ivan Turgenev, *Fathers and Sons*, ed. Ralph E. Matlaw (New York: Norton,
1966), 103.

be certain, like mathematics or physics, but they deny that such knowledge is possible. Both agree that it is all or nothing—one affirming "all" and the other "nothing."

Morson once witnessed a prominent scholar who, in a matter of months, shifted from a long-held adherence to behaviorism to an uncompromising affirmation of radical relativism in truth, value, and meaning. The months of indecision included a wavering between one extreme and the other, but there was never a moment of an in-between position in which, let us say, knowledge was less than certain but could, in some circumstances, be reasonably reliable. Reading an article whose author remarked that, as is often the case with contradictory extremes, the truth is somewhere in the middle, this scholar observed, "That is just what I don't believe. The truth is never in the middle." That, in a nutshell, is the fundamentalist mindset.

In their study *In Praise of Doubt: How to Have Convictions Without Becoming a Fanatic*, Peter Berger and Anton Zijderveld observe that "relativism and fundamentalism are two sides of the same coin . . . in every fundamentalist there's a relativist waiting to be liberated, and in every relativist there's a fundamentalist waiting to be reborn."[61] Negative fundamentalism is entirely different from skepticism. Skeptics might argue that, since science is done by human beings, whose thinking is shaped by cultural presuppositions of which they are unaware, one sometimes needs a sociological perspective on scientific disciplines. Negative fundamentalists regard such a formulation as insufficiently rigorous, if not cowardly, something like the way the Soviets viewed agnostics as those lacking the courage to be atheists. They will rather say, as one sociologist does, that "the natural world has a small or non-existent role in the con-

61. Berger and Zijderveld, *In Praise of Doubt*, 73.

struction of knowledge."[62] Indeed, they drop "small" and keep *what?* "non-existent," as literary theorists are wont to do.

In his book on the nature of science and pseudoscience, *Nonsense on Stilts*, Massimo Pigliucci asks in response: Should one really say that the difference between Copernican and Ptolemaic astronomy is *only* cultural? "Could it really be that the *fact* that the earth rotates around the sun, and not the other way around, played 'a small or non-existent role' in the acceptance and endurance of Copernicus's theory?"[63] Pigliucci goes on to cite a number of thinkers who have argued that "fact" is always relative to a cultural framework, and that objective fact as Pigliucci understands it plays little or no role, and should play little or no role.[64]

Whether one is a positive or a negative fundamentalist, there is no virtue in moderation or indecision. Packer chooses as an epigraph for one chapter: "And Elijah wrote unto all the people, and said, How long halt ye between two opinions? If the Lord be God, follow him" (1 Kings 18:21).[65] Two characters in Dostoevsky's *The Possessed* share their admiration of a passage from the book of Revelation: "I know thy works, thou art neither cold nor hot; I would thou wert cold or hot. So then because thou art lukewarm, I will spue thee out of my mouth" (Rev. 3:15–16).

62. As cited in Massimo Pigliucci, *Nonsense on Stilts: How to Tell Science from Bunk* (Chicago: University of Chicago Press, 2010), 255. Berger and Zijderveld also regard "doubt" (skepticism) as entirely different from "relativism" (negative fundamentalism).

63. Pigliucci, *Nonsense on Stilts*, 255.

64. See also Quentin Skinner, "Introduction: The Return of Grand Theory," in *The Return of Grand Theory in the Human Sciences*, ed. Quentin Skinner (Cambridge: Cambridge University Press, 1997), 1–20.

65. Packer, *Fundamentalism*, 169.

Pierre Bezukhov, the hero of Tolstoy's *War and Peace*, is never lukewarm. Like fundamentalists of both types, he presumes that either knowledge is absolutely certain, or everything is absolutely relative. He alternates between these two possibilities as enthusiastic acceptance of a philosophical system yields, under pressure of some fact or emotional experience it cannot accommodate, to its opposite. Pierre never endorses a system as merely probable, or tries to patch up a system when it falters. No, he falls into profound despair. "They executed Louis XVI because *they* said he was dishonorable and a criminal," he thinks on one such occasion, "and they were right from their point of view, just as right as those who died a martyr's death for him and canonized him. Then Robespierre [in turn] was executed for being a despot. Who is right, and who is to blame? No one. . . . And is it worth tormenting oneself when one has only a moment to live in comparison to eternity?"[66]

Freemasonry, the mystical symbolism of which promises to answer all questions, revives Pierre: "He now felt only too glad to be delivered from his own free will and to submit to those who knew the indubitable truth."[67] But Pierre loses his faith in this system, too, after he gives a controversial speech to his fellow Masons. Curiously, he is shaken not by those who disagree with him, but by those who agree but not perfectly, and what certainty can there be if people cannot even agree on what they agree on? "At this point, Pierre was struck by the endless variety of men's minds, which prevents a truth from ever appearing the

66. Leo Tolstoy, *War and Peace*, trans. Ann Dunnigan (New York: Signet, 1968), 389.

67. Tolstoy, *War and Peace*, 436.

same to any two persons. . . . Pierre again found himself in that state of depression he so dreaded."[68]

Pierre at last achieves wisdom and contentment when this endless variety ceases to bother him. He takes for granted that only imperfect knowledge is possible and delights in the very variety of minds and perspective that fundamentalists find so disturbing. Pierre now recognizes "the impossibility of changing a person's [most basic] convictions by words" and acknowledges "the possibility of every person thinking, feeling and seeing things his own way. This legitimate individuality of every person's views . . . now became the basis of the sympathy he felt for people and the interest he took in them."[69]

Sympathy for, and interest in, those who differ: this is the very opposite of fundamentalism.

Fundamentalist Criterion #2: The Perspicuity of Truth

The Christian fundamentalists believed in the "perspicuity" of truth and of Scripture: both the natural world and the Bible are readily intelligible to the human mind. For those who do not blind themselves, the world is there to be known and nothing stands in the way.

If that were not the case, how could we be certain? We would be immersed in skeptical doubts about the reliability of knowledge.[70] For both secular and Christian fundamentalists, a line

---

68. Tolstoy, 538–39.

69. Tolstoy, 1323.

70. In fact, Midrash, which also proceeds from the assumptions that Scripture is perfectly consistent, free of error, and addressed to people of today, differs from fundamentalism in that it presumes that the Bible speaks cryptically. In Midrash,

of argument extending from John Locke to Kant posed a threat. To simplify: the threat lay in the idea that we do not experience the world directly—rather, we sense impressions presumably produced by external objects but which are themselves experiences in our mind. There is no guarantee that these impressions are accurate, and, what is more, it appears that the mind shapes the world it sees. Hume further argued that we never actually observe the "causal nexus" between happenings; we infer it from their constant conjunction. It is therefore less than certain. Kant resolved Hume's paradoxes with his "Copernican revolution," in which we always see the world in terms that the mind necessarily imposes on it, including space, time, and causation itself. We see only phenomena, not "noumena," or things in themselves.

The argument is actually a lot more complicated, but this summary should indicate why those who believed in the utter perspicuity of the world might find it disturbing.

The Christian fundamentalists relied on Bacon's confidence in induction and, in particular, Thomas Reid's "Common Sense" philosophy. In his *Life of Johnson*, James Boswell tells a story that has since become famous:

> After we came out of church, we stood some time talking together of Bishop Berkeley's ingenious sophistry to prove the non-existence of matter, and that everything in the universe is merely ideal. I observed, that though we are satisfied that his doctrine is not true, it is impossible to refute it. I shall never forget the alacrity with which Johnson answered, striking his foot with mighty force against a large stone, till he

---

then, apparent obscurity does not compromise inerrancy. See Kugel, *How to Read the Bible*, 673.

rebounded from it, "I refute it *thus*." This was a stout exemplification of . . . the *original principles* of Reid and Beattie, without admitting which, we can no more argue in metaphysicks, than we can argue in mathematicks without axioms. To me it is inconceivable how Berkeley can be answered by pure reasoning.[71]

Boswell discovers in this "argument appealing to the stone" (*argumentum ad lapidem*), as some have called it, an "exemplification" of the ideas of Reid and other Common Sense philosophers, who appealed to practice. "No man seeks a reason for believing what he sees or feels; and, if he did, it would be difficult to find one," Reid observes. "But, though he can give no reason for believing his senses, his belief remains as firm as if it were grounded on demonstration." We can be certain of what the principles of common sense tell us: "To reason against any of these kinds of evidence is absurd; nay, to reason for them is absurd. They are first principles; and such fall not within the province of reason, but of common sense."[72]

Marx also invokes practice to refute radical skepticism, while Lenin devotes his *Materialism and Empirio-Criticism* to rejecting any "idealist" philosophy questioning our direct access to things in themselves. He summarily dismisses any argument that we experience only impressions of objects, ideas of objects, or symbols of objects, as he dismisses any observation suggesting that we see not the world, but the world in so far as it conforms

71. As cited in Douglas Lane Patey, "Johnson's Refutation of Berkeley: Kicking the Stone Again," in *Journal of the History of Ideas* 47, no. 1 (January–March, 1986): 139, from *Boswell's Life of Johnson*, vol. 1, ed. G. B. Hill, rev. L. F. Powell, (Oxford: Oxford University Press, 1935), 471.

72. As cited in Harriet A. Harris, *Fundamentalism and Evangelicals* (Oxford: Oxford University Press, 2008), 104.

to our mind.[73] As Gustav Wetter, the authoritative historian of Soviet dialectical materialism, points out, Lenin repeatedly confuses materialism with realism, the idea that there is an external world independent of ourselves, which any Kantian could accept.[74] Nevertheless, Lenin's theory became the unchallengeable basis of Soviet science and philosophy. In his *Dialectical and Historical Materialism*, Stalin explains that Soviet philosophy insists on the uncompromised knowability of the world and so is "contrary to idealism, which . . . does not believe in the authenticity of our knowledge, does not recognize objective truth, and holds that the world is full of 'things in themselves' that can never be known to science."[75] This way of thinking is what led to the temporary rejection of chemical "resonance" (since there is no single configuration to know) and quantum mechanics (for a variety of reasons).

But how can one be so sure that one is sure? Can there be a firm foundation for knowledge, as the great seventeenth-century rationalists tried to establish? Perhaps there is a starting point resembling mathematical axioms, a beginning that cannot be doubted, the role that Descartes assigned to his "cogito"?

Descartes maintained that "I can establish as a general rule that things I perceive very clearly and distinctly are true."[76] "Truth," wrote William Blake, "can never be told so as to be

73. V. I. Lenin, *Materialism and Empirio-Criticism* (Peking: Foreign Languages Press, 1972).

74. See "The Theory of Matter" in Gustav Wetter, *Dialectical Materialism: A Historical and Systematic Survey of Philosophy in the Soviet Union*, trans. Peter Heath (New York: Praeger, 1963), 280–309.

75. As cited in Wetter, *Dialectical Materialism*, 283–4.

76. René Descartes, "Meditations on First Philosophy," in *Discourse on the Method and Meditations on First Philosophy*, ed. David Weissman (New Haven, CT: Yale University Press, 1996), 71.

understood, and not be believ'd."[77] There are some things that no one who, to use Aristotle's phrase, is not "defending a thesis at all costs," would doubt. In Spinoza's view, "he who has a true idea, simultaneously knows he has a true idea, and cannot doubt of the truth of the thing perceived. . . . Even as light displays both itself and darkness, so is truth a standard both of itself and falsity. [T]ruth is its own standard."[78] For Spinoza, the idea of a "self-verifying truth"—truth as its own standard—is crucial, because without it justification faces an infinite regress.

We can now appreciate both the importance and the lineage of the Christian fundamentalist idea that Scripture is self-verifying. In religion, Packer explains, "there are three distinct authorities to which final appeal can be made—Holy Scripture, Church tradition, or Christian reason; that is to say, Scripture as interpreted by itself; Scripture as interpreted (and in some measure amplified) by official ecclesiastical sources; and Scripture as evaluated in terms of extra-biblical principles by individual Christian men."[79] Catholics choose the second, liberal Protestants the third, and fundamentalists, like Packer himself, the first. They regard Scripture as *autopiston*, "authoritative in itself."[80] In so doing, Packer claims to follow the basic idea of the Reformation that, "to learn the mind of God, one must consult His written Word. What Scripture says, God says. The Bible is inspired in the sense of being word-for-word God-given. It is . . . both complete (*sufficient*) and comprehensible (*perspicuous*);

77. William Blake, "The Marriage of Heaven and Hell," in *English Romantic Poetry*, vol. 1, ed. Harold Bloom (Garden City, NY: Doubleday, 1963), 61.

78. Benedict de Spinoza, "Ethics," in *The Chief Works of Benedict de Spinoza*, trans. E. H. Elwes, vol. 2 (New York: Dover, 1951), 115.

79. Packer, *Fundamentalism*, 46.

80. Packer, 121.

that is . . . it contains the principles of its own interpretation within itself."[81] Whether religious or secular, fundamentalists share a deep faith that the mind is adequate for knowing the world; the two are perfectly fitted to each other. For Descartes, the absolute fit of mind and world was insured by the fact that God, who is perfect, cannot be a deceiver, "since the light of nature teaches us that fraud and deception necessarily proceed from some defect."[82]

Here we see one of the most basic differences between hedgehogs and foxes. For hedgehogs, it is just obvious that intelligent people who have cleared their mind of prejudices can reason their way to truth. They must proceed step by step, generation after generation, and they will learn the nature of the world ever more comprehensively and surely. There can be no reason in principle why something cannot be known.

Foxes, by contrast, are profoundly skeptical of the mind. Not only are they attentive to its many cognitive biases and our tendency to self-deception, but they also doubt whether there is a perfect fit between it and the world it examines. Why should there be? Unless one accepts Descartes's reasoning, that God insured that fit, what guarantees it?

God tells Job he simply cannot understand ultimate questions, and Job at last humbles himself. "Therefore have I uttered that I understood not; things too wonderful, which I knew not," he concludes, "wherefore I abhor myself and repent in dust and ashes" (Job 42:3–6). Greek tragedy concurs that we should be modest about our intellectual abilities, as Oedipus, who in his hubris is completely confident in his powers of reasoning,

81. Packer, 47.
82. Descartes, "Meditations on First Philosophy," 83.

learns. The ways of the gods are beyond our ken. Five plays of Euripides end with variations on the following lines:

> The shapes of divinity are many,
> And the gods fulfill many things surprisingly.
> What was expected has not been accomplished,
> And for the unexpected god found a way.
> That is how this affair turned out.[83]

Darwinism also gives good reason for what H. G. Wells called "skepticism of the instrument." When one examines the human mind after studying evolution and comparative anatomy, Wells explains, "a lot of very natural preconceptions" about the powers of human logic are "blown clean out of one's mind. . . . When you have realized to the marrow, that all the physical organs of man and all his physical structure are what they are through a series of adaptations and approximations . . . and that this is true also of his brain and of his instincts and of many of his mental predispositions, you are not going to take his thinking apparatus unquestioningly as being in any way mysterious or better" but will accept their "provisional character."[84] In short, "*the forceps of our mind are clumsy forceps, and crush the truth a little in taking hold of it.*"[85] How ironic, then, that some hedgehogs erect their system on a Darwinian basis!

If the truth is so obvious, why does everyone not agree? We have already seen Gary Becker's confidence that someday

83. As translated in Francis M. Dunn, *Tragedy's End: Innovation and Closure in Euripidean Drama* (New York: Oxford University Press, 1966), 17. The five plays ending this way are *Alcestis, Medea, Andromache, Helen,* and *The Bacchae.*

84. H. G. Wells, "Scepticism of the Instrument," portion of a speech read at the Oxford Philosophical Society, November 8, 1903, included as the appendix to Wells, *A Modern Utopia* (Lincoln: University of Nebraska Press, 1967), 378.

85. Wells, "Scepticism of the Instrument," 382.

people will eventually all agree with him, and his wonder that anyone ever doubted. But postponing agreement to the future does not really solve the problem of why people do not recognize the perspicuous truth now. No one argues about the deductions of Euclidian geometry, so why don't they accept what fundamentalists regard as self-evident or as "science"?

Almost all solutions to this dilemma are variants on one idea: people would see if their judgment were not clouded. Spinoza, who was keenly aware of the dilemma, maintained that careless thinkers allow imagination and prejudice to affect their conclusions; he concluded that the project of knowledge must be to cleanse and purify the mind itself. Many other thinkers resort to "prejudice," which comes in many guises: tradition, conservatism, self-interest, mental disturbance, or that catch-all for beliefs one finds repellent, "superstition."

For Christian fundamentalists, the issue is of the utmost importance. If Scripture is not perspicuous to all, what becomes of the core Protestant argument that, since Scripture is accessible to ordinary people, no mediating ecclesiastical authority is needed to grasp its essential tenets? The Christian fundamentalist Charles Blanchard, who regards it as "impossible for a rational person to disbelieve it [Christianity]," attributes disbelief to the pernicious influence of "ministers and teachers of theology," moral laxity, and the influence of tobacco and alcohol: "It is well known that the critics of our time have been usually men who have poisoned their nervous system and injured their minds by the use of narcotic and other poisons."[86] Ultimately, the problem was that the twentieth century was "an age of insanity."[87]

86. As cited in Marsden, *Fundamentalism and American Culture*, 220.
87. As cited in Marsden, 219.

Some fundamentalists solve the dilemma in advance. They explain from the outset why they are bound not to be accepted except by a few well-trained initiates. If one follows Freud's logic, nonacceptance of psychoanalysis is just what the theory itself predicts and is therefore, instead of a strike against it, yet another vindication of it. The best-known example of this logic, which turns objections into proofs, is the Marxist idea of "false consciousness," a phrase that belongs to Engels: "Ideology [the thought of the dominant class] is a process accomplished by the so-called thinker consciously, indeed, but with a false consciousness. The real motives impelling him remain unknown to him, otherwise it would not be an ideological process at all."[88]

One can always resort to "false consciousness" to parry any objection. Because this sort of answer necessarily posits an elite that can see through the mystifications bedeviling others, it can promise a special sense of superiority. Only those who have accepted Marxism see things as they truly are. Once one does, one experiences the "mental rapture" Koestler describes: "The whole universe falls into pattern like the stray pieces of a jigsaw puzzle assembled by magic at one strike."[89]

Fundamentalist Criterion #3: Foundational Text or Revelation

Fundamentalists often profess belief in an inerrant text or revelation.[90] In the case of rather pacific, secular fundamentalisms, this criterion may be the most important one. Typically, the

88. From Engels to Franz Mehring, July 14, 1893, Marxists Internet Archive, https://www.marxists.org (accessed August 18, 2020).

89. "Arthur Koestler," 23.

90. Is the US Constitution one such inerrant text? While we certainly don't claim to be legal scholars, it is natural to wonder how fundamentalism impacts the law. If some consider the word of God to be sacrosanct, why not the word of the founding

movement recognizes that the sacred text has been distorted, overlaid with false and self-interested readings, or suffered the depredations of criticism that deprive it of its essence. That is why fundamentalism is needed: a reformation, like Luther's, demands a return to the original dispensation. Much as Protestants rejected the authority of church interpretation in favor of direct reading of the Bible itself, so Jewish Karaites cast aside the rabbinic tradition of "oral law" as recorded in Talmud, and accepted only the "written law" of Torah.

The founder of a purported social science may be seen as authoritative in this way. Some—by no means all—Freudians treat Freud's writings as holy writ. In Marxist-Leninist countries, inerrancy is indeed attributed to the writings of Marx, Engels, Lenin, and, outside the Soviet Union, whoever has played the role of local founder (Mao, Kim Il Sung). The present ruler (Stalin, for a quarter century) may be added. That is the significance of the Stalinist slogan "Stalin is Lenin today." If Stalin is the Lenin of today, then his writings could not be mistaken. When Stalin wrote his 1950 essay on language "Marxism

---

fathers? In "The Originalists" (*New York Times Magazine*, March 1, 2020), Emily Bazelon lays out recent debates in an especially insightful way, arguing that originalism in the law is a relatively recent concept, dating only to the aftermath of Roe v. Wade. She asks: Should "judges adhere to the meaning of the Constitution as people understood it when it was ratified?" Yes, said Justice Scalia, adding that originalism should focus not on the intent of the framers, but instead, on the Constitution's original public meaning. Yet, when asked about Justice Thomas's philosophy as a fellow originalist, Scalia said, "I am an originalist, but I am not a nut." On the other hand, Bazelon writes that Scalia also said that "you would have to be an idiot" to conceive of the Constitution as a "living organism." At the other end of the political spectrum, Bazelon reports that Justice Breyer has stated that the Constitution should be placed in context to weigh its underlying purpose and the consequence of different interpretations. To Breyer, "the purpose of the law is to work, to work for the people" (26–33, 46–47).

and Questions of Linguistics," not just linguists, but all disciplines, including hard sciences, devoted conferences and issues of journals to exploring the significance of its revelations. So holy were the texts of Lenin and Stalin that in the 1930s people were imprisoned for misquotations—indeed, for misprints—of their works![91]

Aron Katsenelinboigen—a former colleague of ours at the University of Pennsylvania who once served on the top Soviet economic planning committee—explains that he memorized Marx's work so that, whatever he might want to say, he could find some quotation to justify it. The Sovietologist Wolfgang Leonhard, educated to be a top Communist official and placed in what became the German Democratic Republic, remembers the period when articles not only had to cite the Marxist classics frequently, but also had to follow the "60-30-10" rule: 60 percent of the quotations were to be from Stalin, 30 percent from Lenin, and 10 percent from Marx and Engels. Banners with images of these four sages were ubiquitous.[92]

As Christian fundamentalists rejected Darwinism when it contradicted Scripture, so, as we have seen, the Soviets rejected a variety of scientific theories in biology, chemistry, and physics when they seemed incompatible with the philosophy of the founders. Those who wished such theories to be accepted knew it was insufficient to present scientific evidence for them; they also had to find some way to reconcile them with inerrant texts. For Christians, Jews, Muslims, and Marxists, it is easy to identify

91. See Andrei Sinyavsky, *Soviet Civilization: A Cultural History*, trans. Joanne Turnbill and Nikolai Formozov (New York: Little, Brown and Company, 1990), 112.

92. Wolfgang Leonhard, *Child of the Revolution*, trans. C. M. Woodhouse (Chicago: Henry Regnery, 1958). Morson remembers the 60-30-10 from Leonhard's undergraduate course on Soviet history given at Yale in 1967.

sacred texts, but some Asian "synthetic fundamentalisms," as scholars have called them, have had to create equivalents to the New Testament, the Torah, the Koran, and *Das Kapital.* As the authors of *Strong Religion* explain, adherents tended to "select and canonize a corpus of sacred texts, transforming epics and poems and other open-ended genres into the stuff of 'fundamental,' 'inerrant' Scriptures."[93]

For a text to be taken as inerrant, there must be something that marks it off from all other human, therefore fallible, productions. For the religious, of course, the claim is divine revelation: inspiration from (or even dictation by) the Holy Ghost. The Koran is the word of God that the archangel Gabriel dictated to Muhammed. In Jewish "wisdom literature," Torah and Wisdom existed before Creation.[94] In Proverbs, Wisdom explains, "The Lord possessed me in the beginning of his way, before his works of old. I was set up from everlasting, from the beginning, or ever the earth was. . . . When he prepared the heavens, I was there; when he set a compass upon the face of the earth . . . then I was by him, as one brought up with him, and I was daily his delight, rejoicing always before him" (Prov. 8:22–30). In secular fundamentalisms, the founding text is usually held to be "science," a word used to mean not a continually

---

93. Almond, Appleby, and Sivan, *Strong Religion,* 16.

94. According to "Judaism: The Written Law—Torah" in the Jewish Virtual Library, https://www.jewishvirtuallibrary.org/the-written-law-torah (accessed August 18, 2020): "In rabbinic literature, it was taught that the Torah was one of the six or seven things created prior to the creation of the world. According to Eliezer ben Yose the Galilean, for 974 generations before the creation of the world the Torah lay in God's bosom and joined the ministering angels in song. Simeon ben Lakish taught that the Torah preceded the world by 2,000 years and was written in black fire upon white fire. Akiva called the Torah 'the precious instrument by which the world was created.' Rav said that God created the world by looking into the Torah as an architect builds a palace by looking into blueprints. It was also taught that God took council with the Torah before He created the world."

improving body of knowledge but, on the contrary, an unchanging guarantor of Truth. So understood, the "science" of secular fundamentalists is essentially mystical. Worship of, and confidence in, the founding text or revelation comes in degrees.

It will be appreciated why the "higher criticism" could be so threatening. It treats the sacred text as a *merely* human creation, rife with errors and therefore not to be relied on for ultimate truth. For Marxists and other secular fundamentalists, the ongoing process of science takes the place of the higher criticism; if scientific knowledge changes enough, the sacred texts may turn out to have been wrong. Perhaps Marx and Freud were just men of their times, with all the limitations that implies? Continuing discoveries, at odds with a supposedly final revelation of truth, force a choice between science, supposedly revered, and the "scientific" revelation. In the long run, science divided against itself cannot stand.

Part 2) Alternatives

Assertion and Dialogue

In 1524, the great humanist Desiderius Erasmus wrote a treatise, addressed to Martin Luther, questioning several of Luther's "assertions" (as Luther called them), especially Luther's denial of free will. In 1525, Luther responded. The resulting argument, which they continued to develop, stands as one of the great exchanges in Western thought. For our purposes, it defines two styles of thinking.[95]

---

95. To make a similar point, Berger and Zijderveld cite an exchange between Sebastian Castello and Calvin about toleration and freedom of conscience. See Berger and Zijderveld, *In Praise of Doubt*, 100–102.

The three criteria we employ in defining "fundamentalist" apply to Luther and, indeed, it would be hard to find a better example of what we have in mind. If Luther is the perfect hedgehog, Erasmus is the model fox. Erasmus's way of arguing, not just his specific arguments, illustrates an important alternative to fundamentalist thinking.[96]

Luther and Erasmus differ on several issues. For one thing, Luther expresses an absolute confidence that Scripture is perfectly clear. But Erasmus suggests that we cannot be too certain about the meaning of certain obscure passages. And he had special authority to say so, since he in fact had edited and translated the New Testament, a process that required him to consult differing texts and develop sophisticated methods of textual criticism. It was Erasmus's version of the New Testament that served as the basis for Luther's translation into German and, eventually, for the King James Bible.

To Erasmus, Scripture is far from perspicuous. Observing to Luther that "Holy Scripture contains numerous passages which have puzzled many, without ever anyone succeeding in completely clarifying them," Erasmus suggests that the ineradicable obscurity may even be God's way of inducing us to venerate "Him in mystic silence."[97] Scripture, he advises, "contains secrets into which God does not want us to penetrate too deeply, because, if we attempt to do so, increasing darkness envelops us."[98] We must appreciate "the unfathomable majesty of divine wisdom and the feebleness of the human mind" and so refrain

96. For a recent study of the controversy, see Michael Massing, *Fatal Discord: Erasmus, Luther, and the Fight for the Western Mind* (New York: Harper Collins, 2018).

97. Erasmus-Luther, *Discourse on Free Will*, trans. Ernst F. Winter (New York: Continuum, 1996), 9.

98. Erasmus-Luther, *Discourse on Free Will*, 8.

from trying "to explain what surpasses the measure of the human mind."[99]   *aha !*

Luther would have none of this. God is one thing, Scripture another. "Nobody doubts that in God many things are hidden of which we know nothing," he argues, "but that there are in Scriptures some things abstruse and not quite plain, was spread by the Sophists, whom you echo, Erasmus. They have never yet produced one article to prove this their madness."[100] Like the twentieth-century Christian fundamentalists, the most Luther will allow is that we may occasionally lack knowledge of "grammatical particulars" and "unknown words," but "this ignorance does not in any way prevent our knowing all the contents of the Scriptures."[101]

This difference points to another, more basic one. Erasmus remains deeply skeptical of the powers of the human mind to discern truth, and he is keenly aware of the tendency of people to leap to conclusions, rule out discrepant evidence, and seek only what confirms prior beliefs: "Whatever they read in Holy Scripture, they distort to serve the opinion to which they have once and for all enslaved themselves . . . they are like those who in the heat of battle turn everything at hand, be it a pitcher or a plate, into a missile."[102] "So great is my dislike of [categorical] assertions," Erasmus concludes, "that I prefer the views of the sceptics wherever the inviolable authority of Scripture and the decision of the Church permit."[103] "A skeptic," Erasmus writes in a second tract responding to Luther, "is not someone who

99. Erasmus-Luther, 8.
100. Erasmus-Luther, 103. While Luther refers to the "Sophists," he seems to actually mean the "Scholastics."
101. Erasmus-Luther, 103.
102. Erasmus-Luther, 7.
103. Erasmus-Luther, 6.

doesn't care to know what is true or false . . . but rather someone who does not make a final decision easily or fight to the
death for his own opinion, but rather accepts as probable what
someone else accepts as certain."[104]

Luther famously replies, "Not to delight in assertions is not
the mark of a Christian heart. . . . Take away assertions and you
take away Christianity."[105] For Luther, a Christian does not
doubt, but firmly knows. "Far be it from Christians to be skeptics," he writes,[106] and by this he means that the rejection of
skepticism should apply not only to sacred writings, but also to
the world in general: "A Christian would rather say this: I am so
against the sentiments of skeptics that . . . I shall not only stead-
fastly adhere to the sacred writing everywhere, and in all parts
of them, and assert them, but I also wish to be as positive as
possible on nonessentials that lie outside Scriptures, because
what is more miserable, than uncertainty."[107] "The Holy Spirit,"
he explains in a much quoted aphorism, "is no skeptic, and
what He has written into our hearts are no doubts or opinions,
but assertions, more certain and more firm than all human experience and life itself."[108]

We arrive now at the core difference between these two sorts
of minds: their opposite understanding of what dialogue, like
the one in which they are engaged, is all about. For Luther, it is
about *assertion,* and he defines "assertion" as "a constant adher-

---

104. In his *Hyperaspistes* (A Defensive Shield, 1526), as cited in the article on
Desiderius Erasmus in *The Stanford Encyclopedia of Philosophy,* https://plato.stanford
.edu/entries/erasmus/ (accessed August 18, 2020).

105. Erasmus-Luther, *Discourse,* 100–101.

106. Erasmus-Luther, 101.

107. Erasmus-Luther, 102.

108. Erasmus-Luther, 103.

ing to and affirming of your position, avowing and defending it, and invincibly persevering in it."[109] One's opponent is simply wrong, wittingly or unwittingly serving Satan, and so Luther begins by telling Erasmus that his defense of free will is "a downright lie."[110] It provoked "disgust, indignation, and contempt, which, if I say so, expresses my judgment of your Diatribe."[111] A different point of view should provoke no other emotions and no other judgment. The only reason even to answer opponents is to change their mind. If that is impossible, and if Erasmus cannot be convinced by the plainest arguments, then, writes Luther, "I am the biggest fool, losing words and time on something clearer than the sun."[112]

For Erasmus, by contrast, an exchange can enlighten both parties. If they approach it in the right spirit and regard their positions as fallible opinions, then they can enter each other's viewpoints and appreciate something they had missed. Adjusting their positions accordingly, they can repeat the process again and again. In Erasmus's view, we need not unwavering "assertions," but provisional conjectures: "Therefore I merely want to analyze and not to judge, to inquire and not to dogmatize. I am ready to learn from anyone who advances something more accurate or more reliable."[113]

A real dialogue can be recognized by a few qualities that are anathema to those who think like Luther. First, statements are recognized as *provisional*, to be revised in light of evidence and

109. Erasmus-Luther, 100–101.
110. Erasmus-Luther, 98.
111. Erasmus-Luther, 98.
112. Erasmus-Luther, 101.
113. Erasmus-Luther, 7.

criticism. Second, *the exchange is a vehicle for arriving at the truth*, not just a way of convincing another of a truth already known. It is a process in which both parties adjust their opinions time and again. This process is valuable in itself, because it generates genuinely new and better ideas the participants could not have arrived at on their own.

Finally, a real dialogue is conducted in a spirit of *concord*. Erasmus expresses "a deep-seated aversion to fighting" and regards the mere hurling of contrary assertions as a fruitless endeavor that harms Christian concord more than it helps piety.[114] Luther, who understands just what sort of exchange Erasmus has in mind, refers contemptuously to this "charitable mind and love of peace."[115] Which did martyrs die for, provisional beliefs or unwavering assertions? "What a clown I would hold a man who does not really believe, nor unwaveringly assert the things he is reproving others with! Why, I would send him to Anticyra!"[116] (Anticyra is a place famous for its hellebore, which was reputed to cure stupidity.) For Luther, real belief entails intolerance. For Erasmus, love of truth demands commitment to open-ended exchange.

A real dialogue of the sort that Luther rejects, and Erasmus seeks, is not just a stopgap answer until firm propositions are available. Like free speech in our time, its value goes beyond mere tolerance. Far from being a paltry compromise, it is, in the uncertain world of human affairs, the most reliable way of reaching better solutions. Provisional and valuable in itself, real dialogue both presumes and promotes mutual understanding and concord.

114. Erasmus-Luther, 6.
115. Erasmus-Luther, 100.
116. Erasmus-Luther, 101.

Alternatives: Just in Case

The philosopher Stephen Toulmin has challenged the dominant tradition of post-Renaissance Western philosophy with respect to knowledge, argumentation, and, especially, ethics. In his view modernity has two distinct sources, usually treated mistakenly as moments of the same process: the humanism of sixteenth-century writers including Erasmus, Montaigne, and Shakespeare, and the rationalism of the great seventeenth-century philosophers, including Descartes, Spinoza, and Leibniz, along with their successors, Holbach, Condorcet, and Bentham.[117]

Contrast Leibniz's sense of the rationality and orderliness of things—he denied it was possible even "to conceive of events which are not regular"—with Montaigne's stress on the contingent, accidental, incongruous, impure, and motley:[118]

> We are all patchwork, and so shapeless and diverse in composition that each bit, each moment, plays its own game. And there is as much difference between us and ourselves as between us and others.[119]

> Not only does the wind of accident move me at will, but, besides, I am moved and disturbed as a result of my own unstable posture . . . I give my soul now one face, now another, according to which direction I turn it. If I speak of

117. Stephen Toulmin, *Cosmopolis: The Hidden Agenda of Modernity* (New York: Free Press, 1990).

118. "God does nothing which is not orderly, and it is not even possible to conceive of events which are not regular." Gottfried Wilhelm Leibniz, *Discourse on Metaphysics, Correspondence with Arnauld, Monadology,* trans. George Montgomery (La Salle, IL: Open Court, 1989), 10.

119. *The Complete Essays of Montaigne,* trans. Donald Frame (Stanford: Stanford University Press, 1965), 244.

myself in different ways, that is because I look at myself in different ways . . . the strangeness of our condition makes it happen that we are often driven to do good by vice itself.[120]

Man, in all things and throughout, is but patchwork and motley.[121]

The "strangeness of our condition" makes any attempt at a purely rational account of ethics, or of anything in human life, hopeless. If the rationalists were the perfect hedgehogs, the humanists instantiated foxiness.

 It was the rationalists who won out and set the agenda for modern thought in philosophy and the sciences. Indeed, their understanding of knowledge and ethics triumphed so thoroughly that it became hard to imagine any other. Judging the rationalist perspective to have arrived at last at a dead end, Toulmin counsels a return to the humanist tradition, which might be adapted to current issues in public policy, ethics, and practical affairs generally. Toulmin recounts the story of how he attended a lecture at the University of Chicago entitled "Is It Rational to Be Reasonable?" and realized that the question underlying his life's work was the reverse: Is it reasonable to be rational?[122]

Ethical reasoning has been misconstrued as an essentially deductive science, ideally resembling Euclidian geometry, but we should consider the alternative tradition of reasoning from lived experience rather than from theoretical axioms. Usually called "casuistry," or case-based reasoning, this alternative understands ethical thought not as what Aristotle called theoreti-

---

120. *Complete Essays of Montaigne*, 242.

121. *Complete Essays of Montaigne*, 511.

122. See Morson, "The Tyranny of Theory," in the *New Criterion* 33, no. 6 (February 2015): 8–13.

cal reasoning (*episteme*), but as something quite different: practical reasoning (*phronesis*). The theoretical view creates what
Toulmin calls "the tyranny of principles," while the practical
allows for a subtle appreciation of complexities beyond the
reach of theoretical abstractions.

Geometry, the ancients' model of theoretical reasoning, allows us, if we reason with sufficient rigor, to reach propositions
that are certain. To understand them is to accept them. True
always and everywhere, they never require revision in light of
circumstances. In recent centuries, physics has served as the
model theoretical discipline, which is why so many putative
social sciences have aspired to resemble it. Otherwise, they
could not claim to reach certain conclusions.

But, in many domains of life, including ethics and all clinical
disciplines, theoretical reasoning is inappropriate. We instead
require practical reasoning, which can reach conclusions that
are true, at best, "on the whole and for the most part" (a favorite
phrase of Aristotle's). Uncertainty and openness to revision
pertain to the very nature of clinical disciplines. Aristotle's
point, which today is difficult even to convey, is that we need
not one but two distinct kinds of reasoning. Practical reasoning
is not, as is often assumed, a temporary, barely adequate, substitute to be used when a hard science has not yet established
itself; it is not like "folk physics" that will be replaced by scientific physics. To the contrary, ethics and clinical professions,
though they may make use of scientific and theoretical knowledge, cannot be reduced to it.

In the view of Aristotle and the casuists, it would be as mistaken to treat practical affairs with theoretical reasoning as the
reverse. Anyone who claimed that a triangle may contain two
right angles "on the whole and on the most part" would not
merely be wrong; he would demonstrate a failure to grasp what

mathematical reasoning is all about. But, by the same token, anyone who looked for an ethical algorithm or a clinical formula would demonstrate a failure to grasp what ethical and clinical reasoning are. "It is evidently equally foolish," Aristotle observes, "to accept probable reasoning from a mathematician and to demand from a rhetorician [someone concerned with practical human affairs] scientific proofs."[123]

The seventeenth-century rationalists and their successors thought otherwise. For them, the only real knowledge was theoretical, or, as we would say today, scientific. In his *Discourse on Method*, Descartes explains that he overcame his youthful fascination with ethnography and history, which deal with mere particularities of a given time and place rather than timeless universal truths. Or, as Descartes's aphorism goes: "History is like foreign travel. It broadens the mind, but it does not deepen it."[124]

When applied to ethics, this perspective led to the presumption that any good ethical theory would be a deductive system. It would yield general principles that, when applied to particular cases, would lead to certain results. Its conclusions would be universal, not dependent on a particular culture; permanent, not just timely or the best solution at a given moment; and not open to endless revision, just as the Pythagorean theorem is not open to revision in the light of experience.

Casuists liked to cite Aristotle's critique of this deductive approach to ethics. To do justice by applying abstract principle or law, Aristotle observes, can sometimes lead to manifestly wrong results. One must then adjust the result in favor of "equity":

---

123. Aristotle, "Nichomachean Ethics," in *The Basic Works of Aristotle*, ed. Richard McKeon (New York: Random House, 1941), 936.

124. Cited in Toulmin, *Cosmopolis*, 33.

A law is a general statement, yet there are cases which it is not possible to cover by a general statement. . . . This does not make [the general statement] a *wrong* law: the error is not in the law, nor in the legislator, but in the nature of the case, the stuff of practical conduct being essentially variable. When the law lays down a general rule, and a later case arises that is an exception to the rule, it is appropriate, where the lawgiver's pronouncement was too unqualified and general, to decide as the legislator himself would decide if he were present on this occasion. . . . The essential nature of "equity" is thus to correct the law in situations where it is defective on account of its generality. . . . Like the leaden rule used by builders on Lesbos, which is not rigid but can be bent to the shape of the stone, a ruling is thus made to fit the circumstances of the particular case.[125]

Casuists knew that laws can fail for any number of reasons. To begin with, any law is formulated with a paradigm case in mind, which means that it applies to some cases "centrally and unambiguously," but to others, distant from the paradigm case, "only marginally or ambiguously."[126] Moreover, no rule can be "self-interpreting," in the way fundamentalist Christians thought the Scriptures were self-interpreting, or the rationalist philosophers regarded some truths as self-verifying. No less important, principles sometimes conflict. Two different principles that may be applied to a given case might point in different directions, and, once more, "the considerations that weigh with

125. We cite the translation appearing in Albert R. Jonsen and Stephen Toulmin, *The Abuse of Casuistry* (Berkeley: University of California Press, 1988), 68. For convenience, and because we are following Toulmin's thought in several works, we refer to Toulmin alone when citing or paraphrasing this coauthored book.

126. Jonsen and Toulmin, *Abuse of Casuistry*, 8.

us . . . in balancing the claims of conflicting principles, are never *written into* the rules themselves."[127] According to casuists, what is required in such situations is not some rule of rules, which is bound to have the same problem. Rather, one needs discretion and *judgment*. Good judgment can be developed only through experience and thoughtful reflection. Young people can be good mathematicians, Aristotle observes, but they have not yet had the opportunity to acquire sufficient experience to have good judgment.

One needs to recognize why experience thoughtfully considered, rather than better theory, is required. To begin with, when dealing with theoretical reasoning we know the general rule with greater certainty than we know any particular case, as a physicist knows the laws of motion better than the motion of any particular object. In ethics and clinical reasoning, by contrast, one can know what is right more surely than one knows any general principle to which one might appeal. The hero of Tolstoy's *Anna Karenina*, Konstantin Levin, knows he can no more allow himself to do some things than he can throw a baby in his arms to the ground. And he is more certain of this than he is of any theory he might invoke to justify that conclusion. That is the difference between Levin and his intellectual brother, Sergey Ivanovich Koznyshev, who always tries to reason down from definitions and general principles—a technique that allows him to win arguments, but not to reach wise conclusions.

The statements of theoretical reasoning depend for their certainty on the fact that they treat ideal cases: the perfect triangle of geometry rather than any particular triangular object, or an ideal physical object in an ideal setting. Theoretical statements

127. Jonsen and Toulmin, 8.

are also universal and atemporal. The Pythagorean theorem, and the laws of physics, hold not just in ancient Greece but always and everywhere. In addition, theoretical statements are necessary. If any proposition deduced from them should prove false, that would prove only that the axioms, or the process of reasoning, contained a flaw.[128]

By contrast, ethical statements and other practical judgments are concrete, temporal, and presumptive. The real sample may not coincide with an expected pattern; a diagnosis may hold for one patient and not another; a recommended course of action may be correct now, but not in a few days. Most important, practical judgments are merely presumptive, not certain. When doctors look at the evidence, draw a conclusion about an illness, and then recommend a course of treatment, they presume that the prescribed course of treatment may not work, in which case they would reassess the situation. In the same way, the best-informed ethical judgment may turn out to be wrong. There is always the possibility of rebuttal, and rebuttability is an essential feature of practical reasoning.

The very goals of theoretical and practical reasoning differ. A case may interest a scientist insofar as it might contribute to theoretical knowledge. There is no rush and no interest in other particulars. But you want your doctor to help here and now. To do so, the doctor must have experience in dealing with many particular patients in a variety of typical and atypical situations. Knowledge of biology is not enough. Physicians learn to recognize complexes of symptoms (syndromes), just as casuists are trained to recognize situations that often present themselves. Both learn a taxonomy. They learn to reason by analogy.

128. We follow the argument in Toulmin, *Cosmopolis*, 5–44; and in Jonsen and Toulmin, *Abuse of Casuistry*, 23–46.

⁊. *Avoiding Extremisms*

So long as we think of ethical decisions theoretically, we face a choice between positive and negative fundamentalism. "Once we accept rules and principles as the heart and soul of ethics," Toulmin observes, "no middle way can be found between absolutism and relativism."[129] It follows that "the deadlock between ethical dogmatists, whose absolute principles admit of no exceptions, and moral relativists, who see no room for anything but local custom and individual taste, is inescapable so long as we remain on the theoretical level; but in practical medicine this deadlock is easily resolved."[130] Much as in clinical medicine, decisions are neither necessary consequences of biology, nor merely matters of personal taste, so "by taking a practical view of ethics we can avoid the unpalatable choice between a strict 'moral geometry' and the appeal to 'personal preferences.'"[131]

If extreme positions are the only options, disagreements become unresolvable. In a democracy, one needs to compromise, which means not everything can be a matter of principle allowing no middle way, as is all too often the case today. The same may be true of addressing too many issues as matters of fundamental rights.[132] When issues are matters of principles or fundamental rights, those who disagree are simply evil, and people are driven from extreme to greater extreme. Moderates will be called unprincipled (or worse), so the dynamic, once underway, becomes almost irresistible. Call it the vicious

129. Jonsen and Toulmin, 6.

130. Jonsen and Toulmin, 43.

131. Jonsen and Toulmin, 44.

132. On the dangers of excessive "rights talk," see Mary Ann Glendon, *Rights Talk: The Impoverishment of Political Discourse* (New York: Free Press, 1991).

circle of noble principles: once ensnared in this circle, society becomes hopelessly riven, and the preconditions of a democratic polity are lost. As we discuss in chapter 3 on politics, we believe that danger is clear and present during this age of rabid factionalism.

But it doesn't have to be that way. The essential feature of casuistry, and of practical reasoning generally, is that judgments are presumptive and revisable. They are matters of *opinion*— informed opinion, we hope, but nevertheless opinion—not of infallible moral logic. There may therefore be honest and conscientious disagreement.

Alternatives: The Wisdom of the Novel

When the logic of rationalism came to dominate philosophy, the tradition of casuistry did not disappear. Rather, it found another home: the realist novel. Consider, for instance, Daniel Defoe, often considered the first English novelist. His novels grew out of what we would today call advice columns in the *Athenian Mercury*, an explicitly casuistical periodical. People would write in with difficult moral problems, much as they would write to advice columnists today.[133]

Often enough, these letters pose cases in the first-person singular. Even if all the letters were genuine, which is doubtful, it would have been possible to transcribe them into third-person accounts, as in other casuistical cases, but then one would have had a summary rather than a plea with personal immediacy. The result was an enormous abundance of detail, even more than usual in casuistical presentations that tried to include all

---

133. See G. A. Starr, *Defoe and Casuistry* (Princeton, NJ: Princeton University Press, 1971). See also the references to Defoe in Toulmin, *Cosmopolis*, 134, 135, 148.

relevant circumstances.[134] And the author approached what would soon be recognizable as a novelistic character or narrator.

If one reads Defoe's classic novel *Moll Flanders*, a first-person narrative, one can readily see it as a series of cases of conscience that arise for the same person.[135] The heroine justifies morally questionable actions, and it often takes some thinking to identify why her justification fails. Sometimes, the key fact is one that her narrative has mentioned, but that her justification overlooks. For the reader, the story becomes a moral exercise.

As we shall have occasion to observe, every literary genre depends on enabling assumptions about human life. If you don't believe in heroism, you don't write epics, and saints' lives presume there is such a thing as sanctity. If you think events usually develop gradually without significant moments deciding everything, you don't write adventure stories, and, if you doubt the power of human rationality to solve all problems, you avoid detective stories. The realist novel as a genre presumes the world, and the people in it, are far more complex than could be described by any theory. In ethical matters, realist novels are relentlessly casuistical.

Occasionally, the casuistic opposition to theory becomes explicit. In part 8 of *Anna Karenina*, conversation turns to the Eastern War against Turkey, which was popular with Russians

134. Starr, *Defoe and Casuistry*, 18.

135. In *Defoe and Casuistry*, Starr notes that, as early as 1895, George A. Aitken, commenting on the remarkable similarity of Defoe's novels to casuistical conduct manuals, argued that the novel emerged from the conduct manual by reversing its priorities. If the story existed primarily for the moral in the conduct manuals, the reverse was true of the novels, although the difference, according to Aitken, "was one of degree rather than kind. The difference lay chiefly in the prominence now given the story, which took the leading place, hitherto occupied by the moral" (cited in Starr, 34).

across the political spectrum because it was viewed as an attempt to rescue the Balkan Slavs from Turkish atrocities. All the guests at Levin's estate share that general opinion, but Levin does not. His brother, Sergey Ivanovich, who is "practiced in dialectics," challenges Levin with a tendentious question.[136] Suppose you were to see *right in front of you* drunken men beating a woman or child, Sergey Ivanovich asks. "I think you would . . . throw yourself on them, and protect the victim." "But I would not kill them," Levin responds. "Yes," says Sergey Ivanovich, "you would kill them." Levin replies, "I don't know. If I saw that, I might give way to my impulse of the moment, but I can't say beforehand."[137]

This answer does not satisfy Sergey Ivanovich, because Levin enunciates no *principle* for deciding, but, from Tolstoy's point of view, Levin's answer is correct: no principle *should* decide. The consequences of a wrong decision either way are terrible, and there are too many unknown particulars that cannot even be imagined in advance. One needs to rely on one's ethical judgment, on the "impulse" shaped by a lifetime of reflection on moral questions, such as Levin has practiced throughout the novel.

Acquiring Wisdom

Dr. Lydgate, one of the heroes of George Eliot's *Middlemarch*, begins the novel with confidence that, using reason, he can make good medical decisions and behave ethically. He has derived his sense of the world from the sciences, to which he

136. Leo Tolstoy, *Anna Karenina*, trans. Constance Garnett, rev. ed. by Leonard J. Kent and Nina Berberova (New York: Modern Library, 1965), 841.

137. Tolstoy, *Anna Karenina*, 839.

hopes to contribute. Lydgate aspires to reveal the "minute processes" that are the source of disease and uncover those "subtle
actions inaccessible by any sort of lens, but tracked in that outer
darkness through long pathways of necessary sequence . . .
capable of bathing even the ethereal atoms in its ideally illuminated space."[138] Lydgate, however, lives not in "ideally illuminated
space" but in Middlemarch, among flawed human beings with
all their baffling unwillingness or inability to accede to the clear,
logical arguments that, as a physician and reformer, Lydgate
presents to them.

To his surprise, Lydgate everywhere encounters what Eliot
calls life's "retarding friction," which he regards as unfortunate
annoyances, as bad luck rather than as a basic fact of life.[139]
When he needs to make ethical decisions, such as whom to vote
for as the hospital's clergyman, Lydgate can find no way to apply
his principles in a tangle of circumstances so unlike the straightforward situations he has always imagined: "One would know
much better what to do if men's characters were more consistent, and especially if one's friends were invariably fit for any
function they desired to undertake! . . . Lydgate was feeling the
hampering threadlike pressure of small social conditions, and
their frustrating complexity."[140] He resents being placed in such
situations because he has not yet learned that they are what life
is all about. Eliot writes, "It would have seemed beforehand like
a ridiculous piece of bad logic that he, with his unmixed resolu-
tions . . . would find himself at the very outset in the grasp of
petty alternatives, each of which was repugnant to him. In his

138. George Eliot, *Middlemarch* (New York: Modern Library, 1984), 159.
139. Eliot, *Middlemarch*, 142.
140. Eliot, 174–75.

student's chambers, he had prearranged his social action quite differently."[141]   *? read ?*

As *Middlemarch* proceeds, Lydgate and the novel's heroine Dorothea face difficult ethical dilemmas that require not abstract philosophy, but prosaic wisdom, to resolve—if not perfectly, then as well as possible under the circumstances. Bit by bit, both characters grow wiser. Some others, like the clergyman Farebrother, appreciate the casuistical view of ethics and the irreducible complexity of the world from the outset, while those like the wealthy evangelical Bulstrode, deceive themselves with abstract precepts. The novel, taken as a whole, offers a range of lessons in casuistry.   *? means*

So does *War and Peace*. Near the end of the novel, Pierre learns he can at last make moral judgments that eluded him when he relied on theoretical reasoning, and Tolstoy offers a long list of the sticky dilemmas he resolves. A quite similar passage occurs in *Anna Karenina*: Levin, who has been living rightly even when thinking wrongly, at last ceases to trust in abstractions and relies instead on the wisdom of practice, and then "it seemed as though he knew both what he was and why he was living, for he acted resolutely and without hesitation."[142] He knows, too, where to direct his attention and efforts. His judgment, not his principles, tells him what is "incontestably necessary":

> These things occupied him now not because he justified them to himself by any general principles, as he had done in former days; on the contrary, disappointed by the failure of his former efforts for the general welfare . . . he busied himself

141. Eliot, 175.
142. Tolstoy, *Anna Karenina*, 839.

with all this work because it seemed to him . . . that he could not do otherwise. In former days . . . when he had to do anything that would be good for all, for humanity, for Russia . . . he had noticed that the idea of it had been pleasant, but the work . . . vanished into nothing. But now . . . though he experienced no delight at all at the thought of the work he was doing, he felt absolutely convinced of its necessity [and] saw that it succeeded far better.[143]

Reading the lists of the moral decisions Pierre and Levin can now solve, readers may be tempted to ask: Why doesn't Tolstoy specify the rule by which they decide? The answer is that there is no rule, and, if there were, they would either decide less well, or be unable to decide at all. By relying on educated judgment, and making each act of judging the occasion for still more reflection, they make good decisions and grow wiser in the process. Both Eliot and Tolstoy make explicit the casuistical view the genre presumes and teaches.

Alternatives: Dialogue and Truth

It is quite possible to imagine . . . a unified truth that requires a plurality of consciousnesses, one that in principle cannot be fitted within the bounds of a single consciousness, one that is, so to speak, by its very nature *full of event potential* and is born at the point of contact among various consciousnesses.

—MIKHAIL BAKHTIN, PROBLEMS OF
DOSTOEVSKY'S POETICS[144]

143. Tolstoy, 823.

144. Mikhail Bakhtin, *Problems of Dostoevsky's Poetics*, ed. and trans. Caryl Emerson (Minneapolis: University of Minnesota Press, 1984), 81.

Along with its skepticism of abstract theory and devotion to practical judgment, the realist novel also presumes the value of dialogue, in the sense that the Russian philosopher and literary theorist Mikhail Bakhtin used the term.[145] The world the novelist describes consists not only of people and events, but also of points of view about people and events. We see occurrences from the irreducibly particular perspectives of different characters from different walks of life. The novelist also allows us to see each character's perspective on other characters' perspectives, and so on. While some points of view are truer and more moral than others, none is unquestionably right.

When novelistic authors speak, they do not pretend to offer a final word. Rather, they present their observations as just their perspective, which they may offer as wise but not infallible.[146] Compare, for instance, two famous first sentences:

There was a man in the land of Uz, whose name was Job; and that man was perfect and upright, and one that feared God, and eschewed evil. (Job 1:1)

It is a truth universally acknowledged, that a single man in possession of a good fortune, must be in want of a wife. (Jane Austen, *Pride and Prejudice*)[147]

145. For an overall account of Bakhtin's thought, and the role of dialogue in it, see Gary Saul Morson and Caryl Emerson, *Mikhail Bakhtin: Creation of a Prosaics* (Stanford, CA: Stanford University Press, 1990).

146. Precisely because novels do not tolerate absolute language, Tolstoy was occasionally able to gain considerable rhetorical power from using it. On his reasons for doing so, see Gary Saul Morson, "Tolstoy's Absolute Language," in *Hidden in Plain View: Narrative and Creative Potentials in* War and Peace (Stanford, CA: Stanford University Press, 1987), 9–36.

147. Jane Austen, *Pride and Prejudice*, ed. Donald Gray (New York: Norton, 2001), 1.

The narrator of Job speaks with absolute authority, and he knows things that no ordinary person could know—for instance, that Job is perfect. If a realist novel began this way, we would suspect that the narrator is mentally deficient, since perfect people do not exist. But to read the book of Job as it was written, one must accept the narrator's absolute authority.

Jane Austen's witty sentence pretends to utter universal truths as well, but the irony is palpable. The "universe" that acknowledges this "truth" turns out to consist of nearby families with marriageable daughters. The next sentence reads: "However little known the feelings or views of such a man may be on first entering a neighborhood, this truth is so well fixed in the minds of the surrounding families, that he is considered as the rightful property of some one or other of their daughters." No one states the truth—to do so would open it to question—and so the opening sentence turns out to paraphrase what is tacitly assumed. It is an axiom established by a shared wish.

There is no place in the realist novel for the sort of absolute statements found in the Bible, because, in the novel, every truth is someone's truth. The overarching truth of the novelistic world—or as much as a given novel can present—consists of a plurality of dramatized viewpoints. One cannot sum up the import of such a work by adopting any single point of view. A paraphrase of the work's moral would be wrong, not only because it would be a gross oversimplification, but also because it is a statement instead of an exchange. To understand the world of realist novels, one must trace a process consisting of many points of view in interaction. Or, as Bakhtin expresses the point, novelistic truth is inherently "dialogic."

By "dialogue" Bakhtin has in mind a lot more than one person answering another, or a sequence of statements by two people, as in a drama or, for that matter, a catechism. Instead, one must begin with what Bakhtin calls a "Galilean" rather than "Ptolemaic" consciousness—that is, one must stop regarding one's own perspective as the unchallengeable center of things, like the Ptolemaic earth around which everything revolves, and enter instead into a world where one's own point of view is but one among many, like one planet among many. Using the term "language" in his special sense of "point of view" (along with the language usually employed to express it), Bakhtin observes: "The novel is the expression of a Galilean perception of language, one that denies the absolutism of a single and unitary language—that is, it refuses to acknowledge its own language as the sole verbal and semantic center of the ideological world. It is a perception that has been made conscious of the vast plenitude . . . of languages. . . . The novel begins by presuming a . . . decentering of the ideological world."[148] In such a world, wisdom includes appreciating other perspectives. The genre developed special techniques for allowing readers to enter into the thought processes of characters as they unfold and so to sense them from within as we can never sense another person in real life. In this way, the process of reading becomes practice in empathy and pluralism.

A true dialogue is, in Bakhtin's words, "eventnessful" (or "full of event potential"). In other words, it has no predetermined end, and each participant may wind up saying things he had not known before. The process produces surprises. In principle, that process can continue indefinitely, or, as Bakhtin likes to say, it is "unfinalizable."

148. Mikhail Bakhtin, "Discourse in the Novel," in *The Dialogic Imagination: Four Essays*, ed. Michael Holquist, trans. Caryl Emerson and Michael Holquist (Austin: University of Texas Press, 1981), 366–67.

If we understood culture and society as dialogic in this sense, we would be eager not just to tolerate, but also to learn from others who think differently from ourselves. We would be aware that we never have the final answer, and that all solutions are revisable in light of unforeseeable outcomes. To learn how to do better next time, we would seek out, not just allow, criticism from those with different experiences. We would adopt not Luther's unshakeable confidence in his own "assertions," but Erasmus's intellectual humility in offering tentative suggestions.

The dialogic way of thinking is especially important in a democracy. If ideologically based authoritarian societies are Ptolemaic, democracies are Galilean. As the former relies on truths held to be certain, the latter depends on an acknowledgment of the fallibility of all, including ourselves. That is why we would be wise to see ethics and politics as arenas where we engage in case-based thinking and practical reasoning; where we seek not to impose final truths, but to educate our judgment; and where we cultivate the skills needed for sincere, productive dialogue.

That kind of dialogue is exactly what we try to promote in the following chapters. We begin with politics, where the emergence of factions consumed by hate is threatening our all-too-vulnerable democratic ideals. The dialogic sphere is as fragile as it is valuable. We turn, then, to economics, where fundamentalist ideologies increasingly obscure basic facts and truths. In a book on fundamentalism, it is natural that we turn next to religion, the source of that very term. And, finally, we consider literature—perhaps a surprising topic for those outside the academy, but one we hope to convince all of our readers is of vital importance.

3

Divided We Stand

THE POLITICS OF HATE

Joined Together by Hatred of the "Other"

In the mid-1990s Schapiro had a friend who was a fanatically proud graduate of Auburn University. His man cave was a shrine to Auburn football—Tigers everywhere, "War Eagle" written on the ceiling. Not all that rare, we suppose, given the extent of passions in big-time college sports. But one day he admitted something disturbing: as much as he loved watching his Tigers win, he took even greater satisfaction watching the Alabama Crimson Tide lose. The hatred he had for his rival was more powerful than the love he had for his alma mater.[1]

Welcome to the world of American politics today.

A poll by the Public Religion Research Institute, a highly respected nonprofit, nonpartisan organization, found that 82 percent of Republicans say that the Democratic Party has been taken over by socialists, while 80 percent of Democrats

---

1. When Schapiro was at USC, he enjoyed the ubiquitous cocktail napkins that said "My second favorite team is whoever is playing UCLA." Second favorite is one thing; favorite team is quite another.

say that the Republican Party has been taken over by racists.[2] When asked for their views on President Trump, 86 percent of Democrats say that he has encouraged white supremacist groups, while only 17 percent of Republicans agree. Of the nearly six in ten Americans who report becoming more strongly partisan following the election of 2016, 86 percent of the Republicans say they more strongly identify as Republican and 89 percent of the Democrats say they more strongly identify as Democrats. So it's no surprise that one of the press accounts detailing these results was subtitled "In a Deeply Divided Nation, Democrats and Republicans Don't Just Disagree, They Hate Each Other."[3]

Disagreement is what a healthy democracy is all about. We argue, we listen, we deliberate, we vote. We are supposed to consider the best arguments and evidence for whatever position we take, or we would not be justifying our conclusions by arguments and evidence at all. In a democracy, people think or are encouraged to think. When it looks like they are behaving mechanically—automatically endorsing whatever their party does and condemning whatever the other party does—we recoil. A well-known anecdote tells how a reporter once asked president John F. Kennedy if he had any response to the Republican National Committee's resolution branding his administration

2. "Fractured Nation: Widening Partisan Polarization and Key Issues in 2020 Presidential Elections," PRRI, October 21, 2019, https://www.prri.org/research /fractured-nation-widening-partisan-polarization-and-key-issues-in-2020-presidential -elections/.

3. Susan Milligan, "Democrats, Republicans, and the New Politics of Hate: In a Deeply Divided Nation, Democrats and Republicans Don't Just Disagree, They Hate Each Other," *U.S. News and World Report*, October 21, 2019, https://www.usnews .com/news/elections/articles/2019-10-21/democrats-republicans-and-the-new -politics-of-hate.

"a failure." Kennedy replied, "I presume the vote was unanimous?" The point, of course, was that such automatic condemnation cannot have been the product of thought. It was a foregone conclusion: the outcome was a given no matter the evidence. Unanimity testifies to thoughtlessness, because in politics there are always arguments on both sides. Our laughter at this anecdote testifies to our expectation that political judgment should not be reflexive but deliberative.

But when the difference between factions is based on hatred rather than honest disagreement, there is nothing to laugh at. In that world, people are supposed to line up unanimously and unquestioningly against the other faction. Not to do so becomes a form of treason. Lenin and Stalin, for instance, made it perfectly clear that one had to accept the entire package of Party doctrines without the slightest deviation. Their slogan was "He who is not with us is against us." In other words, no middle ground existed. That was because the enemy was irredeemably evil and the Bolsheviks were, as the chosen force of History, *guaranteed* to be right on all issues.

This is what we call political fundamentalism: a vision of the political world in which all goodness and truth lie on one side. The other side is not just misguided, but damned. Such hatred divides the world into two camps. As in the Apocalypse, all the good are on one side, and all the evil on the other. The "other" is always completely wrong. There is never an in-between space, and there can be no compromise. Democracy, by contrast, views politics as a matter of give-and-take, of negotiation, of persuasion. Lyndon Johnson loved to cite his favorite line from the Bible: "Come, let us reason together." But one does not reason with the devil. Instead of the give-and-take of democratic politics, there is a struggle to destroy the other: come, let us annihilate each other.

aha!

Tables Turned

In such situations, one can easily wind up among the hated others. We turn again to Arthur Koestler, whose celebrated novel *Darkness at Noon* recounts how one former Bolshevik leader, Rubashov, finds himself under arrest for positions once under discussion, but now regarded as unacceptable.[4] It no longer matters whether you acted in good faith when advocating potassium- rather than nitrogen-based fertilizers, or when favoring the construction of a few large submarines over many small ones; it only matters that the other side won out. You turned out to be wrong, which means your position was objectively counterrevolutionary and therefore worthy of death.

Like George Orwell's *1984*, Koestler's novel pertains not only to the Soviet experience, but to the kind of thinking represented by the Soviet regime. Those who imagine that they, and they alone, walk in the bright sunlight, can soon experience darkness at noon. People with a reasonably long career are bound to have taken positions that can now be held against them. To have been wrong in the past is as bad as to be wrong in the present, and, since no one can tell which position will win out next, the logic of hatred threatens everyone. Once politics is apocalyptic, and the world is divided into saints and sinners, anyone can find himself in the wrong category when approved opinion shifts. Many who imagine themselves on the side of the angels, and who righteously expose the machinations of demonic opponents, find themselves consigned to the burning lake.

4. Arthur Koestler, *Darkness at Noon*, ed. Michael Scammel, trans. Philip Boem (New York: Scribner, 2019).

Rubashov discovers that, when this kind of thinking predominates, there are no small mistakes. The logical consequence of
disagreement of any sort is civil war, or other violence against
the forces of goodness and truth, and one is responsible for
what one's bad idea *could* entail. After all, bad actions flow from
bad thoughts, each disagreement is a "potential schism," and so
one is guilty of what one might have done or, for that matter,
what others whom one might have influenced might have
done.[5] As Rubashov expresses the point, he is even responsible
for "the deeds he had neglected to perform."[6]

In theory, the Bolshevik Party worked by "democratic centralism": there could be open discussion and disagreement until
a decision was made, and only then was it absolutely binding
on all Party members. But once the Bolsheviks were safely in
power, they banned all disagreement (or "factions") within the
Party, not only in the present but also retrospectively, in the past.
After Lenin's death, Stalin used this weapon against all the other
original Bolshevik leaders. Koestler's Rubashov is based on one
of the original Bolshevik leaders, Nikolai Bukharin.

What's more, these disgraced leaders had no grounds for
complaint, since each of them had behaved the same way to
earlier opponents and had invoked the same revolutionary logic
in doing so. They were all committed to the morality followed
by Stalin. Those who had enthusiastically suppressed conservatives, liberals, anarchists, and other socialists soon found themselves under interrogation in the torture chamber, condemned
to execution on the same basis they had used to condemn many
others. Or, as Rubashov comes to understand, they were all

5. Koestler, *Darkness at Noon*, 169.
6. Koestler, 195.

"caught in the web they themselves had spun according to their circuitous logic and convoluted morality."[7]

As the revolutionary Girondist Pierre Verginaud remarked at his own trial, the revolution devours its children.[8] As soon as one side has won, the logic of hatred is applied to divergences among the victors, and, when one faction of the victors wins out, it divides in the same way. Soon Robespierre himself is guillotined. Reading of such events—of the execution of Robespierre and of Stalin's secret police chiefs—one experiences a grim satisfaction at just deserts. But surely it would be better if politics as hatred had not been practiced at all.

Recall that headline: "Democrats and Republicans Don't Just Disagree, They Hate Each Other." If that doesn't scare you, try this one. A poll of likely New Hampshire Democratic voters taken on the eve of their primary found that 95 percent disapproved of the job President Trump has been doing.[9] Not at all surprising. But, when asked which of the following outcomes they would prefer on election day the following November, "Donald Trump wins re-election," or "a giant meteor strikes the earth, extinguishing all human life," 62 percent picked the me-

---

7. Koestler, 226.

8. At his trial during the terror of 1793, Verginaud famously observed, "There is reason to fear that the Revolution may, like Saturn, devour each of her children one by one." *The Yale Book of Quotations*, ed. Fred R. Shapiro (New Haven, CT: Yale University Press, 2006), 788.

9. Madeleine Carlisle, "Majority of New Hampshire Democrats Would Prefer a Meteor Extinguish 'All Human Life' Than Trump Get Re-Elected: Poll," *Time*, February 8, 2020, https://time.com/5780556/meteor-poll-trump-new-hampshire/. A detailed description of the polling methodology can be found in Joshua J. Dyck and John Cluverius, "UMass Lowell: Survey of New Hampshire Democratic Primary Voters," Field Dates, January 28–31, 2020, Center for Public Opinion, University of Massachusetts Lowell.

teor. Okay, you lose a presidential election. It might feel like the end of the world, but you make the best of it for the next four years. To actually *prefer* the end of the world as opposed to four more years of President Trump is mind-boggling. We hope, of course, that respondents were exaggerating, but, these days, who really knows for sure?

Most likely, the people who answered this way did not really mean it. But that consideration does not dispose of the significance of their answer; it is still frightening that people would answer as they did. They were willing to endorse an obviously absurd statement simply because it condemned the other side. They may not even have seriously asked themselves whether they actually believed what they were saying. Perhaps they had long ago decided to sign on to *whatever* their side endorsed, as long as it went against their opponents. Perhaps they just said what they were expected to say, or didn't dare to object and be labeled a "compromiser." If one has ever wondered how an entire nation could have followed a murderous leader, one needs to understand that it doesn't take that many people actually believing what the leader says. They just need to be willing to repeat whatever their side is saying.

That sort of repetition may have been at work when, as a *Newsweek* article reported, a column by Bert Farias on a leading Christian website associated with the magazine *Charisma* argued that Pete Buttigieg's "abominable lifestyle" is bringing the "death rattle of a nation."[10] Farias writes, "In fact, when those

10. Ewan Palmer, "Top Evangelical Christian Website Says Pete Buttigieg's Homosexuality Makes Him 'Deserving of Death,'" *Newsweek*, February 15, 2020, https://www.newsweek.com/pete-buttigieg-christian-death-bert-farias-charisma-1487477.

who practice such things that are 'deserving of death' also approve of others who practice them (Rom. 1:32), it is one of God's final signs of His wrath on a society."[11] Of course, there are those who regard the beliefs and lifestyle favored by Farias as abominable.

So is it any wonder that, when people who think this way obtain full control of government, there is a tendency for things to get more and more extreme, as happened in both the French and Russian revolutions? Call it "the slide." Once one has signed on to *every*thing, *any*thing might happen. History suggests that when it is too dangerous to say a certain step goes too far, that step—and the next—will be taken. The point is not just that people are afraid to object, although many are; it is that, afraid or not, they realize they have bought into a way of thinking that condemns them if they do object, as they have condemned others. For Koestler, it is this realization, not just torture, that

11. The article goes on to point out that Farias criticizes Christians who reinterpret the Bible: "The constant compromising of preachers to avoid controversy is creating much damage—not only to the world, which is looking for a clear sound from preachers, but also to believers who have little discernment or are growing tired of ambiguity." He continues, "For example, one very influential and popular minister who has millions of followers was asked if homosexuality was wrong, and his general response was that his views were evolving. Evolving? That's like saying the Bible is evolving. How pathetic of an answer." In fact, the passage in Romans characterizes *all* sin as in principle worthy of death. All those "being filled with all unrighteousness, fornication, wickedness, covetousness, maliciousness; full of envy, murder, debate, deceit, malignity, whisperers, backbiters, haters of God, despiteful, proud, boasters, inventors of evil things, disobedient to parents, without understanding, covenant-breakers, without natural affection, implacable, unmerciful: who knowing the judgment of God, that they which commit such things are worthy of death, not only do the same, but have pleasure in them that do them" (Rom. 1:28–32). In chapter 5 we take a very different view, not just on biblical commentaries on homosexuality, but on the general question of when it is appropriate to reinterpret the holy texts.

explains why so many old Bolshevik leaders confessed to crimes that they could not possibly have committed. Once one's whole life is the Party, one above all does not wish to be isolated. Who does? The last thing such committed people want is to be forced to seek allies from the other side, which they believe consists only of wicked people. And they likely suspect that in objecting to one extreme step, when they have endorsed so many others, it is they themselves who are in the wrong.

In short, it does not take a majority of people to believe in mass cruelty or destruction to make it happen. We have witnessed that horrible tale all too often. It takes only a dynamic in which the other side is unequivocally evil, where people belonging to one faction feel that they are not just in a particular party, but are part of a congregation of the blessed, fighting demonic forces. There will then be a tendency for greater and greater hatred, as more and more extreme positions will prevail. Once the slide begins, everything accelerates. Positions that are inconceivable one year become merely fringe the next, and then mainstream soon after. That is what is so scary about the meteor response: it is *not* that people believe it literally. Rather, the mere fact they would say they do indicates a mentality that, given time, could lead to anything.

Democracy cannot survive when parties or factions view each other in this way. One cannot acknowledge the legitimacy of any victory by the other side, or trust that, since power shifts back and forth, one's own time will come (and then be over). No—one plays for keeps. Hatred on the playing fields of athletics is one thing, hatred on the playing fields of politics quite another. The former might make for some difficult viewing in a stadium or a sports bar; the latter might be tearing apart our nation, destroying both democracy and the rule of law.

Fundamentalism and Democracy in Tension

> For this is not the liberty which we can hope, that no
> grievance ever should arise in the Commonwealth—that let
> no man in this world expect; but when complaints are freely
> heard, deeply considered, and speedily reformed, then is the
> utmost bound of civil liberty attained that wise men look for.
>
> —JOHN MILTON, *AREOPAGITICA*[12]

Let us consider why this fundamentalist mindset and democracy cannot coexist for long. To begin with, democracy depends on the idea of legitimate disagreement. It gives a strong meaning to the concept of *opinion*. No matter how deeply one believes in one's preferred policy recommendations, one knows that they just might be mistaken. After all, if one looks back, people who were just as committed to justice as we are have sometimes adopted positions that proved disastrous and anything but just. Think of how many intelligent, well-intentioned people apologized for Mussolini, Stalin, and Mao!

The lesson to learn from these mistakes is not just that it was wrong to support Bolsheviks and Maoists, but also that however convincing a theory may be, it could turn out to be wrong. One cannot be absolutely certain that the other's view may not turn out to be correct. For John Stuart Mill, that was one reason he believed democracy *needs* a diversity of opinions. The only way humanity learns from its mistakes is by having them pointed out; positions *benefit* from criticism. Mill writes, "Very few facts are able to tell their own story, without comments to bring out their meaning. The whole strength and value, then, of

---

12. John Milton, "Areopagitica," *Complete Poems and Major Prose*, ed. Merritt Y. Hughes (New York: Odyssey, 1957), 718.

human judgment, depending on the one property, that it can be set right when it is wrong, reliance can be placed on it only when the means of setting it right are kept constantly at hand." In any human endeavor, we are likely to make mistakes, and we get wiser only with "the steady habit of correcting and completing" one's opinion "by collating it with those of others."[13]

Fundamentalists, as we defined the term in chapter 2, believe their views are infallible. They do not live in a world of opinion. In that uncertain world, one believes that one is right, but not in a way that precludes the possibility of error. One cannot be certain that one should be so certain. As Mill explains, "We can never be sure that the opinion we are endeavoring to stifle is a false opinion. . . . To refuse a hearing to an opinion, because they are sure that it is false, is to assume that *their* certainty is the same thing as *absolute* certainty. All silencing of discussion is an assumption of infallibility."[14] And what if, in one's certainty, one has helped create a system that does not allow itself to be criticized, let alone voted out of office? Then there can be no corrective when policies fail. Even when their policies lead to disaster, the infallible do not admit they were wrong. Rather, they claim sabotage, ascribe failure to those who point it out, and punish critics as traitors. Failure proves one has not been intolerant enough! When that response to failure leads to still more failure, they repeat it.

And so the slide accelerates. The very fact that more repression makes matters even worse proves that there has been still more sabotage, requiring still more repression. Since there is no visible resistance, it must be hidden, and so people must be

13. John Stuart Mill, *On Liberty* (Buffalo, NY: Prometheus, 1986), 27. The essay was originally published in 1859.
14. Mill, *On Liberty*, 23–24.

watched all the more carefully and encouraged to monitor each other. No amount of vigilance is sufficient. One might have thought that once the counterrevolution has been decisively beaten, things might ease up, but, if one follows the logic of the slide, one appreciates why the very opposite is the case, and why, as we pointed out in chapter 1, Stalin proclaimed "the intensification of the class struggle" *after* the Revolution.

The crucial point is: If one is absolutely certain of one's certainty, if one believes that one's beliefs cannot possibly be incorrect, and if the only explanation for why others differ is that they are stupid, venal, or evil, then why should one allow more than one party or point of view to exist? After all, one does not allow for two opinions on the correctness of the Pythagorean theorem, and one does not vote on the validity of Newton's laws. If only one side can be right in a controversy, if its rightness is certain, if there is no middle ground, and if there is no possibility that the other side just might turn out to be correct, then there is no reason *not* to have a one-party state.

This is why it is so dangerous to believe (as many have) that their political ideas are *scientific*. Since the seventeenth century, countless thinkers have been guided by the faith that what Newton had done for astronomy could also be done for human affairs. It should be possible, they reasoned, to establish a hard science of humanity—a true social *science* in the strong sense of that term. As we observed in chapter 2, it is a small leap from believing that such a science is possible, to the claim that one has actually arrived at it.

Auguste Comte, we have noted, called his new discipline "sociology," after planning to name it "social physics." Bronislaw Malinowski thought his discovery of "functionalism" had established anthropology as a true science, which means that, like physics, anthropology precludes the possibility of "adventitious and fortuitous happenings" and is capable of "prediction of the future."[15] Taking his model of a science from chemistry, the structuralist anthropologist Claude Lévi-Strauss enthused about the ability of social scientists to formulate a table of human possibilities "that would be comparable to the table of elements which Mendeleieff introduced." With the aid of such a table, we would "discover the place of languages that have disappeared or are yet unknown, yet to come, or simply possible."[16]

Readers are sometimes puzzled that Freud was not satisfied with saying that *some* errors arise from an unconscious intention to err and instead insisted, from *The Psychopathology of Everyday Life* (1901) onward, that *all* errors are intentional in this way. There can be no exceptions because "nothing in the mind is arbitrary and undetermined."[17] Nothing at all: Freud is absolutely categorical in ruling out the possibility that anything can be attributed to chance, or that the mind can be anything less than perfectly efficient: "Every change in the clothing worn, every small sign of carelessness—such as an unfastened button—every piece of exposure, is intended to express something which the wearer of the clothes does not want to say outright and of which he is for the most part unaware."[18] In his final book, *Civilization and Its Discontents* (1930), Freud repeats the

15. Bronislaw Malinowski, *A Scientific Theory of Culture and Other Essays* (Chapel Hill: University of North Carolina Press, 1944), 8.

16. Claude Lévi-Strauss, *Structural Anthropology*, trans. Claire Jacobson and Brooke Grundfest Schoepf (New York: Basic Books, 1963), 58.

17. Sigmund Freud, *The Psychopathology of Everyday Life*, ed. James Strachey, trans. Alan Tyson (New York: Norton, 1965), 242.

18. Cited from *The Psychopathology of Everyday Life* in the Standard Edition of Freud's works (SE:256–65), in John Farrell, *Freud's Paranoid Quest: Psychoanalysis and Modern Suspicion* (New York: New York University Press, 1996), 47.

point: "Since we overcame the error of supposing that the for-
getting we are familiar with signified a destruction of the
memory-trace—that is, its annihilation—we have been inclined to take the opposite view, that in mental life nothing
which has once formed can perish—that everything is somehow preserved and that in suitable circumstances . . . it can
once more be brought to light."[19]

Why does Freud insist there can be absolutely no exceptions? How could the brain, unique among biological creations,
be perfectly efficient? Wouldn't it be a remarkable enough discovery that *some* apparently unintentional actions are actually
at some level intended? The reason, we surmise, is that Freud
thought of psychoanalysis as a science like physics, and physical
laws do not work just some of the time. Marx and Engels also
insisted that while other forms of socialism were "utopian,"
theirs was truly "scientific." In the same spirit, Marx likens "the
laws of capitalist production" that he discovered to those of "the
physicist" and so can be certain that they work "with iron necessity towards an inevitable result."[20] Many social Darwinists regarded their theory as a mere extension of Darwinism that
rested on just as firm a scientific basis.[21]

Although each purported science has turned out to be a
pseudoscience, very few learn the lesson that such claims need
to be treated skeptically in light of past experience. Should the
believers in such a claim, however flimsy it may be, achieve political power, they can make actual testing of the claim, weigh-
ing it against counterevidence and skeptical questioning, im-

19. Sigmund Freud, *Civilization and Its Discontents*, ed. and trans. James Strachey
(New York: Norton, 1961), 17.

20. From Marx's preface to the first edition of *Capital* in Karl Marx and Friedrich
Engels, *Basic Writings on Politics and Philosophy*, ed. Lewis S. Feuer (Garden City,
NY: Doubleday, 1959), 135.

21. B. F. Skinner, Gary Becker, and Jared Diamond also claimed scientific status.

possible. What we call the spirit of fundamentalism, Mill referred to as "the spirit of Puritanism," and he, too, discovered it in the followers of the putative social sciences. Some reformers who completely reject religion, he observes, "have been noway behind either churches or sects in their assertion of the right of spiritual domination. M. Comte, in particular . . . aims at establishing . . . a despotism of society over the individual, surpassing anything contemplated in the political ideal of the most rigid disciplinarian among the ancient philosophers."[22]

The appeal, and the danger, of advancing such claims is that one does not have to answer opponents. One silences them or, if that is not possible, ignores them. Nothing they say is worth considering, and some of it might corrupt those less pure than oneself. One knows in advance: opponents are simply ignorant, like those who believe the earth is flat or still accept Aristotelian physics. If not ignorant, they may hope to profit at the expense of those who are. Or they may simply be "insane." In the Brezhnev era, Soviet dissidents were sometimes confined to asylums (the diagnosis was "sluggish schizophrenia"), because doubting Marxism-Leninism was like doubting the law of gravity.

In a world governed by such beliefs, the only valid election would be one that the right side was guaranteed to win. The Soviets expressed this idea by staging "elections" where people "chose" from a slate of exactly one candidate. And everyone had to vote, because abstaining from correctness meant supporting incorrectness. By the same token, although one could in theory leave the ballot blank—in effect, abstaining—no one did so, partly because there was no secret ballot, partly because there was no point in doing so, and partly because if one disagreed with everyone else, how could one be right?

22. Mill, *On Liberty*, 20.

Pseudoscience

The claim of scientific status serves the same function as the claim of religious revelation: it places one in a world of *certainty* rather than of *opinion*. It works as a God substitute, and we are referring to God and revelation as fundamentalists understand them. It precludes the possibility that one could be wrong, or one's opponent right. Therefore, all such claims must be treated with the greatest possible caution.

So enticing is it to claim scientific status, so readily are intellectuals tempted, and so dangerous is it when such claims silence all objections in advance, that it pays to be on the lookout for them, and recognize when they are unwarranted. One sign of an unwarranted claim is a misunderstanding of what science is. To the pseudoscientist, it is a body of unquestionable dogma, rather than a series of falsifiable propositions continually tested, or at least subject to testing, against evidence and open to modification. Unfortunately, when science is taught from textbooks, students may take it as a set of unchangeable dogmatic propositions. The very presentation encourages such an understanding. Could it be that science education is itself a principal propagator of essentially antiscientific attitudes?

Even when one dogmatically accepts propositions currently held to be correct and unlikely to be changed, one has still misunderstood the very nature of scientific reasoning. As John Milton once observed, "A man may be a heretic in the truth; and if he believe things only because his pastor says so, or the Assembly so determines, without knowing other reason, though his belief be true, yet the very truth he holds becomes his heresy."[23] By the same token, it is possible to accept science superstitiously.

---

23. Milton, "Areopagitica," 739.

If one accepts it as unchallengeable and unchangeable dogma, if one takes it as a fundamentalist takes the infallible tenets of his sect, then one is false to the very spirit of science itself. Wince when you hear people who profess that they "believe in science," as if it were one solid block of doctrines to be accepted uncritically and all with equal confidence.

It would be far better, when teaching scientific achievements, to explain *how* they were arrived at: what was the earlier or rival theory, and why it was accepted by intelligent people; what unexpected evidence dislodged it; and on what basis the current theory rests. What alternative theories were available and how did the one that prevailed establish its superiority? What sort of experiment, should it take place, might disconfirm the current consensus? If no such experiment can even be imagined, then one is not dealing with a scientific proposition at all. The metaphysical conclusions drawn by scientists are not themselves part of their science. If students were taught science in this spirit—if they were taught not just the conclusions but the process of scientific reasoning itself—they would be less susceptible to the charms of a fashionable pseudoscience. Students would then understand that, at any given moment, some parts of a science are less likely to be changed than others. There are foundations that have survived for a long time and have been repeatedly tested in different, unexpected ways. To be sure, even these foundations—like Newton's laws—might eventually be overturned or reclassified as special cases, but it would make little sense to question them except for very strong reasons, like the Michelson-Morley experiment and Albert Einstein's conclusions from it, which were themselves falsifiable and testable.

But not all parts of a science are foundational. There is a *spectrum of certainty* extending from the foundations to the latest hypotheses and computer models, which are plausible enough and may have passed some tests, but might readily be questioned in light of evidence to come. Darwin's idea that species have evolved and were not created all at once has proven more durable than his understanding of the mechanisms of change, or his insistence that all change must be gradual ("nature takes no leaps").

The point is that in *any* science, some propositions are more firmly established than others. If that were not the case, science couldn't develop at all except by total revolutions. From Francis Bacon to the present, the essence of the scientific enterprise has been a gradual building of one person's work on that of others, with additions, corrections, and changes accumulating over time. But it is characteristic of those who view science superstitiously to treat it as a whole, as a body of equally unshakeable dogma. Anyone who questions even the most recent hypotheses instantly becomes "anti-science" and is told that "science is real."

One can also recognize pseudoscientific reasoning when its conclusions are extended outside of their proper domain, beyond where they have been properly tested (or are even testable). This is immediately evident when a conclusion from a hard science is applied to human affairs. The social Darwinists were quite convinced that only religious bigots, who insisted on the biblical story of creation, would doubt their application of Darwinism to society. Some progressive intellectuals believed that eugenics was a conclusion dictated by science itself. But, in fact, it was the progressive social Darwinists who turned out to be the fundamentalists.

It is therefore especially important to distinguish social, ethical, or political conclusions inspired by a science from the science itself. In retrospect, it is obvious that social Darwinism was not itself scientific, but that was by no means so obvious at the time. The sciences of each age, especially those that have made impressive new discoveries, are always apt to be "social-Darwinized" so that those who object to essentially political assertions are dismissed as ignorant or worse. The more a science seems to endorse policies we would advocate in any case, the more we should suspect "social-Darwinization."

Reasoning in much the same way as the social Darwinists to very different conclusions, Marxists regarded Darwinism as proof of the Marxist theory of history, leading to an inevitable Communist revolution in the near future. Speaking at Marx's funeral, Engels declared: "Just as Darwin had discovered the law of development of organic nature so did Marx discover the law of human history."[24] Engels repeatedly argued that science, especially geology and Darwinian biology, had proven that human history had an inbuilt direction to progress.[25] As it developed, Marxist fundamentalism proved no less rigid than the biblical. It led, for instance, to the rejection of genetics, relativity, the chemical theory of resonance, and quantum theory, all on the grounds that they contradicted Marxist-Leninist "science" and so had to be incorrect.[26] These rejections followed from Lenin's belief that Marxism, as a hard science, is a monolithic

24. As cited in Richard Pipes, *Communism: A History* (New York: Modern Library, 2001), 9.

25. In *Ludwig Feuerbach and the End of Classical German Philosophy*, for instance, Engels argues that a historical view of nature (as in geology and Darwinism) establishes the historical (by which he means progressive) view of society: "Human society . . . no less than nature has its history of development and its science. It was therefore a question of bringing the science of society . . . into harmony with the materialist foundation and of reconstructing it thereupon," as Marx did. Marx and Engels, *Basic Writings*, 213–14.

26. See Gustav A. Wetter, *Dialectical Materialism: A Historical and Systematic Survey of Philosophy in the Soviet Union*, trans. Peter Heath (New York: Praeger, 1963).

system, with each of its tenets built on an equally firm foundation. "From this Marxist philosophy, which is cast from a single piece of steel," he insisted, "you cannot eliminate one essential part, without departing from objective truth, without falling prey to bourgeois-reactionary falsehood."[27]

Closer to our time, Paul Ehrlich, claiming to speak with the certainty of science, has repeatedly predicted economic disasters that have not happened. Beginning with his 1968 blockbuster, *The Population Bomb*, along with testimony before Congress and in many other venues, he insisted that overpopulation would cause a billion people to starve to death within ten years.[28] No doubt was possible without doubting science itself. Ehrlich's claim was widely accepted, leading to the foundation of Zero Population Growth and the Club of Rome, with its widely circulated study *The Limits of Growth*.[29] In 1965, the *New Republic* had already claimed that "world population has passed the food supply. The famine has begun."[30]

Of course, the exact opposite proved to be the case. Not only did mass starvation fail to take place, but the "green revolution" led to a dramatic increase in food production that has continued to outpace population growth, with hundreds of millions drawn out of poverty. Famine was soon confined to areas like

27. As cited in Neil Harding, *Leninism* (Durham, NC: Duke University Press, 1996), 225.

28. See our discussion of Ehrlich in Morson and Schapiro, *Cents and Sensibility: What Economics Can Learn from the Humanities* (Princeton, NJ: Princeton University Press, 2018), 53–56.

29. Donella H. Meadows, Dennis L. Meadows, Jorgen Randers, and William W. Behrens III, *The Limits to Growth: A Report for the Club of Rome's Project on the Predicament of Mankind* (New York: Macmillan, 1979).

30. As cited in Paul Sabin, *The Bet: Paul Ehrlich, Julian Simon, and Our Gamble over Earth's Future* (New Haven, CT: Yale University Press, 2013), 23.

North Korea and Somalia, where the cause was purely political. And yet Ehrlich continued to repeat his predictions and claim that earlier ones had been verified! What made him so sure? Whence his unshakeable confidence that contrary evidence could be ignored? The answer is that he was an expert in butterflies and imagined that the conclusions he drew from their "demography" would necessarily apply to humans. If economists thought in terms of resource substitution, incentives for better production methods, or the impact of technology—if they treated people as essentially different from butterflies— that only proved that economists did not understand science.

In recent years, senator Sheldon Whitehouse, New York attorney general Eric Schneiderman, and others properly concerned with climate change have called for criminalizing any expressed doubts of the climate change consensus.[31] One can fully appreciate the danger of climate change and still realize that there are several things terribly wrong with this proposal. To begin with, it treats all of climate science as on an equal footing. That is not true of any science; quite the contrary, the spectrum of uncertainty is one mark of a science. Science is not Scripture as fundamentalists take it, nor "a single piece of steel," as Lenin presumed. It is one thing to deny the greenhouse effect, and quite another to point out that we need to understand feedback mechanisms better to make accurate predictions.

---

31. Hans A. von Spakovsky, "Prosecuting Climate Change 'Deniers' is an Abuse of Power," Heritage, April 22, 2016, https://www.heritage.org/environment /commentary/prosecuting-climate-change-deniers-abuse-power#main-content. For Whitehouse's argument calling for the use of the RICO law against "deniers," see his article "The Fossil-Fuel Industry's Campaign to Mislead the American People," *Washington Post*, May 29, 2015, https://www.washingtonpost.com/opinions/the -fossil-fuel-industrys-campaign-to-mislead-the-american-people/2015/05/29 /04a2c448-0574-11e5-8bda-c7b4e9a8f7ac_story.html.

What is more, it is common to call people "denialists" who object to a particular treaty or method of reducing carbon emissions, whereas a moment's thought will make clear that whether a given treaty will be effective, or whether an outright ban or cap-and-trade will work better, is a question that involves politics and economics, which are not themselves hard sciences and leave room for intelligent disagreement.

Still worse, Whitehouse's method solidifies a misunderstanding of science itself. What if a few of the many ideas of modern climate science should prove untrue and in need of revision? Indeed, that would *have* to happen if climate science is to progress. By Whitehouse's understanding of science, which treats it as a whole block only an antiscientific outlook could question, science itself would have been overturned! If those calling for prosecution are so careless in their understanding of science, it is easy to see that many areas of legitimate disagreement will soon be criminalized. And then "the slide" will accelerate.

Science enjoys prestige precisely because it is not a matter of dogma to be taken as a whole, on faith, like the catechism. The ones who bring it into greatest disrepute are the ones who, like the social Darwinists, take it beyond its proper domain and treat all questioning as heresy. Not all fundamentalists are in churches.

Something similar has happened with the recent pandemic. The prediction of Neil Ferguson and his team at Imperial College in London, which was widely reported and influenced British and American responses, proved dramatically wrong. Ferguson predicted that an uncontrolled spread of the disease could cause as many as 510,000 deaths in the United Kingdom and 2.2 million in the United States.[32] As we write on October 3,

---

32. See Mark Landler and Stephen Castle, "Behind the Virus Report That Jarred the U.S. and the U.K. to Action," *New York Times,* March 17, 2020, https://www

// false predictions

2020, total British deaths are officially 42,268 and US deaths are 211,975. One might reasonably argue that death tolls were smaller because Ferguson's advice was in fact taken, but it is hard to believe that his recommendations prevented more than 90 percent of the predicted fatalities.

Moreover, Ferguson also predicted that Sweden, which did not take his advice, would see 40,000 deaths by the beginning of May and 96,000 by the beginning of June. As of October 3, the actual tally is 5,895 deaths.[33] By the same token, Vox reported on May 2, 2020, that the next-day death predictions for

---

.nytimes.com/2020/03/17/world/europe/coronavirus-imperial-college-johnson.html.

33. Ferguson based his predictions on several assumptions that turned out to be badly mistaken: that 0.9 percent of those infected with the disease would die from it (Oxford's Center for Evidence-Based Medicine puts the figure at between 0.1 and 0.26 per cent); that two out of three infected people would experience symptoms; and that, if left unchecked 81 percent of the UK population would catch the disease. Ferguson's latest prediction follows a series of similar failures. "Around 40 million people died in 1918 Spanish flu outbreak," Ferguson reasoned in developing his mortality prediction for H5N1 avian flu in 2005. "There are six times more people on the planet now so you could scale it up to around 200 million people probably." The actual toll, according to the World Health Organization, turned out to be 455. In 2009, his prediction of the mortality rate (between 0.3 to 1.5 percent, and most likely 0.4 percent) from swine flu led to the calculation that, in a reasonable worst case scenario, Britain would see 65,000 deaths, whereas the actual mortality rate turned out to be .0026 percent. See Ross Clark, "Neil Ferguson's Lockdown Predictions Are So Dodgy That You Wouldn't Even Ask Him What Day Christmas Is On," *Daily Mail*, May 6, 2020, https://www.dailymail.co.uk/news/article-8294439/ROSS-CLARK-Neil-Fergusons-lockdown-predictions-dodgy.html. Moreover, according to John Fund ("'Professor Lockdown' Modeler Resigns in Disgrace," *National Review*, May 6, 2020, https://www.nationalreview.com/corner/professor-lockdown-modeler-resigns-in-disgrace/), "Last March, Ferguson admitted that his Imperial College model of the COVID-19 disease was based on undocumented, 13-year-old computer code that was intended to be used for a feared influenza pandemic, rather than a coronavirus. Ferguson declined to release his original code so other scientists could check his results. He only released a heavily revised set of code last week, after a six-week delay." Fund quotes Johan Giesecke, former chief scientist for the European

each state advanced by the University of Washington's Institute for Health Metrics and Evaluation, which also shaped government policy, "were outside its 95% confidence interval 70% of the time."[34] Predictions of the overwhelming of emergency rooms have also largely proven badly mistaken.

Examining several influential models, a paper written by a team of health economists and published by the National Bureau of Economic Research pointed out that the Imperial College London prediction among others presumed unrealistically (and, as it turns out, falsely) that people would not change their behavior in response to the disease. The paper concludes: "In sum, the language of these papers suggests a degree of certainty that is simply not justified. Even if the parameter values are representative of a wide range of cases within the context of the given model, none of these authors attempts to quantify uncertainty about the validity of their broader modeling choices."[35]

 Real-time mistakes during a crisis are to be expected, and are not in themselves disturbing. What is disturbing is a claim of more certainty than is warranted and, still worse, that questioning such claims is to be antiscience and dangerous to human life.[36] Quite the contrary is the case. As one commentator has observed:

Center for Disease Control and Prevention, as saying that Ferguson's model was both "the most influential scientific paper" in memory, and "one of the most wrong."

34. Kelsey Piper, "This Coronavirus Model Keeps Being Wrong. Why Are We Still Listening to It?" Vox, May 2, 2020, https://www.vox.com/future-perfect/2020/5/2/21241261/coronavirus-modeling-us-deaths-ihme-pandemic.

35. For a discussion of that paper and others, see Philip W. Magnes, "How Wrong Were the Models and Why?" American Institute for Economic Research, April 23, 2020, https://www.aier.org/article/how-wrong-were-the-models-and-why/.

36. As early as February 27, Washington governor Jay Inslee claimed that his policies were based on "science," whereas those in the White House who disagreed are not sticking to science and not telling "the truth." Whatever one may think of White

One of the paradoxes of the coronavirus crisis is that the need for public scrutiny of government policy has never been greater, but there's less tolerance for dissent than usual. That's particularly true of the work of Professor Neil Ferguson and his team at Imperial College.... Witness the furious reaction provoked by Professor Sunetra Gupta and her team at Oxford when they published a paper suggesting that the Imperial model might have underestimated the percentage of the population that has already been infected. The *Financial Times* printed a critical letter co-signed by a group of scientists that ... used the word "dangerous" in their description of the Oxford research, as if merely challenging Imperial's model would cost lives, and Professor Ferguson has made the same argument to condemn other critics of his work.[37]

A more sensible method, this commentator continues, would be not to rely too heavily on any single model or set of models, but to instead encourage teams of experts working independently to develop their own models and to challenge others based on actual experience: "That's the tried-and-tested scientific method and it has been bizarre to see respected pundits simultaneously argue that we should be strictly guided by 'the science' and that any scientist expressing dissent from the prevailing orthodoxy is behaving 'irresponsibly.' That was the same

---

House decision-making, at that point, scientists had not determined how contagious the disease was, what percentage of carriers were asymptomatic, what the true mortality rate was, and what was a safe distance, so it is hard to see why Governor Inslee's "scientific" assumptions rule out alternative possibilities. See Todd Meyers, "When Covid 'Science' Is a Smokescreen," *Wall Street Journal*, May 28, 2020, A17.

37. "How Reliable Is Imperial College's Modelling?," Lockdown Sceptics, April 4, 2020, https://lockdownsceptics.org/how-reliable-is-imperial-colleges-modelling/.

argument used by the Chinese authorities for silencing the doctors who first raised the alarm in Wuhan."[38]

What lives really depend on, and real science demands, is the continual correcting of models against facts in an atmosphere free of fundamentalist intimidation. The real enemies of science, once again, include some who claim to speak in its name.

Criticism and the Experience of Others

The role of criticism in the world of opinion bears no resemblance to its role in the world of certainty. When beliefs are recognized as fallible, criticism plays a constructive role. Opponents point out where a given policy is likely to fail, or where similar policies have had unintended and undesirable outcomes in the past, and so one is able to adjust a policy to avoid those outcomes. One can thereby learn from experience.

Without such criticism, one cannot distinguish a genuinely sound position from one that appeals because of habit and prejudice, or because of the comfort of agreeing with one's acquaintances. Much as a scientist or philosopher can establish a theory only by seeing if it survives tests that might disconfirm it, so a proponent of a political position can discover its soundness only by considering the strongest objections to it. Or, as Mill famously puts the point, "he who knows only his own side of the case, knows little of that . . . if he is equally unable to refute the reasons on the other side; if he does not so much as know what they are, he has no ground for preferring either opinion."[39]

In any complex issue of human affairs, "on every subject on which difference of opinion is possible," Mill explains, "the

38. "How Reliable Is Imperial College's Modelling?"
39. Mill, *On Liberty*, 43.

truth depends on a balance to be struck between two sets of conflicting reasons."[40] Therefore, anyone really interested in finding the best policy will not just tolerate criticism, but will actively seek it out. "Nor is it enough," Mill writes, "that he should hear the arguments of adversaries from his own teachers, presented as they state them, and accompanied by what they offer as refutations. That is not the way to do justice to the arguments or bring them into real contact with his own mind."[41]

To bring arguments "into real contact" with one's own mind, one has to grasp what makes them persuasive to an intelligent, well-intentioned person. People who do not make the effort to do that may by chance hold a true opinion, "but it might be false for anything they know; they have never thrown themselves into the mental position of those who think differently from them . . . and consequently they do not, in any proper sense, know the doctrine which they themselves profess."[42] They do not know whether a fact that apparently contradicts their position actually does so, or how their position might be amended to take account of it: "All that part of the truth which turns the scale, and decides the judgment of a completely informed mind, they are strangers to; nor is it ever really known, but to those who have attended equally and impartially to both sides, and endeavoured to see the reasons of both in the strongest light."[43]

If people do not make the effort to seek out intelligent criticism, if they do not bother to find out if the policies they are

40. Mill, 43.
41. Mill, 44.
42. Mill, 44.
43. Mill, 44.

inclined to favor are really the best, and if they remain content with a weaker version of a position or policy than they could have, then they cannot properly say that their chief concern is the policy's professed purpose. One's actual behavior shows that one's professed goal is not one's actual goal, an insight from the field of economics that we discuss at length in chapter 4. If, for instance, a person advocates a reform designed to reduce poverty but does not bother to inquire whether similar reforms have backfired, or ascertain whether a modification of the reform might make it more effective, then the reduction of poverty is a lesser concern than remaining at one's intellectual ease or avoiding the discomfort of disagreeing with one's acquaintances. As Tolstoy would say, one is not thinking authentically. And, if that is the case, one has no business pretending to occupy the moral high ground.

In *Anna Karenina*, Tolstoy examines not just *what* people believe, but also *how* they believe, and he distinguishes between those who truly think from those who arrange to remain comfortable with their positions. His hero, Konstantin Levin, wants to improve the productivity of agriculture and the condition of the peasants. He knows from experience that the doctrines of received liberal opinion do not work. So he seeks out alternative viewpoints; he tries to expand the compass of his experience. By contrast, his friend Sviazhsky makes sure to dismiss in advance any arguments that might lead away from the opinions an up-to-date nobleman is supposed to hold. When a conservative landowner offers criticisms of those opinions, Sviazhsky dismisses them out of hand just because they are "reactionary," while Levin, who has not heard these criticisms before, attends to them.

While Sviazhsky "makes a faint gesture of irony" (get a load of that, you conservative!), Levin, whose main concern is to find out what will really improve the condition of the peasants, listens carefully to the landowner even though he does not share his conclusions. The reason is that the landowner thinks authentically, and that one can learn from his reflections: "The landowner unmistakably spoke his own individual thought—a thing that rarely happens—and a thought to which he had been brought not by a desire of finding some exercise for an idle brain, but a thought which had grown out of the conditions of his life, which he had brooded over in the solitude of his village, and considered in its every aspect."[44]

Since the landowner's opinions derive from real experience, and have not been adjusted to accord with prevailing opinion, Levin can, by entering into the landowner's train of thought, graft that experience onto his own. Without drawing the same conclusions as the landowner, he can enrich his own understanding by considering pertinent facts that have not previously come to his attention. Sviazhsky, and those many people who are like him, cannot do that. Even when criticism is readily available, only those whose real goals are their professed goals—whose concern is to arrive at the truth and not to defend the position shared by their group—can learn from it.

Criticism and Certainty

In the world of opinion, one at least pays lip service to the value of diverse opinions, a free press, and the need to be well informed of all sides of an issue. That is not at all the case in the world of certainty. Attending to views that must be false can only show a failure to appreciate one's own position. It demonstrates that

44. Leo Tolstoy, *Anna Karenina*, trans. Constance Garnett, rev. ed. Leonard J. Kent and Nina Berberova (New York: Modern Library, 1965), 350.

you accept your views as mere belief, rather than as mathematical certainty. In such a climate, the availability of opposing positions is not freedom but mystification.

Morson distinctly recalls being told by a Soviet citizen: "Of course we have complete freedom of speech. We just do not allow people to lie." A lie, of course, was any position at odds with that of the Party, which everyone can be certain is always right. Criticism in such a world performs an entirely different function. It is not an instrument for ascertaining truth, which is already known, but a tool employed against evil and falsity. As Marx observed, it "is not a scalpel but a weapon. Its object is the enemy, [whom] it wishes not to refute but to destroy."[45]

Lenin took this position seriously and extended it. His language of destruction served as a model and was taught as such in Soviet schools. In Lenin's view, a true revolutionary did not establish the correctness of his beliefs by appealing to evidence or logic; the truth of his position was a given. Rather, one engaged in "blackening an opponent's mug so well it takes him ages to get it clean again."[46] Nikolay Valentinov, a Bolshevik who knew Lenin well before becoming disillusioned, reports him saying, "There is only one answer to revisionism: smash its face in!"[47] When the other Russian Marxist party, the Mensheviks, objected to Lenin's personal attacks, he replied frankly that his purpose was not to convince but to destroy his opponent. In work after work, Lenin does not offer arguments refuting other Social Democrats, but brands them as "renegades" from

45. Cited in Pipes, *Communism*, 10.

46. Nikolay Valentinov (N. V. Volsky), *Encounters with Lenin*, trans. Paul Rosta and Brian Pearce (London: Oxford University Press, 1968), 243.

47. Valentinov, *Encounters with Lenin*, 184.

Marxism.[48] Marxists who disagreed with his naïve epistemology were "philosophic scum." Object to his brutality, and your arguments are "moralizing vomit."[49]

The point was to assault the reader and intimidate the opposition. Any observer of Lenin, or of those who imitated him, will recognize a style consisting of name calling and personal invective. Lenin does not just advance a claim—he insists that it is absolutely certain and, for good measure, says the same thing again in other words. It is absolutely certain, beyond any possible doubt, perfectly clear to anyone not dull-witted: "This is beyond doubt. . . . All this is beyond the slightest possible doubt."[50] Nothing is true unless it is absolutely, indubitably so; if a position is wrong, it is entirely and irredeemably wrong; if something must be done, it must be done "immediately, without any delay"; Party representatives are to make no concessions whatsoever.[51]

In this mindset, compromise is ruled out in principle. Truth does not compromise with falsehood, as if there were some middle ground, nor does goodness make any concessions to evil, as if there might be some gain from splitting the difference. Everything is a zero-sum game: to the extent the other side prospers, goodness suffers. Therefore, if the opportunity exists to annihilate one's opponent, it would be criminal not to do

48. To take just one example, there is his reply to Karl Kautsky, entitled "The Proletarian Revolution and the Renegade Kautsky."

49. Valentinov, *Encounters with Lenin*, 242.

50. Lenin, "Two Tactics of Social Democracy in the Democratic Revolution," in *A Documentary History of Communism*, vol. 1, ed. Robert V. Daniels (New York: Vintage, 1960), 40.

51. Lenin, "Draft Resolution on Party Unity," in *The Lenin Anthology*, ed. Robert C. Tucker (New York: Norton, 1975), 501.

so—or, if not criminal, then literally insane. When foreign commissar Georgy Chicherin suggested moderation in repressing the Mensheviks, Lenin called him a "lunatic," and, when in 1922 Chicherin proposed a minor concession in negotiations with the Americans, Lenin made clear he meant the charge of insanity literally.[52] Chicherin, he decided, was "ill and seriously so" and concluded, "We will be fools if we do not immediately and forcibly send him to a sanatorium."[53] Also in 1922, Lenin doubted the sanity of Politburo members Lev Kamenev, Leon Trotsky, and Aleksei Rykov and "ordered the lot of them to be subjected to examination by a visiting specialist in 'nervous diseases.'"[54]

Critics objected that Lenin argued by mere assertion. They observed that he disproved a position simply by showing that it was different from his own. In his attack on the epistemology of the philosophers Ernst Mach and Richard Avenarius, for instance, every argument contrary to dialectical materialism is rejected *for that reason alone*. Valentinov, who saw Lenin frequently when he was crafting this treatise, reports that Lenin glanced through their works for a few hours at most. It was easy enough to attribute to them views they did not hold, associate them with disreputable people they had never heard of, or ascribe political purposes they had never imagined. These were Lenin's usual techniques, and he made no bones about it.

Valentinov was appalled that both Lenin and Plekhanov, the first Russian Marxist, insisted that there was no need to under-

52. Robert Conquest, *V. I. Lenin* (New York: Viking, 1972), 108.
53. Richard Pipes, ed., *The Unknown Lenin: From the Secret Archive*, trans. Catherine A. Fitzpatrick (New Haven, CT: Yale University Press, 1998), 156.
54. Pipes, *Unknown Lenin*, 9.

Today?

stand opposing views before denouncing them, since the very
fact that they were opposing views proved them wrong, and
therefore criminal. He quotes Lenin:

> Marxism is a monolithic conception of the world, it does not
> tolerate dilution and vulgarization by means of various inser-
> tions and additions. Plekhanov once said to me about a critic
> of Marxism . . . : "First, let's stick the convict's badge on him,
> and then after that we'll examine his case." And I think we
> must stick the "convict's badge" on anyone and everyone
> who tries to undermine Marxism, even if we don't go on to
> examine his case. That's how every sound revolutionary
> should react. When you see a stinking heap on the road you
> don't have to poke around in it to see what it is. Your nose
> tells you it's shit, and you give it a wide berth.[55]

"Lenin's words took my breath away," Valentinov recalls.[56]

If one is certain one's beliefs are correct, then it is entirely
logical to refute an idea just by showing that it differs from one's
own. In fact, this was to become a standard form of argument
in the Soviet Union. One could refute a theory of chemistry in
two ways: either do what "bourgeois" scientists would do and
show that chemical experiments do not substantiate it, or show
that it is inconsistent with Marxism-Leninism.

Lenin and his followers fully recognized the consequence of
regarding all truth and goodness as lying on one side. Certain
was certain, and infallible was just that. The converse is also
often true: people who use this sort of argument may do so
because of an essentially Leninist way of thinking. One can

55. Valentinov, *Encounters with Lenin*, 182.
56. Valentinov, 182.

recognize a move toward Leninist thinking in the following circumstances, all of which are consequences of locating all truth and goodness in one's own position:

1. The view of politics as a zero-sum game. In that case, anything that hurts the other side is good. Compromise is ruled out in principle.

2. The monitoring of the members of one's own side for any deviation in the wrong direction, any concession that the other side might have a point. A culture of denunciation arises, at first to silence conservatives, then to deny a forum to liberals, and at last to ensure purity in one's own group. A similar dynamic, of course, can exist on the right and work in the opposite direction. Addressing the fourteenth Party Congress in 1925, S. I. Gusev declared, "Lenin once taught us that every member of the Party must be an agent of the Cheka [secret police], that is, we must watch and inform. . . . If we suffer from anything it is not from denunciation but from non-denunciation. We might be the best of friends, but once we start to differ in politics, we must not only break off our friendships, we must go further and start informing."[57] When people hesitate to express doubts to friends or colleagues, or to express them in writing that someday might be discovered, the move toward Leninism is in process.

3. The choice of rhetoric or tactics designed not to refute but to destroy opponents or, at least, to silence them.

---

57. Dmitri Volkogonov, *Lenin: A New Biography*, trans. Harold Shukman (New York: Free Press, 1994), xxxviii.

4. The willingness to charge opponents without evidence of the most heinous attitudes or crimes. They are all whatever-is-most-evil-today-ists, in the pay of whatever foreign power is most heinous, or guilty of the most obscene perversions.

5. A culture of what the Soviets called "self-criticism" (*samokritika*), in which someone who has advocated a view now regarded as wrong must abase himself, denounce his deviations with no loophole or room to doubt his sincerity, pledge never to deviate in the future, and call for condemnation if he should ever do so. To preserve one's job, and eventually one's life, one must humiliate oneself.[58]

6. An interpretive practice in which even apparently innocent remarks by an opponent may be shown to be coded heresy (as we would say, a "dog whistle") designed to pass unnoticed except by other opponents. When this practice becomes common, no utterance is safe.

7. Above all, when the predominant appeal and most prevalent emotion is not happiness about the good being accomplished, but hatred of those who stand in its way. The plans of one's own side may be vague, and the ways in which they will be implemented or paid for left unspecified, but the evil of those on the other side becomes the chief focus. It is of course a lot easier to destroy others than to create justice.

---

58. For an example of self-criticism in English, see Sergei Eisenstein, "My Worthless and Vicious Film," in *Readings in Russian Civilization*, vol. 3, ed. Thomas Riha (Chicago: University of Chicago Press, 1964), 705–7.

Novels and Utopias

We do not live in a world of certainty, but some literary genres try to persuade us that we do. In literary utopias, for instance, anyone who maintains that we cannot be absolutely certain must be a defender of the old capitalist world. The idea of "opinion" serves the existing order and must be rejected.

By convention, most literary utopias tell the story of a person from our world, with all the beliefs presently regarded as common sense, who somehow (say, after a century's sleep) finds himself in the world of utopia, where today's common sense seems preposterous. "Looking backward," it seems hard to believe that all the old truisms—like the constancy of human nature, the need for incentives, the inevitability of different points of view—were ever accepted.[59] In such classics as Edward Bellamy's *Looking Backward, 2000–1887* and William Morris's *News from Nowhere*, the traveler to utopia discovers that human nature is not complex, that social problems have a ready solution, that ethical problems are simple, and that there is no more disagreement about anything, just as no one disagrees about arithmetic. At some point the traveler asks the sort of question that readers might ask, but the question itself shows the corruption or foolishness of anyone who would pose it. Should the traveler inquire about how criminals are treated, he will discover that only a fool would believe that there would be any crime in a socialist society; should he ask about utopian politics, he will meet with incomprehension as to what that term could possibly mean. Horror, shock, or lack of understanding reveal what might be called a self-implicating question:

59. See Gary Saul Morson, *The Boundaries of Genre: Dostoevsky's Diary of a Writer and the Traditions of Literary Utopia* (Austin: University of Texas Press, 1981).

"Oh, Stranger! That last question of yours finally reveals to me the last depths of your country's wretchedness."

—DENIS DIDEROT, SUPPLEMENT TO
BOUGAINVILLE'S "VOYAGE"[60]

As soon as the words were out of my mouth, I felt I had made a mistake, for Dick flushed red and frowned, and the old men looked surprised and pained; and presently Dick said angrily, yet as if restraining himself somewhat—

"Man alive! How can you ask such a question?"

—WILLIAM MORRIS, *NEWS FROM NOWHERE*[61]

"I am glad that it is of *me* that you ask that question. I do believe that anybody else would make you explain yourself, or try to do so, till you were sickened of asking questions."

—WILLIAM MORRIS, *NEWS FROM NOWHERE*[62]

By contrast, realist novels presume that absolute truth about human affairs cannot be had. Even when the narrator expresses a strongly held opinion, as George Eliot often does, she speaks as one human conversing with others, as someone who, like all humans, generalizes from necessarily partial experience and so could turn out to be wrong.

Time and again, realist novels tell a story the exact opposite of that told in utopias. In utopias, we see the light; in novels, the twilight. The hero and readers of utopias learn that the world is not as complex as they supposed, while their novelistic counterparts

60. Denis Diderot, "Supplement to Bougainville's 'Voyage,'" "Rameau's Nephew," *and Other Works*, trans. Jacques Barzun and Ralph H. Bowen (Indianapolis: Bobbs-Merrill, 1956), 202.

61. William Morris, *News from Nowhere, or An Epoch of Rest, Being Some Chapters from a Utopian Romance* (New York: Longmans, 1910), 47–48.

62. Morris, *News from Nowhere*, 94.

learn that it is not as simple. As we read great realist novels we recognize that our minds focus on one line of causation, but there are many; we see only what is most noticeable, while countless barely perceptible events acting together may be more important; moral questions appear simple only to people who are ignorant of the intricate weave of circumstances and conflicting imperatives; choices are often difficult because to get one good thing, one must forego another, and no one can tell which is better; all actions have unintended consequences, and no one can foresee the unintended consequences of unintended consequences; a sensible decision in one social milieu, culture, or age may prove foolish in another, for reasons no one can specify.

These novelistic lessons, pertaining to the world in which all people live, are complicated by others pertaining to ourselves. It is not just that the world is hard to understand; our processes of understanding themselves mislead us. We think we see clearly, but we select and shade according to our "pride and prejudice" and, with unearned confidence in our own perception, wonder why others do not see as we do. In a famous passage in *Middlemarch*, George Eliot explains the trick by which our ego shapes the perceptions we regard as objective:

> Your pier-glass or extensive surface of polished steel made to be rubbed by a housemaid, will be minutely and multitudinously scratched in all directions; but place now against it a lighted candle as a centre of illumination, and lo! the scratches will seem to arrange themselves in a fine series of concentric circles round that little sun. It is demonstrable that the scratches are going everywhere impartially, and it is only your candle which produces the flattering illusion of a

concentric arrangement, its light falling with an exclusive optical selection. These things are a parable. The scratches are events, and the candle is the egoism of any person now absent.[63]

Even the candle parable turns out to be too simple, because candles closely resemble each other, but all of us are vain in our own way: "Our vanities differ as our noses do: all conceit is not the same conceit, but varies in correspondence with the minutiae of mental make in which one of us differs from another."[64]

Utopians and political fundamentalists generally treat people as essentially interchangeable. As Turgenev's ideological materialist, Evgeny Bazarov, puts the point, they all have the same spleen. That is one reason why political solutions seem so obvious. But, for the great realist novelists, wisdom consists in recognizing that small differences—"the minutiae of mental make" and of social conditions—can make all the difference. We do not know the single right answer to difficult moral questions, but we can be confident that to the extent we see them as simple, we are deceiving ourselves. Indeed, at least since Jane Austen, the realist novel's great theme is self-deception. Ideologues and fundamentalists do not suspect its importance, and if it enters their vocabulary, it is only to accuse their opponents of it.

In much the way that utopias transport believers in complexity into a world where everything is simple, realist novels of ideas place believers in a single comprehensive simple truth in a world where such truths are not to be had. There are two main

63. George Eliot, *Middlemarch* (New York: Modern Library, 1984), 255.

64. Eliot, *Middlemarch*, 145.

ways in which novels cast an ironic shadow on all ideologues. First, the authors subject their belief to what might be called an "irony of origins": readers detect what eludes the ideological hero or heroine, that the beliefs regarded as certain appear so because they satisfy a psychological need. Second, ideological heroes and heroines encounter an irony of *outcomes*: their beliefs lead to disaster precisely because of complexities they had not imagined. A materialist hero who rejects art, sees the world entirely in terms of natural laws, rejects any talk of nature's "beauty" and regards love as a merely physiological process—finds himself hopelessly in love with a woman who knows how to use all kinds of beauty to bewitch him (Turgenev's *Fathers and Children*). An atheist who rejects the existence of absolute moral norms, and who maintains that whatever moral norms may exist pertain only to actions and not to wishes, ends up consumed by guilt for a murder he has enabled only by desiring it (Dostoevsky's *The Brothers Karamazov*).

Reality ambushes those who think they have grasped it. But not until it is too late. If one asks political fundamentalists to examine their own need for certainty or moral purity, or if one points to the disasters caused by earlier ideologues who were as certain as they are, they will regard such questions as tricks and not consider them seriously. If they were capable of considering them, they would not be political fundamentalists in the first place.

It is probably no accident that the only nineteenth-century work to have foreseen what we have come to call "totalitarianism" was not a political disquisition or a philosophical treatise, but a realist novel about revolutionaries: Dostoevsky's *The Possessed*. Predictions regarded as mad at the time—for example, that communist revolutionaries in power would "remove a hundred million heads"—have proven to be, if anything, under-stated.[65] During Mao's Cultural Revolution, when the Chinese Communist Party destroyed traditional art, some readers re-called Dostoevsky's revolutionary Pyotr Stepanovich's promise of a universal "system of spying" to enforce "equality": "Cicero will have his tongue cut out, Copernicus will have his eyes put out, Shakespeare will be stoned. . . . We'll reduce all to a com-mon denominator! Complete equality!"[66] It was as if Dosto-evsky, and Dostoevsky alone, had seen into the future!

Dostoevsky wanted to dramatize not just where ideological thinking could lead, but also the sort of mindset that produces it. Especially well-known is the exposition of one ideologue, Shigalev:

> I've come to the conviction that all [earlier] makers of social systems from ancient times up to the present year, 187-, have been dreamers, tellers of fairy-tales, fools who contradicted themselves, who understood nothing of natural science. . . . In order to avoid further uncertainty, I propose my own sys-tem of world-organization. . . . I am perplexed by my own data and my conclusion is a direct contradiction of the origi-nal idea with which I start. Starting from unlimited freedom, I arrive at absolute despotism. I will add, however, that there can be no solution of the social problem but mine.[67]

It has proven eerily correct that ideologies promising the great-est freedom and equality have produced the greatest despo-tisms. Dostoevsky's point is that such an outcome is what one

65. Fyodor Dostoevsky, *The Possessed*, trans. Constance Garnett (New York: Modern Library, 1963), 413.

66. Dostoevsky, *Possessed*, 424–25.

67. Dostoevsky, 411.

might expect from fundamentalist ideology encountering no resistance. The most absurd programs will be put into practice with the absolute assurance that "there can be no solution of the social problem but mine."

Satire and Systems

As we have seen, every literary genre proceeds from guiding assumptions. In presuming that individual people, society, and the world as a whole are far more complex than any theory, realist novels continue the tradition of another genre: satire. In satire, that conclusion is not the main point, as it is in realist novels. Rather, it is the consequence of satire's suspicion of *all* grandiose human claims, especially claims of virtue we do not have and knowledge we cannot possess.

As the great satirists have represented them, people endlessly succumb to belief in their own virtue and wisdom. Any doctrine that flatters their self-regard in either respect is almost guaranteed to gain adherents. Such doctrines typically divide the world into adherents who are good and wise, and opponents who are evil and ignorant. In the most savage satires, this division is taken to the extreme and leaves no middle ground: vanity persuades people that if only the good people (those like themselves) had absolute power, they could bring utopia to earth.

From the perspective of the great satirists, such hubristic beliefs derive from the worst vice of all: pride. Satires may be directed against any human failing; name your sin—lust, gluttony, greed, envy, and there are satires about it.[68] But pride occupies a special status, since it is the vice that makes us deny

---

68. One might think that sloth would be an exception, inasmuch as it is difficult to construct a plot where the hero does nothing, but Ivan Goncharov's magnificent

other vices. It is therefore often accompanied by hypocrisy and self-deception. Pride goes so deep that we can never escape it. As La Rochefoucauld observed, "Self-love is cleverer than the cleverest person in the world."[69] It is always one step ahead of us. We pride ourselves on having overcome it. We cannot outwit it and therefore succumb all the more readily to every other vice. No genre has a more profound sense of ineradicable human fallibility than satire. It is the genre of original sin, and, as the old saw has it, original sin is the only theological doctrine that can be proven empirically.

Satire's favorite targets are those who imagine that they are wiser or better than others. In some periods that means sanctimonious clergy, who flaunt their purported superiority to the laity. Since the age of reason, the intelligentsia—the stupidly learned, foolishly theoretical, and pseudoscientifically smug— plays the same role. Intellectuals gravitate to theories that offer the key to human affairs, and they almost always imagine that theoretical knowledge is far superior to practical wisdom. From the satirist's perspective, the reason is obvious: if theory rules the world, then theorists should rule the world. As Tolstoy puts it, it is "natural and agreeable" for learned people to think "that their class is the basis of the movement of all humanity," and if we have histories that trace the cause of events to men of ideas, but none to the activity of merchants or shoemakers, that is only because merchants and shoemakers do not write histories.[70] The worldly success of merely practical people therefore

---

Oblomov, whose hero does not get out of bed for the first hundred pages, shows it can be done!

69. La Rochefoucauld, *The Maxims of La Rochefoucauld*, trans. Louis Kronenberger (New York: Random House, 1959), 33.

70. Leo Tolstoy, *War and Peace*, trans. Ann Dunnigan (New York: Signet, 1965), 1420.

seems to them an injustice to be remedied. The wealth of those who do or produce things, seems like some sort of trick, if not theft.

Some satires mock thinkers whose palpably absurd systems seem to hang in thin air, as Socrates literally does in Aristophanes's *The Clouds*. Suspended in a basket over the stage—as if he is up in the clouds—he ponders such conundrums as the end through which a gnat breaks wind. In Laurence Sterne's classic satire *Tristram Shandy*, Tristram's father, Walter Shandy, is ever on the lookout for some new system, each more preposterous than the previous one, since Sterne's target is the systematizing mind itself. Walter believes, for instance, that a person's name determines his or her character, so that "there was a strange kind of magick bias, which good or bad names, as he called them, irresistibly impress'd upon our characters and conduct."[71] "By mere inspiration of the names," people called Caesar or Pompey would become worthy of them.

Walter "proves" his theories by a series of specious arguments that, we recognize, are common to defenders of many more plausible systems. To begin with, he offers illustrations of a theory as demonstrations of it, whereas, of course, a theory must be tested against counterexamples. Any cockamamie idea can be illustrated. Or he takes an extreme, and emotionally charged, example. "In that soft *piano* of voice, which the nature of the *argumentum ad hominem* absolutely requires," he would ask his opponent whether for any sum of money he would consent to have his son named Judas?[72] Sterne goes through fallacy after fallacy in Walter's argument, to the point where *Tristram*

---

71. Laurence Sterne, *The Life and Opinions of Tristram Shandy, Gentleman*, ed. James Aiken Work (New York: Odyssey, 1940), 50.

72. Sterne, *Tristram Shandy*, 51.

Shandy could serve as a go-to book for anyone puzzled by the way systematizers argue.

Tristram presents his father's case as "a warning to the learned." His point is that educated people are predisposed to such reasoning because it flatters their importance. They begin innocently enough to entertain a comprehensive explanation as a mere hypothesis, but it soon becomes an unshakeable truth: "Such guests ... after a free and undisturbed entrance, for some years, into our brains,—at length claim a kind of settlement there, working like yeast." And so the learned person soon becomes "the dupe of his wit."[73] Or, as the great satirist Orwell once remarked, "One has to belong to the intelligentsia to believe things like that; no ordinary man would be such a fool."[74] Sterne intends for Tristram's famous characterization of his father to apply to adherents of all systems, past, present, and to come: "He was serious;—he was all uniformity; he was systematical, and, like all systematick reasoners, he would move both heaven and earth, and twist and torture every thing in nature, to support his hypothesis."[75]

The first part of Dostoevsky's *Notes from Underground*— a satire embedded in a novel—ridicules nineteenth-century systems purporting to explain the world, specifically utilitarianism as an explanation of all human behavior and the rationalistic "law of progress" guaranteeing that later is better. Both of these systems reflect an optimism that no actual experience of the world, and no self-knowledge, could justify. Neither individuals nor the world can be described as "rational," the underground

73. Sterne, 53.
74. From "Notes on Nationalism," as cited in *The Yale Book of Quotations*, ed. Fred R. Shapiro (New Haven, CT: Yale University Press, 2006), 569.
75. Sterne, *Tristram Shandy*, 53.

man argues, unless one arbitrarily excludes counterevidence or resorts to sheer tautology. There are countless things one can say about the history of the world, he remarks, "anything that might enter the most disordered imagination. The only thing one cannot say is that it is rational. The very word sticks in one's throat."[76]

The underground man knows in advance, as satirists traditionally do, that his arguments will make no difference. That is because the great systems include answers to any logical objections and can explain away any possible evidence; they are masters of what might be called "preemptive epistemology." In short, the underground man observes, "man is so fond of systems and abstract deductions that he is ready to distort the truth intentionally, he is ready to deny what he can see and hear just to justify his logic."[77]

Systems like Walter Shandy's are more ridiculous than dangerous. But when utopian theorists actually gain political power, the destructiveness concatenates. It turns out that nothing causes more evil than the attempt to abolish evil once and for all, and that no corrupt thug occasions as much horror as an ideological fundamentalist in power. "Madmen in authority who hear voices in the air," writes John Maynard Keynes, "are distilling their frenzy from some academic scribbler a few years back."[78]

The great satirists of our time—Orwell, Bulgakov, Solzhenitsyn—are considerably more savage than Sterne. They have had occasion to examine political fundamentalism in power. In one celebrated passage, Solzhenitsyn poses a question: Why is it

76. Fyodor Dostoevsky, "Notes from Underground" and "The Grand Inquisitor," ed. Ralph Matlaw (New York: Dutton, 1960), 27.

77. Dostoevsky, Notes from Underground, 21.

78. As cited in Yale Book of Quotations, 425–26.

that Macbeth and other Shakespearean villains "stopped short at a dozen corpses," while Lenin and Stalin were able to motivate the killing of millions? The answer is that Macbeth and Iago had no *ideology*: *what ?*

> Ideology—that is what gives evil-doing its long-sought justification and gives the evildoer the necessary steadfastness and determination. That is the social theory which helps to make his acts seem good instead of bad in his own and others' eyes, so that he won't hear reproaches and curses but will receive praise and honors.... Thanks to *ideology*, the twentieth century was fated to experience evil-doing on a scale calculated in the millions.... That is the precise line the Shakespearean evildoer could not cross. But the evildoer with ideology does cross it, and his eyes remain dry and clear.[79]

No matter how much evil they do, ideological fundamentalists imagine they are doing good, and that it is the other side that commits evil. *today*

The Silo

How is it possible to believe that one's opponents are not just mistaken about policy, but are actively evil? What makes one suppose that they are not well-intentioned believers in policies

what ?

79. *The Solzhenitsyn Reader: New and Essential Writings, 1947–2005*, ed. Edward E. Ericson Jr. and Daniel J. Mahoney (Wilmington, DE: ISI, 2015), 234 (from *The Gulag Archipelago*). Solzhenitsyn's savagery as a satirist is present throughout *The Gulag Archipelago*, *In the First Circle* (see, e.g., the chapters "The Trial of Prince Igor" and "The Ark," and the descriptions of Stalin writing his essay on linguistics), and *The Red Wheel*. In *August 1914*, the first part of *The Red Wheel*, see especially the long passage in which two aunts persuade their daughter not to disgrace the family tradition of terrorism by devoting herself to art, which the aunts call "nihilism."

bound to fail, but deliberate abettors of harm? In totalitarian regimes, people can easily be educated from birth to think of others they have never met as demons, since, after all, one never hears the other side make its case. Others cannot speak for themselves, but are characterized by those who hate them. It is as if juries first heard the prosecution's case, and then, instead of hearing from a defense attorney, heard the prosecutor describe what the defense would have said.

In a democracy, a plethora of voices is always available, and so, one would think, accusations against opponents could not stray into the fantastic. And yet when people are in the grip of fundamentalist politics, they do.

Before racial integration, it was possible to demonize people of other races in ways that would appear ridiculous once one encountered them daily. Then they proved to have similar concerns and worries, and their differences from ourselves did not seem greater than their differences among themselves. It follows that the more one group of people is segregated from another, the more extreme views can seem plausible. Fundamentalists favor silos.

The *New Yorker* film critic Pauline Kael supposedly said about Nixon's 1972 landslide electoral victory, "I can't believe Nixon won. I don't know anyone who voted for him." That version apparently shortens her actual words: "I live in a rather special world. I only know one person who voted for Nixon. Where they are I don't know. They're outside my ken. But sometimes when I'm in a theater I can feel them."[80] And Morson recalls overhearing one Stanford professor commenting to an-

80. John Podhoretz, "The Actual Pauline Kael Quote—Not as Bad, and Worse," *Commentary*, February 27, 2011, https://www.commentarymagazine.com/john-podhoretz/the-actual-pauline-kael-quote%E2%80%94not-as-bad-and-worse/.

other during the election of 1988, "I don't believe the polls that say Bush is going to beat Dukakis. I don't know a single person voting for Bush."

The problem here is not just a failure to grasp the concept of a biased sample. It is, rather, the consequence of living in a milieu where only one point of view exists. In such a milieu, if someone offers a false characterization of the other side, there is no one to correct him, and so, after frequent repetition, the falsehood will be taken as fact that no sane person could doubt; then it will make plausible another characterization still further from the truth. Soon one's political opponents become sinister, as Kael's comment that "sometimes when I'm in a theater I can feel them" suggests. Like demons, they lurk in the dark.

When we began to teach more than four decades ago, it was common enough for Catholics to say they would never marry a Protestant, and vice versa. When we asked that question some five years ago, we were pleased to discover that no one admitted feeling that way anymore, until we realized that that was likely due to the fact that many of our students did not care about religion at all. It's very easy to be tolerant when you don't give a damn. Where they actually cared, they were *more* intolerant than their predecessors. Many agreed that they would never marry a Republican. Evidently, party identification had taken the place of religion as an unbridgeable gap. And the reason for such intolerance was not a devoted adherence to one's own faith, as it was for many earlier Catholics and Protestants, but a belief in the irredeemable evil of the other party. One suspects that, in an environment where everyone is a Republican, Democrats might occupy the same demonic position. One would not invite a "mixed couple"—a Democrat and a Republican—to dinner.

It is much easier now to live in a silo not just because people often dwell among people like themselves, but also because it is so easy to shut out news sources offering a different perspective. The idea that responsible journalists explain the positions of each side in a way its adherents would deem accurate now seems passé. One never has to acknowledge that issues are not black and white, or that events have shown one's views to have been mistaken. The world of CNN or Fox News can be so reassuring. The more people dwell in silos, the more others seem hateful and therefore worthy of hate. Democracy dies in silos. How odd that people who make a point of never listening to the other side accuse their opponents of being closed-minded!

United by Hatred or Hope?

The vanity of the selfless . . . is boundless.

—ERIC HOFFER, THE TRUE BELIEVER

Back in the supposedly simpler days of the early 1950s, Eric Hoffer explored the causes of fanaticism in his masterpiece, *The True Believer: Thoughts on the Nature of Mass Movements*.[81] Having rejected culture and traditions, discontented people who regard their lives as without meaning readily embrace mass

---

81. Eric Hoffer, *The True Believer: Thoughts on The Nature of Mass Movements* (New York: Harper & Row, 1951). The page numbers below are from the Perennial Classics, HarperCollins, Kindle edition. The epigraph to this section is from Hoffer, *True Believer*, 15. James Hohmann, in "The Daily 202: The Reading List That Helped Hillary Clinton Cope," *Washington Post*, September 18, 2017, https://www .washingtonpost.com/news/powerpost/paloma/daily-202/2017/09/18/daily-202 -the-reading-list-that-helped-hillary-clinton-cope/59bf19ad30fb045176650d02/, reports that Hillary Clinton was well aware of this book when she ran for president in 2016: "During the campaign, she writes that she and her husband Bill both read *The True Believer*, the 1951 classic by Eric Hofer [*sic*] about the psychology behind fanaticism and mass movements. She says she even told her senior staff that they should read it too."

movements promising drastic change; individuals trade their independent goals and capacity to judge for "united action and self-sacrifice."[82] One comes to identify as "a member of a certain tribe or family," Hoffer observes, and rituals designed to make the individual feel overwhelmed and awed by their membership in the tribe become commonplace. The past might be idealized, but the present certainly is not: "The radical and the reactionary loathe the present."[83]

"The effectiveness of [such] a doctrine," Hoffer observes, "does not come from its meaning but from its certitude."[84] In one way or another, doctrines "interpose a fact proof screen between the faithful and the realities of the word."[85] Hoffer stresses the psychological appeal of such screens, which lies precisely in their capacity to banish doubt. Here he echoes Dostoevsky's famous argument in the Grand Inquisitor chapter of *The Brothers Karamazov.* The inquisitor contrasts Jesus's desire for people to choose faith freely with his own insistence that people do not want freedom because it inevitably entails the agony of uncertainty. "So long as man remains free he strives for nothing so incessantly and so painfully as to find someone to [blindly] worship," the Inquisitor explains. "But man seeks to worship what is established beyond dispute, so that all men would agree at once to worship it."[86] All people must agree, because, where there is disagreement, there is doubt, and so all mass movements have tried to impose a uniform belief system. "I tell thee that man is tormented by no greater anxiety than to

82. Hoffer, *True Believer,* 84.
83. Hoffer, 74.
84. Hoffer, 80.
85. Hoffer, 79.
86. Fyodor Dostoevsky, *The Brothers Karamazov,* trans. Constance Garnett (New York: Modern Library, 1996), 282.

find someone to whom he can hand over the gift of freedom with which the ill-fated creature is born," the Inquisitor argues. "Nothing is more seductive for man than his freedom of conscience, but nothing is a greater cause of suffering."[87]

A doctrine banishing doubt, Hoffer observes, must not be too clear. "We can be absolutely certain only about things we do not understand" because what is understood can be closely examined. "A doctrine that is [fully] understood is shorn of its strength."[88] Here, too, Hoffer follows Dostoevsky's Inquisitor, who seeks to establish a world in thrall to "miracle, mystery, and authority," with "mystery" understood as a vagueness precluding close questioning and precluding doubt.[89] People flock to such movements because it is much more comforting to accept the truths of the social group to which one belongs than to live the skeptic's lonely life of doubt. The world of opinion may bring us closer to genuine truth, but it runs against deep currents of our nature, since we intuitively prefer a finalized doctrine to an endless series of approximations.

Certitude works best if fed by hatred. At the extreme, all opponents are evil, and all evil is at root the same. Hoffer quotes Hitler's observation that the great leader concentrates hatred so that "even adversaries far removed from one another seem to belong to a single category."[90] Hoffer also cites Luther's confession that, when his faith cools, he can always summon up hatred: "When my heart is cold and I cannot pray as I should, I scourge myself with the thought of the impiety and ingratitude

87. Dostoevsky, *Brothers Karamazov*, 282.

88. Hoffer, *True Believer*, 81.

89. Dostoevsky, *Brothers Karamazov*, 283.

90. Hoffer, *True Believer*, 92–93, citing Adolf Hitler, *Mein Kampf* (Boston: Houghton Mifflin, 1943), 118.

of my enemies, the Pope and his accomplices and vermin, and Zwingli, so that my heart swells with righteous indignation and hatred and I can say with warmth and vehemence: 'Holy be Thy Name, Thy Kingdom come, Thy Will be done!' And the hotter I grow the more ardent do my prayers become."[91]

Participants in movements that regard opponents as necessarily evil may not believe in a god, but they readily believe in a devil. It is hatred, not love or respect, that unifies the true believers. In the famous comic chapter of *The Brothers Karamazov*, in which Satan visits Ivan in a nightmare, the devil relates how he once tried to publish a letter of thanks to someone who had done him a service, but discovered that the newspapers would not print it, since belief in the supernatural is hopelessly conservative. "I laughed with the men at the newspaper office, 'it's reactionary to believe in God in our days,' I said, 'but I am the devil, so I may be believed in.' 'We quite understand that,' they said. 'Who doesn't believe in the devil? Yet it won't do, it might injure our reputation.'"[92] Dostoevsky's point is that even materialists and extreme relativists often accept the absolute evil of their opponents. Given human nature, hatred is a stronger motivator than respect and decency, let alone love.

Was Hoffer ever prescient! The devil for some is President Trump; for others it is the Squad. The other party is described as disgraceful, shameless, cruel, and utterly corrupt. And each side copies the worst tactics of the other. One proclaims sanctuary cities for immigrants sought by the immigration service, and the other responds with sanctuaries from state gun control laws. We have Antifa; how long before Antiso? What unifies

91. Hoffer, 99, who in turn is citing Luther's "Table Talk," in Frantz Funck-Bertano, *Luther* (London: Jonathan Cape, 1939), 319.

92. Dostoevsky, *Brothers Karamazov*, 750.

political true believers isn't what they are, but what they are not and whom they despise. Is it really surprising that in 2016 one estimate said that more than 20 percent of Bernie Sanders supporters refused to vote for Hillary Clinton, thereby helping elect Donald Trump?[93] Or that Republican Never-Trumpers declared in 2020 that they would rather vote for Sanders, whose views they have always regarded as atrocious?

The tradition of literary satire offers little hope. "We have just Religion enough to make us *hate*, but not enough to make us *love* one another," observes Jonathan Swift, but satire is, after all, a genre of exaggeration.[94] Hoffer, by contrast, doesn't give up hope. On occasion great leaders emerge who "harness man's hungers and fears to weld a following and make it zealous unto death in service of a holy cause; but unlike a Hitler, a Stalin, or even a Luther and a Calvin, they are not tempted to use the slime of frustrated souls as mortar in the building of a new world. . . . They know that no one can be honorable unless he honors mankind."[95]

Honoring mankind; finding and speaking to what is good in all of us; encouraging our regard for those with different views! What a novel idea—one that we need desperately to rediscover today, before the political meteor strikes.

93. Cass R. Sunstein, "Why Sanders Supporters Are So Tenacious," Bloomberg, February 20, 2020, https://www.bloomberg.com/opinion/articles/2020-02-20/bernie-sanders-supporters-driven-by-outrage. The article goes on to ask why so many of those who supported Sanders in the primaries didn't in the end support the Democratic candidate for president: "Much of the answer lies in one word: outrage. Trump supporters and Sanders supporters have that, at least, in common. Their outrage is fueled by the dynamics of '*group polarization*,' which means that when like-minded people speak mostly with one another, they usually end up more confident and more unified—and more extreme."

94. From "Thoughts on Various Subjects," as cited in *Yale Book of Quotations*, 740.

95. Hoffer, *True Believer*, 149.

4

Price and Prejudice

ECONOMICS AND THE QUEST FOR TRUTH

economics

Another Kind of Fundamentalism

Fundamentalism is not limited to the political arena. Alas, it is flourishing in economics as well. There are those whose faith in free markets is absolute and unwavering. To them, the role of government should be as small as possible, limited to such things as establishing and protecting property rights, which a market needs to function, and to providing "public" goods and internalizing externalities, called for by market theory itself.[1]

---

1. "Public goods" are goods and services that are socially valuable but that for-profit firms fail to provide, especially when, as in the case of many parks and local roads, it is difficult to exclude those who refuse to pay for using them. Externalities are created when a person's or a firm's production or consumption affects someone else's production or consumption. A positive externality arises when the marginal social benefit exceeds the marginal private benefit, thereby leading to a situation where goods and services are underproduced from the point of view of a social optimum. An example is an inoculation against the flu: society benefits more than an individual, so too few get flu shots unless the government subsidizes the price. A negative externality arises when the marginal social cost exceeds the marginal private

Market failures are rare, and there is a tendency to find failure where it is not really present, so the best that government can do is to leave the market pretty much alone.

So far as we can determine, the phrase "market fundamentalism" entered the public consciousness upon the 1998 publication of George Soros's book *The Crisis of Global Capitalism: Open Society Endangered*, where it is used repeatedly.[2] Soros does not explicitly define the term, but his usage suggests that he means it to apply not to a general preference for market solutions, but to a categorical commitment to them deduced from first principles and impervious to counterevidence. Market fundamentalists, as he describes them, believe their conclusions to be certain, because they are based on a hard science. To make such a claim when it is not warranted is to propound a pseudoscience, which does not mean those making the claim have nothing valuable to say—not all pseudosciences resemble astrology—but that, whatever their merits, their claim of scientific status is spurious.

At the heart of Soros's philosophy is a deeply held belief in human fallibility and occasional irrationality, which make a hard science of human behavior impossible. Consciousness of

---

cost, leading to overproduction—for example, with pollution. In each case, the government should step in to internalize the externality, leading to a situation where the marginal social benefit of each good or service is equal to its marginal social cost. The brilliant insight of the Coase theorem is that, while the assignment of property rights has an impact on income, a social optimum can be achieved regardless of who owns those rights. For example, if producers under capitalism have a right to maximize profit regardless of what they do to the environment, they should be rewarded if they pollute less. If the rest of us have a right to clean air and water, polluters should be subject to effluent fees to clean up the environment, or compensate those who suffer from their activities. Ronald Coase, "The Problem of Social Cost," *Journal of Law and Economics* 3, no. 1 (1960): 1–44.

2. George Soros, *The Crisis of Global Capitalism: Open Society Endangered* (New York: PublicAffairs, 1998).

human fallibility should also make us aware that solutions are not logically necessary, but they do work in particular contexts, and at particular times. That is, Soros thinks economics should be reconceived in terms of practical, not theoretical, reasoning, where solutions may be true "on the whole and for the most part." Correct solutions on any given occasion cannot be determined by theory alone: "Exactly what is right can be discovered only by a process of trial and error."[3]

Market fundamentalists, as described by Soros, also tend to see economic models as applicable to other disciplines, which can, by replacing traditional methods, also attain scientific status. He seems to have in mind the sort of application for which Gary Becker became famous. Market fundamentalists pretend they do not make value judgments, but in fact they smuggle into their analyses a moral theory according to which self-interest is not only a sound description of human behavior, but also a proper moral norm in itself. However, no society can exist for long unless people also share other values that allow for collective purposes and make sense of self-sacrifice.

Market fundamentalism, at the extreme, demands only an individualist morality, whereas, Soros explains, "there *are* common interests, including the preservation of free markets, that are not served by free markets."[4] In China, Confucian values, which stress the role of the family, provide another source of value, much as Lee Kuan Yew stressed the need for nonmarket, nonindividualist values as essential to a successful market economy. In this respect, Soros echoes a traditional conservative critique of libertarianism and extreme individualism.[5] While

3. Soros, *Crisis of Global Capitalism*, 96.
4. Soros, 95.
5. See, for instance, Roger Scruton, *The Meaning of Conservatism*, 3rd ed. (Houndmills, UK: Palgrave, [1980] 2001).

some libertarians see religion as oppressive superstition, many conservatives see religious values as essential for making a market economy work in an ethical way.

It is not necessary to accept Soros's specific critiques of capitalism, or his proposed solutions, to recognize that what he calls "market fundamentalism" satisfies our three criteria for fundamentalist thinking. Market fundamentalism exists, and, even if it is incomparably less dangerous than its polar opposite, the totalitarian philosophies of Marxist-Leninist command economies, it may still mislead. With the supreme confidence of scientists addressing the laity, market fundamentalists contend that markets lead not only to the most efficient allocation of scarce resources but also, quite often, to fairness as well. After all, don't we often call the price where supply and demand are equal the "fair" market price?[6] Here, as elsewhere, they smuggle in a moral conclusion as an objective description. Laissez-faire becomes laissez-"fair."

These fundamentalists suppose they worship at the foot of the founder of modern economics, Adam Smith. Smith's *The Wealth of Nations*, which they rarely read and present as it is typically summarized in basic textbooks, serves as a quasi-sacred text or, at least, as a founding revelation, before which all was darkness. Smith's notion of the "invisible hand" is a powerful metaphor attesting to the proposition that, in a free market economy, individual self-interest, operating through unseen forces, ends up serving the best interests of society. Rational actors, governed solely by their selfishness, will lead us to opti-

6. Language matters. The "fair" market price or value is actually the price for which the number of willing buyers is equal to the number of willing sellers. Whether or not that is in fact "fair," as a philosopher would define the term, certainly depends on the income distribution, access to education, and much more.

mality, assuming the government is smart enough to refrain from unnecessary interference.

Not surprisingly, some economists cringe at such unregulated, laissez-faire policies. One illustrious example is Joseph Stiglitz, who in his 2001 Nobel Prize lecture took a highly critical look at unbridled faith in market outcomes. Raising the specter of fundamentalism, Stiglitz took the International Monetary Fund, among others, to task:

> I believe that some of the huge mistakes which have been made in policy in the last decade, in for instance the management of the East Asia crisis or the transition of the former communist countries to a market, might have been avoided if there had been a better understanding of issues, like bankruptcy and corporate governance, to which the new information economics called attention. And the so-called Washington consensus policies, which have predominated in the policy advice of the international financial institutions over the past quarter century, have been based on market fundamentalist policies which ignored the information-theoretic concerns, and this explains at least in part their widespread failures.[7]

Calling out Adam Smith by name, Stiglitz states that "many of the major political debates over the past two decades have centered around one key issue: the efficiency of the market economy,

7. Joseph E. Stiglitz, "Information and the Change in the Paradigm in Economics," Nobel Lecture, December 8, 2001, 3. Stiglitz remains an active contributor to discussions of economic policy. One example is his response to President Trump's January 2020 speech at the World Economic Forum in Davos, Switzerland. See Max Zahn, "Donald Trump Is 'Just Wrong' about the Economy, Says Nobel-Prize Winner Joseph Stiglitz," Yahoo Finance, January 29, 2020, https://money.yahoo.com/donald -trump-wrong-economy-nobel-prize-joseph-stiglitz-202041681.html.

and the appropriate relationship between the market and the government. The argument of Adam Smith (1776), the founder of modern economics, that free markets led to efficient outcomes, 'as if by an invisible hand,' has played a central role in these debates: it suggested that we could, by and large, rely on markets *without government intervention.*"[8] On the other hand, if there is one thing worse than placing *complete* faith in market outcomes, it is having *no* faith. However foolish it may be to presume that the free market always leads to efficient and equitable solutions, it is still more foolish to presume that an intrusive government can always lead to a better result.[9]

In *Cents and Sensibility*, we urge economic policy makers to display less hubris and more common sense.[10] If they learned more about real people from the humanities and humanistically oriented social sciences, their strategies to enhance the human condition would prove more realizable. With a little less *Cents*, and a little more *Sensibility*, economists could better determine

---

8. Stiglitz, Nobel Lecture, 1. Italics are in the original text.

9. In an op-ed in the *Wall Street Journal*, William McGurn, former chief speechwriter for president George W. Bush and a member of the *Journal's* editorial board, lamented the use of "market fundamentalism" and "laissez-faire" in a derisive way: "At a time when many Americans regard capitalism as having failed, a debate over first principles is a good thing. But referring to critics as 'market fundamentalists' isn't aimed at encouraging debate. It's aimed at stacking it—in the same way progressives use 'anti-science' to tar anyone who dissents from their pet orthodoxies." Similarly, he writes that "*Laissez-faire* has become a dirty word. Today it serves as shorthand for a soulless, anything-goes approach to life in which government makes no contribution to a thriving economy and the market is the solution to every problem." William McGurn, "And Now a Word for *Laissez-Faire*," *Wall Street Journal*, March 10, 2020, A15. McGurn's point is that "market fundamentalism" and "laissez-faire" should not be used as all-purpose pejoratives. That is why we have offered a strict definition so debate could proceed responsibly.

10. Gary Saul Morson and Morton Schapiro, *Cents and Sensibility: What Economics Can Learn from the Humanities* (Princeton, NJ: Princeton University Press, 2017).

when and where to interfere with the market, thereby maximizing the chance that their policies will have their intended impact. In making recommendations to developing or post-
communist economies, they could, by considering local culture
and history, offer solutions more likely to succeed in a given
context.

But the reverse is also true. Humanists, and those who think
the way they do, would do well to become economically literate. It is one thing for faculty members in the humanities to
ignore the basic tenets of economics; it is much worse to see
citizens, and the politicians they elect, acting as if the ideas of
incentives, opportunity costs, and objective empirical analyses
lacked merit. Their *Prejudice* against the belief that a *Price* may
matter, makes it much less likely that their lofty aspirations will
ever be met and much more likely that their policies will make
things still worse. From recognizing and dealing with climate
change to addressing income inequality and its consequences,
to allocating budgets at the federal, state, local, and college
level, you ignore economics at your peril.

Not so long ago it seemed that, with the failure of the Soviet
Union, the dangers of a command economy were well understood. Never again, it was assumed, would people fail to grasp
that government officials have interests of their own, which
they pursue under the guise of helping the public.[11] Their solutions may be worse than the problems they presume to remedy.
The socialist formula (in the sense of government control of the

11. This argument became associated with former Yugoslav Communist leader
Milovan Djilas. See Milovan Djilas, *The New Class: An Analysis of the Communist
System* (San Diego, CA: Harcourt Brace, 1957). One can find a version of it in James
Burnham, *The Managerial Revolution: What Is Happening in the World* (New York:
John Day, 1941). Beginning with Bakunin, the Russian anarchists predicted just such
an outcome should Marxists gain power.

means of production and distribution) was supposedly dead forever. That is what Francis Fukuyama meant by "the end of history," and almost everyone seemed to share the sense that, even if history were not over, the debate between markets and command economies had been settled.[12] It is therefore dispiriting to see a resurrection, among humanists and others, of these not so dearly departed concepts. "Capitalism," "neoliberalism," and other all-purpose pejoratives are, as in the early twentieth century, once again the source of all evil. If market fundamentalism is a mistake, so is a failure to understand the benefits of markets.

Sometimes the ignorance and naïveté regarding basic economic concepts borders on the quaint. Morson once attended a meeting of humanities department chairs at a prestigious private university. Knowing that the chairs had stressed the importance of improving the pay of nontenure eligible faculty, the dean asked them how the money available for raises should be divided: What share should go to the non–tenure track faculty, who typically teach large numbers of classes at salaries far below tenure-line faculty, and what share should go to their tenured and tenure-track counterparts? Since the chairs were themselves tenured and elected by other tenured faculty, the question put them in the uncomfortable position of choosing between their professed principles and their self-interest. By choosing to unduly reward themselves, the chairs would be revealed as hypocrites, while the opposite choice would entail personal cost.

Economists assess preferences not by what people say, but by what they do. In other words, it is behavior, not pronouncements, that reveals underlying preferences. That is, they rely on

12. Francis Fukuyama, *The End of History and the Last Man* (New York: Free Press, [1992] 2006).

"revealed preferences," an important concept in the field of economics. So what did these chairs do? Anyone who knows how humanists often argue will not be surprised that, after a long pause, one declared: "We reject the false choice based on the notion that resources are limited."

Of course, no matter how big the pie, it is always finite, and priorities must be set somehow—if not explicitly, then implicitly by what one actually chooses. Economics, after all, is the study of how *scarce* resources are allocated. But, to these humanists, and those who have imbibed their ethos, scarce resources are merely an illusion. One only receives, never forgoes.[13] Their revealed preference was to preserve at all costs their image as high-minded agents without sacrificing their self-interest, either as administrators or as faculty members.

Alas, we believe such ways of thinking are now all too common. Despite efforts to deny it, scarcity exists. A horn of plenty that constantly replenishes itself occurs only in fairy tales. You can't redistribute what isn't produced. Consequently, there is

13. We bet readers will not be surprised by the skepticism among some faculty about economic trade-offs and the like. After all, aren't faculty these days supposed to be paragons of far-left antimarket thinking? One might ask how much truth there is in this characterization—is it overstated or perhaps even understated? A survey of Harvard University faculty taken on the eve of the Massachusetts primary is quite illuminating. James S. Bikales and Jasper G. Goodman ("Plurality of Surveyed Harvard Faculty Support Warren in Presidential Race," *Harvard Crimson*, March 3, 2020, https://www.thecrimson.com/article/2020/3/3/faculty-support-warren-president/) report that only 1 percent consider themselves either "conservative" or "very conservative," with 19 percent saying they are "moderate," 41 percent "liberal," and 38 percent "very liberal." How many of the 260 respondents said they support President Trump in his reelection campaign? Three. Of course, Harvard faculty may not be representative politically of the more than a million and a half faculty currently employed in the United States, and saying you are "very liberal" doesn't necessarily mean you reject market capitalism, but these numbers are a bit shocking even to us.

an economic imperative to allocate resources as efficiently as possible in order to address a society's needs.

Efficiency is also a moral imperative. No matter what one's goals, waste should be avoided. To dismiss economic principles and analyses as some form of "neoliberalism," without bothering to understand their potential power, is impossible to defend on *ethical* grounds. If deploying resources one way would save a thousand lives and another only ten, 990 lives depend on reaching the right decision. And this is a point that great literature, as well as great economics, has illustrated over and over again.

Anton Chekhov never tired of pointing out the self-indulgence of failing to allocate time, money, and energy effectively. Waste is one of his great themes. In his plays and stories, intellectuals regularly posture about their compassion, while wasting resources needed to help others. In this way, otherwise well-intentioned people cause serious but avoidable damage. They do not properly appreciate that if poverty is bad, then wasting resources capable of alleviating poverty is also bad, no matter how uplifting and morally gratifying a wasteful activity may be. In Chekhov's *Uncle Vanya*, Doctor Astrov eloquently describes the ongoing destruction of the natural environment, having traced decades of diminishing forests, wild elk, swans, and grouse. Astrov is disturbed not only because he loves nature and believes that people have an obligation to protect it, but also because the destruction has been entirely pointless. At least there might have been "in place of these devastated forests . . . highways, railroads, if there were factories, mills, schools, and the people had become healthier, richer, more intelligent—but you see, there is nothing of the sort!"[14] The

14. Anton Chekhov, "Uncle Vanya," in *Chekhov: The Major Plays*, ed. Ann Dunnigan (New York: Signet, 1964), 208.

same is true of human relations. If only we economized on human suffering! If only it were limited to the minimum necessary for the greater good! Indeed, we would be better off if it resulted entirely from self-interest; in that case, there would be a lot less of it than there is. Chekhov's stories and plays dramatize sheer waste, opportunities for kindness that are simply neglected. In the economy of things or personal relations, waste may be the greatest tragedy and is in itself immoral.

Much waste comes from the refusal to acknowledge the necessity of trade-offs. Those department chairs faced a choice on how to allocate resources. In Chekhov's final play, *The Cherry Orchard*, Madame Ranevskaya and her family, who have spent a lifetime wasting resources for no purpose, now must at last choose between having their estate sold at auction to pay the mortgage, or accepting the suggestion of the merchant Lopakhin, who proposes to save the estate by replacing the orchard with summer cottages for tourists. However sad it would be to lose the beautiful orchard, where the family spent so many wonderful hours in childhood, it will be destroyed in any case by anyone who buys the estate. But the family dreamily refuses to acknowledge that they simply *must* make a choice. This failure to face a real dilemma, which cannot be dismissed as a "false choice," creates avoidable waste. Instead of preserving something, they lose everything. Indeed, it has been their failure to recognize that resources are limited that has led to the inability to pay the mortgage in the first place.

It is no less true today that to regard efficiency and maximizing utility as vulgar, or ideologically suspect, entails harm to the very people about whom one professes to care. But try to explain "marginal utility" to most humanists, or, these days, to many politicians and voters. Chekhov's characters are still everywhere.

Recall the poll results summarized in the preceding chapter: 82 percent of Republicans said that the Democratic Party has been taken over by socialists. Any surprise, given that one of its standard-bearers, Bernie Sanders, is a self-described "democratic socialist"? And that he not only spent his honeymoon in the Soviet Union (no one goes there for the weather); he also served as an elector for the Socialist Workers' Party, which explicitly endorses Marxism-Leninism?[15]

The Economics of Hate?

Unfortunately, there is ample evidence that in Western countries people on the political extremes have a common goal: to tear down the status quo, sometimes with little notion of what should come after.[16] Even those closer to the center may act that way unwittingly. As Soros observes, sometimes even moderation can be taken to an extreme.[17]

Extremists tend to have more in common than just the idea that elites are bad. From the radical left to the far right, they often reject the application of basic economics, as if ideas like "scarce resources" and "trade-offs" were some conspiracy of the wealthy to defraud others. The very idea of assessing costs as well as benefits becomes suspect.

15. Not surprisingly, Sanders argues that many of his proposed policies, and his personal history, have been misrepresented in the media. For some valuable insight, see Robert Draper, "Left Behind: Bernie Sanders Believes America Misjudged Him. Did He Misjudge America?" *New York Times Magazine*, March 22, 2020, 28–31, 47–48.

16. See, for example, "Europeans Sour on Elites and the EU, but Agree on Little Else," *Economist*, December 1, 2018, https://www.economist.com/graphic-detail/2018/12/01/europeans-sour-on-elites-and-the-eu-but-agree-on-little-else.

17. Soros, *Crisis of Global Capitalism*, 96.

And this neglect of basic economics comes at a substantial price.[18] As icebergs melt, wealth inequality rises, and personal and governmental debt balloons, wouldn't it be wise to recommit ourselves to prudence and a concern for truthfulness—to choose reforms that work, over rhetoric that sounds good and policies that feel good? Wouldn't it be better to act on the basis not of self-righteous indignation but of careful consideration of facts in the light of experience? Should one choose a policy advertised as reducing income inequality or carbon emissions that basic economic analysis and past experience show is likely to have little effect—or, worse, the opposite effect? Objectivity and good judgment may not be as stimulating as hyperpartisanship, or as emotionally satisfying as the enthusiastic embrace of pseudoscience, but they sure do lead to better outcomes.

Yet such an approach isn't easy to adopt in what some have described as a "posttruth" era. In an insightful op-ed, University of London political economy professor William Davies spoke of an "oversupply of facts in the 21st century" while trying to understand the surprise (especially among academics!) of the Brexit and Trump votes.[19] Max Boot, once a conservative, warns the Left not to emulate the Right by trampling facts: "For both the far left and the far right, facts are an irksome 'detail' of scant importance. What really matters [to them] is being 'morally

---

18. For an excellent description of how well-crafted government policies can enhance a population's general welfare, see Bjorn Lomborg, "Making Government Smarter," *Foreign Affairs*, September–October 2017, 90–98. What is the magic formula? Not so tricky: simply employ basic cost-benefit analysis to identify which policies provide the greatest investment return.

19. William Davies, "The Age of Post-Truth Politics," *New York Times*, August 24, 2016, https://www.nytimes.com/2016/08/24/opinion/campaign-stops/the-age-of-post-truth-politics.html.

right.'"[20] In practice, that means admitting only evidence—
without inquiring too closely as to its soundness—that supports positions one presumes in advance to be correct.
~~The posttruth approach is getting us~~ nowhere. But how to
replace it?

Learning from Objective Analyses

It is clear that the mere recitation of facts doesn't work very
well. For one thing, with the birth of "alternative" facts, how
does one know whom to believe? For another, when "fact-
checkers" themselves become opinionated voices, the very
word "fact" becomes ideologically charged. This perversion of
the very idea of fact-checking is more distressing than merely
misrepresenting facts, for much the same reason it is worse
when the police themselves commit crimes. What economists
might call a version of Gresham's law all too often prevails: as
bad money drives out good, so do bad ideas drive out better
ones. And sensational pseudofacts drive out real ones, while
tendentious interpretations of statements are said to be the
statements actually made.

Moreover, as long-time faculty, we know from sad experience that delivering lessons doesn't always capture the attention, much less the soul, of the listener. Morson once had the
dispiriting experience of telling students they should think, not
just take notes to memorize, and then discovering a forgotten

20. Max Boot, "Alexandra Ocasio-Cortez Shouldn't Approach Her Facts the Way
Trump Does," *Washington Post*, January 8, 2019, https://www.washingtonpost.com
/opinions/2019/01/08/alexandria-ocasio-cortez-shouldnt-approach-her-facts-way
-trump-does/.

notebook where a student had written: "Reminder for exam—don't forget! You can't just memorize!"

As for the presentation of objective truths, we believe Neil Postman, who argued three decades ago—long before the world of Twitter and its ilk—that there are limitations to how modern experts conceive and express ideas.[21] "Many of our psychologists, sociologists, economists and other latter-day cabalists will have numbers to tell them the truth or they will have nothing," Postman writes, critical of what he saw as a prevailing assumption that numbers alone could capture and articulate reality. Jerry Z. Muller's delightful study *The Tyranny of Metrics* makes Postman seem all the more prescient.[22] Muller examines the cultural paradigm "engulfing an ever-widening range of institutions," which he calls a "metric fixation." He cites an oft-quoted dictum wrongly attributed to the brilliant physicist Lord Kelvin ("If you cannot measure it, you cannot improve it") and the more recent adage of management guru Tom Peters ("What gets measured, gets done"). And so more and more things are measured.

One problem with this approach is that what is measurable is often not important, and what is important is often not measurable.[23] Another is that the metric may negatively affect real outcomes. Governments and insurance companies sometimes decide to reward or penalize hospitals and doctors based on the percentage of successful outcomes. As a result, surgeons naturally are less likely to take difficult cases, and so people who

---

21. Neil Postman, *Amusing Ourselves to Death: Public Discourse in the Age of Show Business* (New York: Penguin, 1985).

22. Jerry Z. Muller, *The Tyranny of Metrics* (Princeton, NJ: Princeton University Press, 2018).

23. Muller, *Tyranny of Metrics*, 17.

might have been saved by a risky operation end up dying. If pay depends on how many patients survive thirty days after surgery, resources will be wasted on extending life a few more days to meet the metric. When hospitals are penalized for patients re-admitted soon after a procedure, hospitals reclassify them as outpatients receiving treatments, or send them to the emergency room, potentially wasting resources and endangering the lives of the patients. And when politicians demand that police reduce felonies by a certain percentage, and reward or punish them accordingly, officers reclassify felonies as misdemeanors, report lesser crimes, or simply do not report them at all. The crime rate declines, while crime remains the same (or grows worse).

Postman would not have found these results amusing. He dreamed of ways that "cabalists" might find and convey deeper truths, noting that experts in a past era might have described the economy in the form of poems, parables, or well-chosen proverbs. He might have been thinking of the witty poem W. H. Auden delivered at the 1946 Harvard commencement, "Under Which Lyre: A Reactionary Tract for the Times," which concluded with the memorable commandment: "Thou shalt not sit / With statisticians nor commit / A social science."[24]

Sure, Postman anticipated the scorn this approach would undoubtedly evoke today, much as Auden anticipated similar scorn by subtitling his poem "A Reactionary Tract." We naturally ask, should Stiglitz have acted out his Nobel Lecture rather than read it? Should he have replaced the prose with poetry? Of course not, but, all the same, Postman concluded, while "the truth in economics is believed to be best discovered and expressed

---

24. See Adam Kirsch, "A Poet's Warning," *Harvard Magazine*, November-December 2007, https://harvardmagazine.com/2007/11/a-poets-warning.html.

in numbers," "there is a certain measure of arbitrariness in the forms that truth-telling may take."[25]

In that spirit, we choose a hybrid rhetoric: setting aside both figures and rhymes, metrics and meters, we aim to present often ignored economic truths with *stories*, some taken from our own experience, some drawn from recent events, and some borrowed from great literature. These stories illustrate how an understanding of incentives, trade-offs, marginal utility, revealed preferences, and other core economic concepts, along with the dispassionate analysis of data, could go a long way toward helping the citizens of a democracy make informed choices. We bear in mind that one alternative to informed choices is uninformed ones; another is the end of democracy itself.

[handwritten margin note: how this book was written ?]

Let Justice Be Done, Though the World Perish: Dealing with Climate Change

[handwritten margin note: what]

Here is an example of what we have in mind. Talk with many on the left about reducing carbon emissions, and it soon becomes apparent that they are thinking not practically, but theologically. They regard carbon use as a kind of sin, and so they engage in moral crusades, not well-thought-out policies, against it. Often enough, they resemble those humanities professors allotting salary increases: they reject "false choices" and refuse to think in terms of scarce resources that must be deployed most efficiently to attain the desired end. When they encounter such thinking, they instinctively react to it as morally questionable.

---

25. Postman, *Amusing Ourselves*. Deirdre McCloskey's 1985 classic, *The Rhetoric of Economics* (2nd ed., Madison: University of Wisconsin Press, 1998), provides great insight into how economists make their arguments.

Monks, missionaries, and other moralists do not do cost-benefit analyses designed to reduce the most sin with the least effort. They don't think of trade-offs among the Ten Commandments. Their whole worldview militates against such thinking, which carries a whiff of the neoliberal devil's sulfur.

We recently discussed climate change with a colleague who quoted statistics proving it to be an "existential problem" that we must solve within a decade or so if the planet is not to be ruined irretrievably. No expense, he claimed, could be too great, no effort too strenuous, no policy too draconian, when the stakes are so large; all other problems must be set aside until this one is solved. We naturally assumed, therefore, that our colleague would be a strong proponent of nuclear power, which emits no carbon. But the very suggestion provoked his horror. Don't you realize, he instructed, that there is a problem with safe disposal of nuclear waste products? Don't you know, as President Obama explained, that accumulated nuclear waste may cause serious problems for life on earth in a hundred thousand years?[26] Our colleague went on to echo an article in the *New Republic* criticizing President Obama for not taking more decisive action against nuclear power. The author mocked those who say that "in the fight against climate change, anything is better than dirty coal, right?" and then proceeded to outline several specific problems with nuclear waste disposal.[27]

26. See Jim Inhofe, "Obama Should Embrace Nuclear Energy," CNN Opinion, April 22, 2015, https://www.cnn.com/2015/04/22/opinions/inhofe-obama-nuclear-energy/index.html. President Obama's actual approach to nuclear power was perhaps better described as ambivalent.

27. Zoe Loftus-Farren, "President Obama, Cut Dirty Nuclear Power from Your Climate-Change Talks," *New Republic*, January 25, 2015, https://newrepublic.com/article/120843/obama-must-cut-dirty-nuclear-power-climate-change-talks.

Problems in waste disposal, perhaps a hundred thousand years from now, balanced against an existential threat a decade or so away! But that is just the point: the two threats were not "balanced." One was not weighed against the other, or it would have been apparent which risk to choose over the other. In this kind of thinking, *all* risks are bad in the way that all sins are bad. One does not eliminate one sin by replacing it with another; one renounces sin altogether. Solutions have to be perfectly "green" and "clean," or they are not solutions at all.

An economist naturally prefers trading carbon credits to banning the use of carbon altogether. If one charges for exceeding a given threshold and then allows a market in "permits to pollute" sold by those who do not reach the threshold, one promotes efficiency and ensures that carbon will be used only where the value it produces is greatest. But if one thinks in terms of sin, one wants instead to mandate the total elimination of all "non-renewables." Just set a date when all fossil fuels will be banned and energy will come from the wind and sunlight. And how will it be stored when the source is intermittent and battery technology is still inadequate? Pass a law setting a date for better batteries!

What if a small use of carbon would produce enormous benefit, perhaps saving many lives, or providing the means to pay for more environmental protection? The use could happen under carbon credits but not, of course, under a total ban. We used to see buses with big signs saying that they burned not gasoline but "clean natural gas"—and natural gas does indeed yield more energy per unit of carbon than oil. Has anyone noticed that one seldom sees such buses anymore? Either they are no longer used, or their signs have been painted over: one does not advertise that one has switched from cigarettes to cigars or from whiskey to beer. But if the goal is to reduce carbon use as much as possible, then surely switching from oil to natural gas, at least until a still better source is sufficiently available, makes eminent sense. Doing so may just bring us below the climactic "tipping point" that, we are told, threatens our existence.

There is an old Latin saying, favored by nineteenth-century revolutionaries: *fiat justitia, pereat mundus.* "Let justice be done, though the world perish." This is not an economist's way of thinking. It is what we expect from a utopian dreamer (or a humanistically inclined moralist). All or nothing, purity or death. It is a rejection of trade-offs: we either get it *absolutely* right, or not at all. This is what fundamentalist thinking is all about.

In the real world, nothing is ever pure. Things are better or worse. There are no gains without costs. In short, in discussions of climate change and other problems, we confront not just two theories, but two completely different views of the universe and two ways of thinking. Is one really ready to let the world perish rather than allow the smallest injustice? Is life truly intolerable if the greater good entails a lesser, but still measurable, evil?

In Dostoevsky's novel *The Brothers Karamazov,* Ivan asks his brother Alyosha if, to eliminate the suffering of millions, it was necessary to sacrifice one innocent child, would he do so? Remember that the millions saved from death and torment include millions of children. Alyosha movingly declares that he could never build human happiness on the bones of an innocent child, and that is the answer Ivan desires. For him, the world is morally acceptable only if there is no unjustified suffering at all. Would one appoint Ivan Karamazov as secretary of the interior? As secretary of defense or the treasury?

In response, one could ask who is really more moral: the one who would let earth and everyone on it perish, or the one who would tolerate some injustice to preserve it? The one who would preclude life for all future generations, or the one who would allow some evil so that people still unborn might inherit the earth as we have? Trade-offs of this type are what economics is about, and, by rejecting the economic way of thinking, these problems don't magically go away.

Sometimes it is hard to believe those humanistically inclined moralists who claim to be concerned with an existential threat to the climate. Consider, as an economist would, their revealed preferences: if one refuses to allow nuclear power and natural gas, even at the risk of life itself, can one really be so concerned about the climate? After all, one is choosing not what will minimize risk to the climate, but something else entirely. Whatever that "something else" might be—the purging of the world's sinfulness, the sense of one's moral purity, the triumph of one's own political group—then, all protestations to the contrary notwithstanding, that "something else" is what one really prefers. If someone were to say that the most important thing for him was saving money for his daughter's college education, but then takes an expensive vacation, one might conclude that his preference was not so much for his daughter's education as for feeling good that he valued it highly. The economists' idea of revealed preferences turns out to contain great wisdom, including about moral questions.

Germany has long been a leader in supporting international agreements to reduce carbon emissions. The United States has not. Seriously concerned about climate change, Germany has massively subsidized and mandated the use of renewable energy sources, thus raising the price of energy substantially, a burden that falls particularly hard on the poor. These subsidies could, of course, have been used to promote social welfare elsewhere. Nevertheless, this policy makes good sense, insofar as we face a dire threat from carbon to our lives. And yet Germany's

carbon use has remained stable since 2009, while American use
has been reduced substantially. Why is that?

For one thing, Germany also decided simultaneously to
phase out nuclear power. One might imagine that those who
profess concern about climate change would have opposed
such a policy bound to increase carbon emissions, but the opposite is the case. If one thinks in terms of revealed preferences,
one might ask: Can they really be as concerned about climate
change as they say? Interestingly enough, the Finnish Green
Party supports nuclear power; in contrast to the Germans, they,
if judged by revealed preferences, prefer what they say they profess to prefer. One reason the United States has reduced carbon
use, despite its withdrawal from climate treaties, is that fracking
has dramatically increased the supply of natural gas and so by
basic economic principles reduced its price, thus incentivizing
its substitution for less carbon-efficient oil and coal. And yet we
have heard colleagues and students condemn the United States,
not Germany, for its carbon sinfulness. What are they really
more concerned with—reducing carbon or making appropriate
pledges?

If one presses humanistically inclined moralists on this
point, one is likely to hear that fracking may undermine the
earth and destroy houses built on newly unstable ground. Let
us suppose that is true. How does that danger balance against
an existential threat to the earth? To equate the danger of collapsing houses with the threat of carbon in the atmosphere is to
judge increased carbon to be no more dangerous than some
collapsing houses. If one predicted the sea would rise dramatically in a few years, and then bought beachfront property, what
would one's revealed belief be?

Those of us who do take climate change seriously are bound
to reflect that one does not have to be inordinately selfish, mor-

ally obtuse, or stupidly opposed to science in order to wonder whether such Green activists really believe what they say. The Green New Deal, endorsed by several presidential candidates and many members of Congress, proposed, in addition to phasing out combustion engines and retrofitting all buildings, providing an adequate income for the unemployed as well as suitable housing and healthy food for all, while ensuring that eminent domain is not abused.[28] Surely, if the planet is in grave danger, and resources are limited, one ought to postpone supporting such myriad causes, regardless of how desirable they might be. We may detect among some proponents a refusal, resembling that of those humanities chairs, to acknowledge that resources are limited. Among other proponents, we may discern a lack of real (as opposed to professed) concern about climate change.

Or consider a low-income Appalachian family reading about the enormous amount of energy consumed by the best-selling authors of books about the fragile environment. The members of this family are aware that their *betters*, who hector them about carbon, use air travel to take vacations or other entirely discretionary flights and, in total, use dozens of times more carbon than those they fault for moral obtuseness or hostility to science. And what if it is families that are poor enough that they

28. Noah Smith, "The Green New Deal Would Spend the U.S. into Oblivion," *Bloomberg*, February 8, 2019, https://www.bloomberg.com/opinion/articles/2019 -02-08/alexandria-ocasio-cortez-s-green-new-deal-is-unaffordable; and "A Bold New Plan to Tackle Climate Change Ignores Economic Orthodoxy," *Economist*, February 7, 2019, https://www.newsbreak.com/news/1290604019124/a-bold-new-plan -to-tackle-climate-change-ignores-economic-orthodoxy. The latter article points to the bipartisan list of distinguished economists who favor some form of a carbon tax and refund program that relies on economic analysis. See also Greg Ip, "Upside-Down Economics of Green New Deal," *Wall Street Journal*, February 14, 2019, A2.

will be unable to afford the more expensive fuel to keep their houses at a habitable temperature?

None of this, of course, means that those who warn about climate change dangers are wrong. We have already cited Milton's observation that a person can be a "heretic in the truth." But it does mean that they might stop berating others who take them not at their word, but at their deed. No rational person believes everything he is told, and those of us who are not scientists have to assess beliefs currently held to be respectable. Seeing whether people behave as if they believe what they are saying is one method of assessment we all use, and we would be foolish not to. If doctors widely refused to have their own children vaccinated, would one fault their patients for hesitating? Those who scold, but do not act accordingly, might recognize that by their example they not only make it reasonable to doubt the scientific conclusions they endorse, but also bring the very claim of "science" into disrepute, which means it will have still less persuasiveness in the future. One does not want to be the boy that cried science.

It is important to note that a majority of the American public now considers climate change to be an important concern, a fact that the two of us applaud enthusiastically. A 2020 report from the Pew Research Center shows that, for the first time in that survey's twenty-year history, more than half of respondents said that climate change should be a top priority for the president and Congress, up fourteen percentage points over the preceding four years.[29] But that support differs substantially across

---

29. Nadja Popovich, "Rise in Concern on Climate, but Not for Everyone," *New York Times*, February 21, 2020, A15. The polling figures are from that article. About two-thirds of Americans said that environmental protections were a leading policy priority, roughly the same as those who placed economic growth and jobs in the top spot.

the political spectrum, with more than three-quarters of Democrats citing climate change as a top policy priority in 2020 and fewer than one-quarter of Republicans, with that partisan gap being the largest among the eighteen issues Pew surveyed. As observers have noted, with President Trump having said that "we must reject the perennial prophets of doom and their predictions of the apocalypse,"[30] a sentiment reinforced by some in the conservative media, that finding isn't all that surprising.[31] By contrast, Democratic candidates for president in 2020 repeatedly referred to climate change as an "existential threat," which suggests that, even if they did not really seem to believe it, they thought that most Democratic voters did. Finally, it is of interest that other Pew polling showed a significant generation gap: while only 39 percent of Republicans said that the federal government is not doing enough to reduce the effects of climate change, more than half (52 percent) of Republicans age thirty-eight or younger agreed with that statement.

But a growing consensus, especially among Democrats, doesn't mean agreement on what the government should do. Some liberals scoffed at the Republican climate agenda, which featured a plan to plant one trillion trees by 2050.[32] But is the

30. Heller Cheung, "What Does Trump Actually Believe on Climate Change?," BBC News, Washington DC, January 23, 2020, https://www.bbc.com/news/world-us-canada-51213003.

31. An earlier Pew survey from 2016 found that only 11 percent of conservative Republicans believe that scientists understand the causes of climate change "very well," and only 15 percent trust scientists "a lot" to deliver full and accurate information about the causes of climate change. Pew Research Center, "The Politics of Climate," October 4, 2016, https://www.pewresearch.org/science/2016/10/04/the-politics-of-climate/.

32. One example is Kate Aronoff, "Republicans' Climate Change Plan Is Big Oil's Climate Change Plan," *New Republic*, January 21, 2020, https://newrepublic.com/article/156269/republicans-climate-change-plan-big-oils-climate-change-plan. Her

response from the far left really any more realistic? The title of a *Washington Post* editorial put it pointedly: "Bernie Sanders's Climate Plan Will Take Us Nowhere."[33] $16 trillion in new spending over the next ten years to eliminate the use of fossil fuels in electricity and transportation by 2030; $2 trillion to build new wind, solar, and geothermal electricity-production infrastructure through government-run utilities; $2 trillion to buy people electric cars; $607 billion to link US cities through high-speed rail. Nuclear power? Forget about it. Sanders would halt the building of new plants and deny relicensing to existing ones. The editorial's conclusion is worth quoting at length:

> No central planner can know exactly how and where to invest for an efficient and effective energy transition. That is why economists continue to recommend that the government take a simple, two-pronged approach: invest in scientific research and prime the market to accept new, clean technologies with a substantial and steadily rising carbon tax. People and businesses would find the most effective ways to avoid the increasingly high, tax-inflated costs of using dirty fuels. Maybe that would mean building huge new solar farms throughout the country.

conclusion: "Planting trees, in other words, isn't enough. And the kinds of clean fuel Republicans and their donors say they're interested in supporting are dwarfed by the more traditional ones cooking the planet and lining their pockets." Of course, Republicans can be wrong without "lining their pockets," and it is highly unlikely that is true of most Republicans, including poor ones.

33. Editorial board, "Bernie Sanders's Climate Plan Will Take Us Nowhere," *Washington Post*, August 25, 2019, https://www.washingtonpost.com/opinions /bernie-sanderss-climate-plan-will-take-us-nowhere/2019/08/25/4e780768-c5c3 -11e9-b5e4-54aa56d5b7ce_story.html. The numbers and the quotation that follow are from the editorial.

Maybe it would mean massive energy efficiency gains driven by home retrofits or new appliances. Maybe it would mean continuing to accept some role for nuclear power.

In another piece, Fareed Zakaria points out that, between 2005 and 2016, US carbon emissions fell almost 15 percent.[34] When President Obama was in office, the United States reduced emissions more than any other country. How? Zakaria reports that a major reason was fracking, but about one-third of the reduction was shifting from coal-fired plants to natural gas ones. Solar power? That accounts for a mere 3 percent of the overall reduction.

Yet the Sanders plan not only opposes fracking, but also proposes to shut down all natural gas plants. Zakaria concludes that "the Sanders green energy 'plan' is based on magical thinking." Perhaps, but we think it is based on a different kind of thinking—theological reasoning. Pollution is a sin, so eliminate it. And, should the world perish with it, so be it.

Having a set of policies endorsed by a broad spectrum of economists might just be compelling for most Americans, but the fundamentalists on either side of the spectrum would disagree. On the one hand, pollution is evil and needs to be eradicated regardless of the cost. On the other, if you leave markets alone, the invisible hand will ensure that things will work out for the best. When dealing with a problem beset by negative externalities, that, too, may be a form of "magical thinking."

We, and others concerned with climate change, among current problems, should choose to think economically—and to

34. Fareed Zakaria, "Bernie Sanders's Magical Thinking on Climate Change," *Washington Post*, February 13, 2020, https://fareedzakaria.com/columns/2020/2/13/4z3fpsr38uaodc6dyi2bmfibpoo8hn.

do so for moral reasons. We repeat a difficult truth: if there is a moral imperative to solve a problem, then there is a moral imperative to expend scarce resources most effectively. Discard one's prejudices and consider prices.

Not Just Climate Change

The rejection of the basic principles of Economics 101 when discussing climate change is just one of a number of examples of ideology eclipsing reason. Dealing with growing income inequality is another.

No one, regardless of political perspective, seriously denies that income and wealth inequality in the United States, as in many Western countries, has increased substantially over the past four decades. It is possible, of course, for inequality to rise even when the amount of absolute poverty is decreasing, since relative and absolute poverty are separate issues. In other words, a wealthy society might have growing inequality but, at the same time, even the very poorest could have an acceptable standard of living. In the United States, poverty has indeed lessened as inequality has grown, but it persists at levels that observers consider intolerable. And, even though poverty has lessened, rising inequality breeds jealousy and perhaps social unrest. What's more, poverty, especially when there is intergenerational transmission as is typically the case, wastes resources and is inherently unfair.

In *Bleak House*, Charles Dickens describes a world of poor people neglected by those supposing that they can safely ignore the suffering of others. But they can't, because the infectious diseases bred among the poor cannot be confined to them. The novel's heroine, Esther Summerson, contracts smallpox, almost dies from it, and remains horribly scarred for life.

Dickens means this plot to be an allegory about all neglect of the unfortunate. There but for the grace of God go I.

Directly or indirectly, poverty exacts a price. It is certainly tempting to use the tax system to reduce both income inequality and poverty, even when the proposed solutions might just make the problem worse.

With a cleverness that economists can only dream about, Tolstoy's *Anna Karenina* captures the dilemma faced by those who sincerely want to do something about poverty. Stepan Arkadyevich—who has no trouble with inequality—asks rhetorically why "I receive a bigger salary than my chief clerk, though he knows more about the work than I do."[35] He means that this is just the way things are and have to be. But his friend, the pampered and foppish Vasenka, takes the question to heart: "'Why is it we spend our time riding, drinking, shooting, doing nothing, while they are forever at work?' said Vasenka Veslovsky, obviously for the first time in his life reflecting on the question, and consequently considering it with perfect sincerity."[36] For the first time in his life! Tolstoy wants us to wonder what sort of moral obtuseness it would take for this question *never* to have occurred to someone, and what kind of upbringing could have produced such evidently innocent but woeful ignorance? While we may doubt that many people have begun to reflect on income inequality and poverty for the first time, there is little doubt that many are taking the issue seriously now.[37]

---

35. Leo Tolstoy, *Anna Karenina*, trans. Constance Garnett, rev. ed. by Leonard J. Kent and Nina Berberova (New York: Modern Library, 1965), 615.

36. Leo Tolstoy, *Anna Karenina*, 615.

37. We point to the phenomenal success of Thomas Picketty's monumental review of inequality, *Capital in the Twenty-First Century* (Cambridge, MA: Harvard University Press, 2014).

As they should. "A decent provision for the poor," Samuel Johnson famously observed, "is the true test of civilization."[38] "All the arguments which are brought to represent poverty as no evil," he also remarked, "show it to be evidently a great evil. You never find people labouring to convince you that you may live very happily upon a plentiful fortune."[39] But, as people too often forget, recognizing a problem is one thing; proposing a good solution is quite another. You cannot fairly accuse someone of not caring about the problem just because they reject your solution. And, in this case, some proposed solutions are downright scary.

The vestiges of Occupy Wall Street are upon us, with the yellow-jacketed protesters in France and a growing number of their counterparts in the United States and elsewhere questioning the value of a market economy itself.[40] This seems decidedly odd, after the abject failure of command economies in Russia and Eastern Europe, and after China grew wealthy when it abandoned socialist for market economics. How ironic would it be if previously nonmarket economies adopt the price system as a resource-allocating mechanism while the once proudly capitalist countries go in the opposite direction! Will Prime Minister Macron's attempt to stave off the rioters lead France to adopt policies that will hinder future economic growth? What would have happened if Jeremy Corbyn's plan to nationalize major industries in Britain had been implemented?[41] In all such

38. From Boswell's *Life of Johnson*, as cited in *Bartlett's Familiar Quotations*, 15th ed., ed. Emily Morison Beck (Boston: Little, Brown, 1980), 354.

39. From Boswell's *Life of Johnson*, as cited in *The Oxford Dictionary of Quotations*, ed. Elizabeth Knowles (Oxford: Oxford University Press, 2004), 428.

40. See, for example, "Millennial Socialism," *Economist*, February 14, 2019, https://www.economist.com/leaders/2019/02/14/millennial-socialism.

41. For a favorable take on these plans see the *Guardian*'s "Jeremy Corbyn's Nationalisation Plans Are Music to Ears of Public," October 1, 2017, https://www

cases, one must ask whether a larger share of a shrinking economic pie will satisfy the needs and the desires of the alienated lower and middle classes.

In *Anna Karenina*, Konstantin Levin, the novel's well-off hero, who is concerned about the justifiability of wealth, considers giving away all his property. After much thought, he convinces himself of the folly of that idea. He knows that either the peasants would rapidly dissipate it, or his land would fall into the hands of an unscrupulous owner and conditions would grow far worse.

Finding solutions to alleviate poverty are not easy, but there are some government-funded programs that clearly work: for instance, Head Start and SNAP (the supplemental nutrition assistance program), among others. And there are time-tested policies that work as well. You might never guess this, if you listened to the competing claims espoused by those on both ends of the ideological spectrum, both of which may argue that such reforms cannot work but for different reasons. Nevertheless, examples abound.

The reality is that there is a surprisingly robust consensus among economists, not just about carbon taxes and cap and trade policies, but on much more. When you hear the rhetoric about dramatically lowering taxes, or the recent, equally fervent, rhetoric about dramatically increasing the top marginal tax rate for the rich, take caution. Some conservatives believe that it is possible to raise all boats simply by reducing personal income taxes, not only spurring economic growth and lowering unemployment, as has happened before, but also generating enough revenue to make up for the lower tax rates, which, as the historical record shows, has not. A maximum marginal

---

.theguardian.com/business/2017/oct/01/jeremy-corbyn-nationalisation-plans
-voters-tired-free-markets.

personal income tax rate of, say, 30 percent, would be no less misguided than one of 70 percent. Either would be, in the minds of the vast majority of economists, a disaster, propagated by ideology disguised as economics.

Similarly, some might want to eliminate the minimum wage, which is said to hurt the most vulnerable of workers by pricing them out of the job market. Others might want to triple it so that all workers earn a "living" wage that is high enough to provide for themselves and their families. It is important to realize that at every level, there is always a *trade-off* between the social cost of denying some people jobs and raising the wages of others. Raise the minimum, and some will lose their jobs while others benefit. What is the best balance to strike? Fortunately, the extensive economic literature provides a pretty good idea of the minimum wage's sweet spot.[42] Eliminating the minimum wage would hurt workers with limited education, especially where labor markets are less than competitive. By the same token, raising it too much would reduce employment opportunities for precisely the workers one is trying to help. Our guess is that most economists, in contrast to dogmatists on both sides, would favor a range between $12 and $16 an hour, not $8 or $25.

How about trade policy? Some politicians seem convinced that free trade ends up exporting good jobs to low-wage countries, so we need to protect our economy using tariffs and other barriers to trade. Didn't Japan and South Korea grow in that way, at least for a time? Absolutely wrong, others reply: free

42. The late, great economist Alan Krueger pretty much put the argument to bed long ago. See, for example, David Card and Alan B. Krueger, *Myth and Measurement: The New Economics of the Minimum Wage* (Princeton, NJ: Princeton University Press, 1995).

trade allows us to grow the economy by focusing on goods and services where we have a comparative advantage, with *both* sides ultimately gaining—so just let markets work their guaranteed magic. [*which is ... ?*]

Those opposed to free trade ignore more than two centuries of economic theory and data to the contrary, while free-trade purists gloss over the fact that with benefits come costs, including noneconomic ones that do not appear in their models. These costs may include social dislocations and the destruction of whole communities and ways of life, which it would be both prudent and humane to ameliorate. Could it be that some of the opposition to free trade treaties comes as a result of such dislocations? [*well*]

Neither protectionism, nor free trade without *any* provision for worker retraining or support or concern for disrupting communities, holds much sway with economists. While restricting trade goes against a basic premise underlying economic thought, entirely ignoring the inevitable worker displacements that occur is economically, as well as socially, short-sighted. In sum, protectionism wastes opportunity, while free trade without remediation may prove inefficient and endanger free trade itself. We have little doubt that a large share of economists would endorse that view.[43] [*author's view*]

43. There is certainly widespread skepticism among economists about import tariffs. The University of Chicago's Booth School convenes a panel comprising many of the world's preeminent economists. In 2016, one of the questions was about import duties, asking whether "adding new or higher import duties on products such as air conditioners, cars, and cookies—to encourage producers to make them in the US—would be a good idea." For the results, see Tim Worstall, "100% of Economists Asked Said Import Tariffs Were Not a Good Idea," *Forbes*, December 23, 2016, https://www.forbes.com/sites/timworstall/2016/12/23/100-of-economists-asked -said-import-tariffs-were-not-a-good-idea/#94faffd58c71. In our experience, finding unanimity among academics on any question is rather remarkable!

[*funny?*]

Health policy? That has been a highly contentious issue, even among economists. Still, a survey of two hundred health economists found greater agreement than one might expect.[44] While politicians are eager to share their strongly held views on whether or not Obamacare (the Affordable Care Act) should be dismantled, 89 percent of economists strongly rejected its simple repeal without replacing it with something better to achieve the desired effect. Can it be improved? Here again there is general agreement. 81 percent said that the individual mandate (paying a fine if individuals choose not to be insured) was essential; 80 percent said that premiums should not be raised for those with "genetic defects"; 70 percent recommend charging higher premiums for those who engage in unhealthy behaviors; and 71 percent said that they opposed the idea of converting Medicare into a program based on income (with high-income individuals losing some Medicare benefits). Only 28 percent support raising the age of Medicare eligibility. With almost one-third of these health economists thinking differently than the rest on certain key features of health policy reform, we certainly wouldn't conclude that there is an overriding consensus about exactly what the government should do. But listening to candidates argue about health care, one would think that there is no agreement whatsoever among the experts, and that is simply not the case.

Finally, we turn to a topic close to home for those of us in the academy: student loan debt.[45] There are constant reminders in the press that college debt in the United States now exceeds $1.5

44. These results are described in Austin Frakt, "A Health Plan Economists Approve Of," *New York Times*, February 19, 2020, B5.

45. The *Chronicle of Higher Education* details the situation very clearly in "Who Holds America's $1.5-Trillion Student-Loan Debt," March 4, 2020, https://www.chronicle.com/article/who-holds-americas-1-5-trillion-student-loan-debt/. The numbers below come from that report.

trillion, more even than credit card debt, after having doubled since 2009. 45 million people owe college loans, up from 29 million in 2007, a fact certainly not lost on politicians. Remember those debates? One of the few things the Democratic candidates for president agreed on was the need to do something about this! But what?

Market fundamentalists (and others) undoubtedly cringe at the thought of American taxpayers wiping out loans that students and their families willingly took on. Perhaps they might make an exception if consumers were duped by for-profit private institutions, since markets are not supposed to work by fraud. But good luck convincing them that those with college debt should automatically be bailed out by the rest of us; it would mean that the uneducated poor would be subsidizing better educated others. What's more, it is even more problematic to cancel college debt for everyone, rich and poor alike.

An objective examination of the data might help. A majority of student loan holders—55 percent—owe $20,000 or less. To put that number in perspective, the average loan for a new car is $32,000. But what about those who owe much larger amounts? One-quarter of all borrowers owe more than $40,000, while 7 percent owe more than $100,000. We would never dismiss the worries of those who owe extraordinary amounts; they are real. Yet the media loves to recount the story of baristas struggling to pay off six-figure loans, as if such a scenario were the rule, even though it is the exception. And don't forget that, unlike car loans that paid for a rapidly depreciating consumption good, a student loan typically supports the acquisition of an investment good with an extremely high return—a college degree.[46] While not all loan holders completed their degrees,

---

46. We review data on the economic returns to higher education, and speculate about what the future holds, in chapter 10 of Gary Saul Morson and Morton Schapiro,

69 percent did. And let's not ignore the fact that, of the 45 million with college debt, more than half are in households with incomes high enough to be among the richest 40 percent of Americans—with 25 percent being in the 60–80 percent quintile and 28 percent in the top quintile. Somehow the fact that more than one-quarter of loan holders are in the top fifth of US households never surfaced during those presidential debates. Here again it seems as if the poor are being asked to subsidize those better off. Lastly, while the conversation seems exclusively about the benefits of relieving debt for undergraduates, 31 percent of the trillion and a half in college debt comes from students who enrolled in graduate or professional school programs.

The barista story, and the one about the student tricked into enrolling at some bogus private for-profit school, are a lot more compelling than the story of the person with a business degree, or the physician or lawyer, comfortably residing in the top income quintile. Should taxpayers really subsidize them? Perhaps college debt forgiveness can be justified on ethical grounds, not economic ones? Some might say that debt is like pollution— that is, something fundamentalists might consider a sin that needs to be purged at all costs. But, if that is the case, why stop at college debt? Maybe taxpayers should chip in to pay off mortgages, car loans, and credit cards as well. Try selling *that* to the American public. Economic consequences aside, would it even be morally right? Our point is a simple one: effective public policy should be based on facts, not rhetoric, especially when those facts are clear and readily available. You just need to look for them.

The Fabulous Future? America and the World in 2040 (Evanston, IL: Northwestern University Press, 2015).

To be sure, there are some substantive disagreements among policy makers and researchers that have nothing to do with their underlying politics, and all to do with their understanding of how the economy functions. A good example is the increasingly popular proposal from the Left to tax not just income, but wealth.[47] Some worry about incentives that will be created that would undermine the intent of the tax (rich people, and their accountants, are really good at minimizing their tax bills, and the economy suffers when they invest not for greatest return, but for greatest tax avoidance). Others insist that the government can cleverly anticipate attempts from the very rich to circumvent the tax, thereby generating additional revenues that can better fund some of the intervention programs (such as SNAP) that have a documented record of success. But those disagreements are the exception, not the rule.

Prejudice and Price

Humanists who reject "neoliberal" policies and the market economy often invoke fairness. Is it right that an English professor who took seven years to get a PhD should be paid less than a plumber? Should businessmen really earn more than academics? New drugs should not cost so much. More locales—or all of them!—should have rent control. Life should not be governed by what Carlyle, and then Marx, called "the cash nexus."

Wouldn't it be better if, instead of market chaos produced by the profit motive, well-intentioned government officials set

47. An informative summary can be found in Jim Tankersley and Ben Casselman, "The Liberal Economists behind the Wealth Tax Debate," *New York Times*, February 21, 2020, https://www.nytimes.com/2020/02/21/us/politics/the-liberal-economists-behind-the-wealth-tax-debate.html.

prices and wages (wages being prices for labor)? Economic affairs could then be arranged by experts, not greedy corporations. If that happened, humanity would no longer be battered by blind forces, but would itself shape the world deliberately and rationally. That change is what Engels called "the leap from the kingdom of necessity to the kingdom of freedom."[48]

The appeal of these ideas is obvious. Who can be against fairness? Order is preferable to chaos, human purposes to what Engels called "extraneous historical forces": "Anarchy . . . is replaced by systematic, definite organization."[49] In all walks of life we trust experts over lay people. What can possibly go wrong with their setting prices and directing productive activity? Since experts are well-educated people, it is hardly surprising

---

48. The famous passage from Engels's *Anti-Dühring* (1877) reads: "With the seizing of the means of production by society . . . anarchy in social production is replaced by systematic, definite organization. . . . Then for the first time man, in a certain sense, is finally marked off from the rest of the animal kingdom, and emerges from mere animal conditions of existence into really human ones. The whole sphere of the conditions of life which environ man, and which have hitherto ruled man, now comes under the dominion and control of man who for the first time becomes the real, conscious lord of nature because he has now become master of his own social organisation. The laws of his own social action, hitherto standing face to face with man as laws of nature foreign to, and dominating him, will then be used with full understanding, and so mastered by him. Man's own social organisation, hitherto confronting him as a necessity imposed by nature and history, now becomes the result of his own free action. The extraneous objective forces that have hitherto governed history pass under the control of man himself. Only from that time will man himself, with full consciousness, make his own history—only from that time will the social causes set in movement by him have, in the main and in a constantly growing measure, the results intended by him. It is humanity's leap from the kingdom of necessity to the kingdom of freedom" (https://www.marxists.org/archive/marx/works/1877/anti-duhring/ch24.htm.) A similar passage, ending with the same famous phrase, occurs in Engels's "Socialism: Utopian and Scientific." See Marx and Engels, *Basic Writings*, 109.

49. Engels, "Socialism," in Marx and Engels, *Basic Writings*, 109.

that such thinking has appealed to people with advanced degrees, especially those who have studied neither economics nor the history of countries that exchanged the market for "scientific" rule. As market fundamentalists reduce moral categories to economic ones, so humanists may replace economics with their concept of justice.

Humanists and economists typically approach problems differently. The former look back, see what has happened, and ask what would be the just distribution of rewards. Economists, by contrast, look to the future. If we distribute resources in the suggested way, what incentives will that produce? Perhaps the most fundamental difference between humanists and economists pertains to prices. For the former, prices are a matter of fairness. The latter, by contrast, regard them as signals directing the allocation of resources more efficiently than any central planner could possibly do. No one has to know the many pressures that prices at a given moment reflect or be able to identify what circumstances have caused prices to alter, as they constantly do. One only needs to respond appropriately, using more of a good when it becomes less expensive than alternatives and finding substitutes or efficiencies when prices rise.

What happens when humanist ways of thinking about prices are put into practice? What occurs when prices are set not by the market, but by scientific experts?

In the early decades of the Soviet Union, many thinkers around the world regarded its commitment to replace the market with central planning as the triumph of science. In their book *Our Economic Society and Its Problems*, Rexford Tugwell, president Franklin Roosevelt's secretary of the treasury, and Howard Hill argue that "the challenge of Russia to America . . . lies . . . in the idea of planning, of purposeful, intelligent control over economic affairs. This, it seems to me, we must accept as a guide to our economic life to replace the decadent notions of a laissez-faire philosophy."[50] The "decadent notions of a laissez-faire philosophy": Can you imagine a treasury secretary using those words today?

British evolutionary biologist, eugenicist, and science popularizer Julian Huxley thought it obvious to any well-educated person that "proper planning is itself the application of scientific method to human affairs." Praising the Soviets, he observed that "while the Five-Year Plan is without doubt of the greatest importance, it is in a sense only . . . an incident in a long series of plans; it is a symptom of a new spirit, the spirit of science introduced into politics and industry."[51] Huxley's beliefs in eugenics and planned economies went well together. To him, as to many others, both derive from a deep conviction that life can and should be governed not by the choices of countless uninformed people but by scientifically trained experts.

The Soviets abolished the market and, along with it, market prices. While they at first also tried to eliminate money and replace it with coercion, the result was a famine, after peasants lost all incentive to produce grain that would simply be taken from them. From that point on, the Soviets used money and prices, but, as the system matured, the prices were set not by the market but by the government. We have mentioned the late professor Aron Katsenelinboigen who, before emigrating to the United States, chaired the Soviet bureau tasked with setting the price of all goods in the Soviet Union. Morson remembers him

---

50. As cited in Paul Craig Roberts and Karen LaFolette, *Meltdown: Inside the Soviet Economy* (Washington, DC: Cato, 1990), 3. In the discussion that follows, the examples of how the Soviet economy worked are, unless otherwise stated, taken from *Meltdown*.

51. As cited in Roberts and LaFolette, *Meltdown*, 3.

saying that one year his bureau set the price of one hundred thousand goods, or about fifty per hour. "And do you know how many parts go into one battleship?" Katsenelinboigen asked. "Three million." The task was obviously impossible. Still worse, once prices were set, they were fixed. They were rarely adjusted in response to demand.[52]

On what basis did you set the prices? Morson asked, and Katsenelinboigen replied: according to Marx's labor theory of value. The price of a good was equal to the amount of labor used to produce it, with hours adjusted according to the skill of workers. That is, the price of a good bore no relation to any need for it. The whole point, as Paul Craig Roberts and Karen LaFollette argue, was to strip "prices of their relation to market value."[53] Consumers had no way of influencing what was produced, and, by consumers, Roberts and LaFollette included factories that get goods from other factories.

The economy was measured in terms of gross output, and planners set quotas for each factory. Factory managers did not seek to conserve resources, satisfy demand, or make a profit. They were required to fulfill a quota, punished if they did not, and given a bonus for anything above the quota.

What was the result of such a system? Pretty much what you would expect. Since gross output was all that mattered, quality

---

52. Schapiro once interviewed a prospective graduate student who had worked for the price commission in his home country, Tanzania. When asked how the members of the commission decided to alter prices, the reply was that they drove around Dar es Salaam, noting where there were long lines outside of stores, or, alternatively, where the stores were empty of shoppers. In the first case, they raised prices; in the second, they lowered them. Not exactly a formula for market efficiency, but at least they tried!

53. Roberts and LaFolette, *Meltdown*, 14.

suffered. Appliances did not work. Refrigerators did not cool.[54] Since one factory's output was another's input, poor quality was passed down the line of production. A factory could not reject goods as inferior, or discuss needs with suppliers, since such negotiations would preempt central planning. A steel factory satisfying its quota with poor-quality steel sent its product to a nail factory, with the result being that the nails produced broke when hammered too hard and could not withstand standard loads for long periods of time.[55] Shoddy buildings, in turn, were erected with these nails and other materials of equally poor quality. It is hardly surprising, then, that an earthquake in Soviet Armenia measuring only 6.9 on the Richter scale caused a massive collapse of buildings, with whole towns destroyed, along with two-thirds of Leninakan, Armenia's second largest city. Some twenty thousand people were killed. As Paul Craig Roberts and Karen LaFollette observe in their classic study of the Soviet economy, "It didn't take much to collapse multistoried buildings made of unreinforced concrete, low-grade masonry, and prefabricated concrete sections haphazardly linked together."[56]

The petroleum industry measured output as the number of holes drilled, with the result that geologists reacted by drilling only shallow holes. Because construction managers received their payments based on the number of square meters under construction, they began new projects and left old ones unfinished. When premiums were given for finishing buildings before a prescribed deadline, builders declared buildings without roofs and plumbing as being finished. "Unusable buildings are de-

---

54. Roberts and LaFolette, 20.
55. Roberts and LaFolette, 21.
56. Roberts and LaFolette, 13.

problems

clared finished every day, and premiums pocketed for timely performance."[57]

There was always a shortage of spare parts. As one engineer in a plant manufacturing machinery explained, if a factory manager produces one hundred machines with the proper number of spare parts, he gets no bonus, but if he instead produces one hundred and two machines with no spare parts, he does. The result was that, throughout the country, machines could not be repaired. If there was a shortage of some spare part in a market economy, its price would rise and more would be produced, but that feedback mechanism, which depends on varying prices and the initiative to respond to them, is absent in a planned economy.

In theory, abundant food was produced, but a great deal of it was left to rot in the fields because storage and transport facilities for perishable goods were inadequate. Prime minister Nikolay Ryzhkov, prominent in the last years of the USSR, estimated the loss at 25 to 30 percent. It does not matter whether the food can be consumed; the gross output is what counts. Nor is there any possibility that demand for storage facilities will raise their price and so make it profitable to produce them. Entirely useless or outmoded goods were produced year after year. A well-known example is a factory that continued producing foot-pedaled sewing machines. Such goods filled scarce warehouse space, while the plan called for more output and rewarded it with bonuses. In a market economy, falling prices would send a signal to reduce or eliminate production, and no factory would continue indefinitely to produce goods where the inputs cost more than the output could be sold for.

It was common for factories to use expensive materials that were available instead of cheaper ones that would serve the

57. Roberts and LaFolette, 11.

purpose, with the result that the "value added" was often negative. Since factories had trouble getting needed inputs, many
turned to producing their own. They did so inefficiently, but at
least they could be assured of having what they needed. In a
market economy, efficient producers would replace inefficient
ones, but that cannot happen in a planned economy. By the
same token, innovation makes no sense, since in the short run
it would mean missing the output quota. In any case, there is
no reward for doing so. If one factory had a surplus of a good
another factory needed, a legal sale was impossible, because
that would constitute market activity outside the plan. Factory
managers often turned to the service of a *tolkach* (roughly,
"pusher"), someone with good connections to the black market which theft supplied.

With such poor quality and a lack of innovation, the USSR
produced goods that were largely worthless on the world market. Given a choice, who would ever buy a Soviet refrigerator,
appliance, or automobile? Ever-present waste provided a ready
excuse for falling short. Should a manager produce seventy
thousand eggs instead of the mandated one hundred thousand,
he could claim to have produced the higher figure with the difference lost to waste. Everyone knew that figures were padded.
For all these reasons, the leadership itself had no idea what real
productivity was. When the country collapsed, its GDP turned
out to be a small fraction of what Western economists and intelligence agencies had thought. The estimates of the historian
Robert Conquest turned out to be far more accurate. As Conquest explained, others relied on official Soviet figures, even
though they regarded them as distorted and requiring adjustment: "In fact, they were not distorted, they were invented."[58]

58. Robert Conquest, *Reflections on a Ravaged Century* (New York: Norton, 2000), 134.

The right approach was to disregard them entirely and base an estimate on other indicators.

A distinguishing feature of Soviet life was constant shortages. In their book *The Turning Point: Revitalizing the Soviet Economy*, Nikolai Shmelev and Vladimir Popov, hoping that Gorbachev's reforms could save socialism, would characterize Soviet life as, in effect, one endless queue. They tell the story of a long line that formed at Moscow's Women's Department Store because, a rumor had it, pantyhose had arrived. But why should pantyhose be in short supply to begin with? "Opinions varied widely," they deadpan. Some spoke of a closed factory, but there were many pantyhose factories. Or perhaps they could not afford pantyhose imports because oil prices had fallen? Most likely, there was a conspiracy: someone was holding them back for self-interested reasons. But ad hoc explanations will not do, the authors opine, because there are always shortages of one thing or another: "But really—why did pantyhose disappear from the stores? . . . if it's not sheets, it's detergent, or batteries, or meringues, or lozenges, or wallpaper, or thread. Why do people have to put their names on waiting lists in drugstores for crucial drugs? And why is there always a shortage of something? When one thing appears, something else disappears; when that reappears, a third thing disappears from the shelves."[59]

Shortages and waiting in lines came to define Soviet life.[60] Professional people who could not stand in line for hours often hired someone—the domestic equivalent of a *tolkach*—to do

59. Nikolai Shmelev and Vladimir Popov, *The Turning Point: Revitalizing the Soviet Economy*, trans. Michele A. Berdy (New York: Doubleday, 1989), 80.

60. Through it all, it seems that many Russians maintained their ironic sense of humor. An example: in 1980 a Russian woman said to her husband, "Good news! I reached the phone company and they are sending someone to fix the phone. We have an appointment for 4 p.m. on July 13, 1994." Her husband replied, "Call them back, because that isn't going to work. That's when the plumber is coming."

it for them. This job demanded real skill: it required a network of contacts, plied with bribes, to learn when and where shipments of scarce goods would arrive. "This shopping is serious business in the Soviet Union," Roberts and LaFollette observe, "and the successful person must have all the attributes of a top-flight purchasing agent in the West."[61] The root cause of the many shortages, reformers realized, was not some conspiracy, but the absence of market-determined prices and the ability to respond to them. Is there better evidence that individuals respond to incentives than the former Soviet Union?

Prices allow one to respond to contingencies as central planning does not. When an opportunity or obstacle arises, a manager could not send to Moscow for an answer, which would take years to get. Reflecting on these facts, Katsenelinboigen liked to pose a parable. Evolution has designed amazingly elaborate structures—think of the liver—but has never created a quadruped with wheels instead of legs. We all know the advantages of wheels; no one with a car would walk from Chicago to Denver.

The answer to the parable is that the world isn't paved. Wheels are better in a specialized, predictable environment, but imagine a wheeled antelope escaping a predator that encounters a log that legs, but not wheels, could negotiate. Legs are less efficient in specialized environments, but are more adaptable to unforeseeable circumstances. The fact that quadrupeds have legs instead of wheels testifies to the radical uncertainty and unforeseeable contingencies of the world. As Katsenelinboigen concluded, if the world were certain and contingencies rare, quadrupeds would have wheels, prices could be set, and central planning would work.

61. Roberts and LaFolette, *Meltdown*, 44.

If economics is viewed this way, markets work better because no one can foresee everything. We are fallible and make mistakes. Knowledge is always limited. Decisions need constant adjustment in light of contingencies. As we have already argued, these are the very reasons that make practical, rather than theoretical, reasoning appropriate for human affairs.

It is all the more ironic then, that market fundamentalists fail to appreciate this point. Thinking theoretically and categorically, they know in advance that market solutions are guaranteed to be right. But markets themselves work better precisely because there are no guarantees. Sometimes markets fail. At other times, they work but other considerations prove more important. You do not want to import armaments from your potential enemy. And, as became very clear during the coronavirus pandemic, you don't want to rely on an uncertain market for suddenly necessary medical supplies.[62]

In short, there is all the difference in the world between, on the one hand, thinking that because markets generally work better, the burden of proof lies with those who argue for some other approach in a particular case, and, on the other, ruling out exceptions in principle. Fundamentalists notwithstanding, markets work best not inevitably but "on the whole and for the most part." In human affairs, that's as much as one could hope for.

---

62. As reported by Jeremy W. Peters, "New Schism Shakes the Republican Faith in a Supreme Market," *New York Times*, May 6, 2020, A22: "Questions over whether the government should play a more active role in protecting Americans from global shocks like the coronavirus pandemic have exposed a widening divide in the Republican Party over whether the small-government, free-market brand of conservatism at the heart of its agenda—and a top priority of its biggest donors—is out of step with the times."

A Way Forward Based on Facts?

We increasingly face a stark choice: govern by ideology or by sound economic principles. The reality is that we know some programs and policies that work. We also know many others that sound good but don't work. Those on the political extremes may pretend otherwise, but, in topic after topic, there is a striking bipartisan consensus among the experts.[63] Maybe we simply need to get that story out there. To be sure, it will not persuade fundamentalists, but it might register among those whom fundamentalists have persuaded.

Perhaps, as Postman argued, it is the messenger who fails to present a compelling story. Reciting a list of numbers and findings, even when they are firmly established, doesn't necessarily convince. You are competing with marches, signs, slogans, and fearmongers. In a battle with slogans, even the most carefully crafted arguments often lose. It is hard to win an argument with a bumper sticker!

We believe not just in data, but also in stories. They not only are rhetorically more effective; they reveal what generalized theory and data obscure. We favor crafting our own stories, while listening to those of others. Tell us how you are affected by incentives—ones that lead you to relocate to a state or country with lower tax rates, or ones that prompt you to promote the

63. One of the more remarkable recent examples is the support by a wide range of economists for staggering levels of deficit spending by the US government in the wake of soaring unemployment rates resulting from the partial shut-down of the economy due to COVID-19. A front page article in the *New York Times* (Jim Tankersley, "A Giant Deficit, Once Dreaded, Is Now Desired," May 17, 2020, 1 and 11) states that "there is little argument among either conservative or liberal economists that the deficit needs to grow, as tax revenues fall and spending needs rise amid a pandemic that has shuttered business activity."

common good. Or how you are moved by the way some arguments based on objective facts are presented, while others leave you listless. And tell us what the conclusions of specialists—and their general models—leave out.

Economists *can* propose wiser answers to the problems that plague us. Sometimes they fall short, but it would be extremely unwise to ignore them altogether. Even when they do not have all the answers, they can often recognize proposals that run so counter to basic economic principles that they are likely to be counterproductive.

But one thing is very clear: economists need to figure out a better way to make their case.

Back to Adam Smith

In looking for an intellectual forefather who can bridge the chasm between market fundamentalists and anti–market fundamentalists, we have a suggestion: Adam Smith. But isn't he the person the market fundamentalists adore? Yes, but, as we argued earlier, they rarely read him, relying instead on textbook-like summaries of his points that made it into mainstream economic theory. The fundamentalists' founding revelation and the lessons drawn from it are two different things.[64]

The way in which economics textbooks typically represent Smith's great classic *The Wealth of Nations* bears little resemblance to its overall spirit.[65] Far from thinking that it is desirable or even possible to describe economic activity by formulas or

---

64. We suspect that is also true of some other founding revelations.

65. Adam Smith, *An Inquiry into the Nature and Causes of the Wealth of Nations*, ed. R. H. Campbell and A. S. Skinner (Indianapolis: Liberty Classics, 1976). The book was originally published in 1776.

other ahistorical ideas, Smith chooses instead to devote a substantial portion of the book to purely narrative explanations. And, rather than imagine that human behavior can be modeled in terms of rational choices, Smith refers time and again to rationality as exceptional. More often people are guided by what Smith calls mere folly.[66] Speaking of the pernicious influence of "the constitution of the Church of Rome [in England]," for instance, he observes sardonically that it was in no danger from "any assault of human reason. . . . Had this constitution been attacked by no other enemies but the feeble efforts of human reason, it must have endured forever."[67] In this case, as in so many others, purely contingent historical factors, which must be narrated to be understood, accomplished what no principle of reason ever could.

Above all, Smith is far from reducing ethical questions to transactions modeled by most of today's economists. As those who have promoted the importance of asking ethical questions have stressed, Smith was the author not only of *The Wealth of Nations*, but also of *The Theory of Moral Sentiments*.[68] Indeed, moral argument occurs frequently in *The Wealth of Nations* itself. Not only does Smith reject the idea that all human action is guided by perceived self-interest—an idea that in his time was represented by Hobbes—he argues quite the opposite, that

66. Smith notes that wealthy noblemen lost their political and military power when they chose to spend their money on expensive baubles instead of the maintenance of thousands of retainers: "And thus, for the gratification of the most childish, the meanest, and the most sordid of all vanities, they gradually bartered their whole power and authority." Smith, *Wealth of Nations*, 419.

67. Smith, *Wealth of Nations*, 802–3.

68. Adam Smith, *The Theory of Moral Sentiments*, originally published in 1759. The page numbers below are from the D. D. Raphael and A. L. Macfie (Liberty, 1982) edition. Jonathan B. Wright, *Ethics in Economics: An Introduction to Moral Frameworks* (Stanford, CA: Stanford University Press, 2015) presents an illuminating analysis of Smith's two classic works.

a concern for others, as well as for ourselves, lies at the core of human nature. *The Theory of Moral Sentiments* famously begins: "How selfish soever man may be supposed, there are evidently some principles in his nature, which interest him in the fortune of others, and render their happiness necessary to him, though he derives nothing from it except the pleasure of seeing it. Of this kind is pity or compassion, the emotion which we feel for the misery of others, when we either see it, or are made to conceive it in a very lively manner."[69] And Smith makes it clear that our inclination to pity and compassion cannot be reduced to an indirect kind of self-love or self-interest, as a rational-choice theorist might suppose.

Smith evidently regarded the sort of thinking that laid the foundation for modern economic theory as necessary but not sufficient, either to understand how people do behave or to recommend how they should. One needs economics and more. Particularly distasteful to Smith was the mentality of what he called "the man of system"—the intellectual fundamentalist—who

> seems to imagine that he can arrange the different members of a great society with as much ease as the hand arranges the different pieces on a chessboard . . . to insist on establishing, and upon establishing all at once, and in spite of all opposition, everything which that idea may seem to require, must often be the highest degree of arrogance. It is to erect his own judgment into the supreme standard of right and wrong. It is to fancy himself the only wise and worthy man in the commonwealth, and that his fellow-citizens should accommodate themselves to him and not he to them.[70]

69. Smith, *Moral Sentiments*, 9.
70. Smith, *Moral Sentiments*, 234.

The wise person will accommodate himself to people and society that do not accord with his ideas: "The man of system, on the contrary, is apt to be very wise in his own conceit; and is often so enamoured with the supposed beauty of his own ideal plan of government, that he cannot suffer the smallest deviation from any part of it."[71] To Smith, it made little difference what the system was, and market fundamentalists, as contemporary "men of system," demonstrate just the sort of thinking he had in mind. Smith never regarded economic analysis as all we need.

How we agree with that! We need more facts and less rhetoric. We need economics supplemented not just by the humanistic social sciences—history, philosophy, sociology, and the like—but by the humanities as well. And we need to have fundamentalists on both sides, market lovers and haters, focus on objective economic data. As the old saying goes, the plural of anecdote is not data. We know many important answers, if only more of us would put aside our wrath and our a priori certainties and just seek them out.

71. Smith, *Moral Sentiments*, 233–34.

5

Searching for Eternal Truths

RELIGION AND ITS DISCONTENTS

A Rabbi's Parable

A few years back Schapiro heard a memorable sermon about a clock in a village square. A visitor to town observed a workman raising the clock far above eye level and wondered whether this was being done to increase its visibility. No, a villager replied; it is to place it beyond arm's reach. Folks would walk by and continually adjust the hands of the clock. If a person's watch said 11:02 and the clock said 11, the passerby would change the clock. The next person who would come by did the same, until it turned out that there was no reason to believe that the clock told the true time. After the clock was raised, people instead started adjusting their watches to the clock, rather than the re- verse, thereby agreeing on a common time.

The point of the story is that until the clock is raised beyond the reach of human hands, the very reason for having a town clock is lost. If everyone adjusts it as seems fit to him, then it must reflect only subjective judgment, constantly shift, and remain unreliable. Even if the clock had originally been a few minutes off, that would have been a lot better than continual alteration. A standard that changes unpredictably is no longer a standard.

Standards are supposed to be above subjective interpretation, so there is something decidedly wrong-headed about changing them to accord with one's own preference. Doing so resembles correcting the dictionary when it indicates we have spelled a word wrong. In Lewis Carroll's *Through the Looking-Glass*, Humpty Dumpty famously refuses to be guided by the dictionary or any other authority: "'When I use a word,' Humpty Dumpty said, in a rather scornful tone, 'it means just what I choose it to mean—neither more nor less.'" The always sensible Alice replies: "The question is . . . whether you can make words mean so many different things." Humpty Dumpty retorts, "The question is which is to be master—that's all."[1] But if all of us used words in whatever way struck our fancy, language would not work at all. Some things by their nature demand that people acknowledge their authority, even if doing so constrains them. Whenever people correct the town clock, or change language to accord with their whims, they typically justify their actions with the same "rather scornful tone" as Humpty Dumpty's.

The Clock and the Dictionary

The rabbi's parable has its counterparts in arguments over proper use of language. When new "unabridged" dictionaries or new books explaining proper word usage appear, a familiar

---

1. Lewis Carroll, *Through the Looking-Glass and What Alice Found There* in *The Annotated Alice*, ed. Martin Gardner (New York: Bramhall House, 1960), 269.

debate resumes.[2] Linguists are trained to be descriptive, not prescriptive, much as anthropologists describe and analyze but do not judge cultures. They are therefore inclined to disparage any prescriptivist approach to language. Usage guides or dictionaries that distinguish correct from incorrect often strike them as philistine, the work of grouchy grammarians and punctuation puritans. Should a politician be criticized for using the word "literally" to mean "I really mean it!" ("he literally fell to pieces" or "he literally had the future in his hands"),[3] some linguist is sure to observe that in fact the word "literally" now is frequently used that way, and so the usage is correct.[4]

In fact, this conclusion makes no logical sense, because to deem something correct means that it might be incorrect, which is precisely what descriptivism rejects at the outset. It is like hearing an anthropologist argue that cannibalism is moral simply because it is done. One might as well say that murder is not a crime because, from a descriptivist standpoint, it is common.

Such judgments arise from what might be called "the disciplinary fallacy." A discipline makes an enabling assumption to get started, and then its practitioners conclude that it has *proven* what it has in fact assumed. Economists may postulate that choices are rational, and then, since they never encounter anything they

2. See, for instance, Herbert C. Morton, *The Story of Webster's Third: Philip Gove's Controversial Dictionary and Its Critics* (Cambridge: Cambridge University Press, 1995).

3. See, for instance, Alexandra Petri, "Literally, Joe Biden," *Washington Post*, September 7, 2012, https://www.washingtonpost.com/blogs/compost/post/joe-bidens -literally-indefensible-word/2012/09/07/8e35edd8-f8a8-11e1-8398-0327ab83ab91 _blog.html.

4. See John McWhorter, *Words on the Move: Why English Won't—and Can't—Sit Still (Like, Literally)* (New York: Holt, 2016).

deem to be irrational (how could they, if they assume it away?), they assert that economics has demonstrated human rationality. Disciplines ruling out judgments of value eventually tempt their practitioners to conclude that no behavior treated by the discipline can be incorrect.

The proper response to these linguists is that standards of correctness are not themselves linguistic. They are social standards applied to language, and none the less real for that. They are not supposed to describe what people do any more than legal codes do. On the contrary, they *presuppose* that some things people do are incorrect.

But that is not the response one always hears. There are some who go to the opposite extreme and insist that, if standards change, there will soon be no standards at all. And indeed, if standards changed quickly and at whim, or by the fiat of some group, the very purpose of standards would be called into question. They would be as worthless as the constantly altered clock in the rabbi's parable.

However, that objection does not apply to standards that change gradually, at the direction of no one in particular, in response to numerous changes in customs, values, and bodies of knowledge. It is a mistake to think that standards must be absolutely immutable in order to work. To be sure, if each judge could make the law mean whatever she wanted it to mean, there would be no law, but that does not show that law, or the interpretation of it, cannot change at all without ceasing to be law.

Usage standards classify actual behavior as better or worse. One would expect, then, that as the body of speech to be regulated changes, standards, to have the same effect, will have to adjust. If, let us say, 30 percent of common usage is classed as incorrect, and 10 percent as exemplary, criteria will have to alter to maintain the same percentage of changing behavior. In his preface to the first dictionary of the English language, Samuel Johnson explains that he hoped at first to stabilize the language. It was common at the time to fear that as Geoffrey Chaucer was no longer intelligible without annotations, the same fate would eventually befall John Dryden and all recent poets. What creativity adds at one end, linguistic change subtracts at the other. In short, as Johnson explicates this way of thinking, there is an advantage in "steadiness and uniformity"[5]: "Much less ought written language to comply with the corruption of oral utterance, or copy that which every variation of time or place makes different from itself and imitate those changes, which will again be changed."[6] Such considerations lead one to "wish . . . that the instrument might be less apt to decay, and that signs might be permanent like the things they denote."[7]

But such a wish is both vain and misconceived. It is vain because it is a hope that neither reason nor experience can justify. As Johnson writes,

When we see men grow old and die at a certain time one after another, from century to century, we laugh at the elixir that promises long life for a thousand years; and with equal justice may the lexicographer be derided, who, being able to produce no example of a nation that has preserved their words and phrases from mutability, shall imagine that his dictionary can embalm his language . . . that it is within his power to change sublunary nature, and clear the world at once from folly, vanity, and affectation.[8]

5. Samuel Johnson, "Preface to the Dictionary," in *Rasselas, Poems, and Selected Prose*, ed. Bertrand H. Bronson (New York: Holt, Rinehart, 1958), 215.

6. Johnson, "Preface to the Dictionary," 215.

7. Johnson, 216.

8. Johnson, 233.

Academies have been instituted to prevent all change, Johnson explains, "but their vigilance and activity have hitherto been in vain . . . to enchain syllables, and to lash the wind are equally the undertakings of pride."[9] Johnson recounts how he came to recognize that some sources of change are not only inevitable but also legitimate. Only a barbarous nation "secured from strangers" and lacking books could keep out foreign influences and the words they bring.[10] Whenever a book is translated it imparts "something of its native idiom."[11] As sciences develop, they add new words or give a new meaning to existing ones: "The tropes of poetry will make hourly encroachments, and the metaphorical will become the common sense."[12] For all these reasons, usage does and should change. It is indeed possible, and all too common, for standards to suffer corruption, much as a country's morals sometimes get worse, but not every change in either can properly be called decay. As with the rabbi's clock, adjustments should not be too frequent or cavalier, but, as we shall see when we return to this parable in the conclusion of the chapter, they sometimes need to be made.

When Standards Become Mere Prejudice

For believers, the essential truths of religion are a standard. They are something quite different from a statement of personal preference or taste. The Ten Commandments are not ten recommendations or ten fashion tips for today. They convey timeless wisdom or, at least, the wisdom of many ages. If there were

9. Johnson, 233–34.
10. Johnson, 234.
11. Johnson, 236.
12. Johnson, 235.

no sacred texts—and every culture has them, whether written or oral—then there would be nothing against which to measure contemporary preferences and beliefs. Every generation, every group, and every individual would be prone to considering its beliefs infallible precisely because they believed them. Like a person who checks his own spelling, they would verify their opinions by asking if they coincided with their opinions and would of course always find that they did. They would be willfully confined in a prison house of their own moment, social class, and culture, with the rest of human experience forever inaccessible.

The hero of Dostoevsky's novel *Crime and Punishment*, Raskolnikov, thinks in this way. He regards religious tradition, particularly its respect for the sacredness of each human life, as mere "prejudice." A radical utilitarian, he believes that lives should be sacrificed when doing so would cause more good than harm: "One death and a hundred lives in exchange—it's simple arithmetic!"[13] Raskolnikov trusts his subjective judgment because extraordinary people like himself have the "the right to transgress" in the name of the truth as they conceive it.[14] Tradition, scripture, the town clock—those are, for ordinary people, "mere material," as Raskolnikov calls them.[15]

On this basis, Raskolnikov commits a double murder. When at last he realizes his moral error, he has a dream, one of the most famous in world literature, in which humanity is infected by some mysterious plague of trichina worms "endowed with intelligence and will." All infected people regard themselves as

13. Fyodor Dostoevsky, *Crime and Punishment*, trans. Constance Garnett (New York: Modern Library, 1950), 67.

14. Raskolnikov outlines his theory in part 3, chapter 5.

15. Dostoevsky, *Crime and Punishment*, 258.

"completely in possession of the truth . . . never had they considered their decisions, their scientific conclusions, their moral convictions so infallible." But, although everyone is certain, they all see things differently: "Each thought that he alone had the truth . . . they could not agree what to consider evil and what good," and so "men killed each other in a sort of senseless spite."[16] Armies form, but before they can fight others, they break into smaller and smaller groups fighting each other. Of course, this dream reflects Raskolnikov's realization that in moral matters individual certainty, while subjectively powerful, is no guide to truth at all.

The Hebrew Bible contains a famous dream making a similar point. In chapter 2 of the book of Daniel, King Nebuchadnezzar, who has had a disturbing dream, demands that the wise men of Babylon interpret it. To prove that they are not just spinning a clever tale, they must first tell the king what his dream was. When they respond that no one can do that, he orders them all killed. Daniel solves the problem in a way the wise men had not considered. He asks his companions to pray to God for help, and God reveals both the dream and its meaning to him. Daniel can do what no one else can do, give the true interpretation and prove it is correct by telling the King his own dream, precisely because Daniel does *not* rely on his own judgment. He is smart enough to know, as the "infected" intellectuals of Raskolnikov's dream do not, where smartness is not enough.

That is a point people today who do not take this story literally can appreciate. Something beyond any individual judgment—in the Bible, that means God's truth—is needed.

16. Dostoevsky, 528.

Challenging Stories

As the rabbi's parable suggests, today especially it appears that many Jews are troubled by the fact that the Bible does not seem to accord with their own values. Of course, the same is true of many Christians, as well as those of other faiths. Numerous demands seem at odds with our own beliefs. Holy texts speak in a language that is distant from our own. And they tell stories that, as we say today, require "trigger warnings."

Who has not cringed reading the many passages that seem unequivocally antithetical to current social norms? Examples abound. Take the story of Tamar in the book of Genesis. After marrying two of Judah's sons, she is about to marry the third son when Judah intervenes. Tamar then dresses up like a prostitute, seduces her father-in-law, and gives birth to twins. Or in Judges, when Jephthah leads the Israelites against Ammon and in the heat of battle vows that, should he survive, he will sacrifice to God whatever comes out first to greet him when he gets home. Alas, that turns out to be his beloved daughter. Or, again in Judges, where a concubine is gang-raped and left for dead by a group of violent men in the town of Gibeah: in the morning, when her husband finds her, he chops her up into twelve pieces. These stories make Jacob bribing Esau or tricking Isaac seem trivial.

Or consider the story of God demanding that Abraham sacrifice his son Isaac.[17] We have a friend, a superb philosopher

17. Jewish Midrashic interpretation also reflects how disturbing this story was to rabbis. They found ingenious ways to show that, in spite of what the text seems to say, God knew the outcome of the test in advance and that Abraham did not, responding truthfully to Isaac's question that he was to be the sacrifice. See James L. Kugel, *How to Read the Bible: A Guide to Scripture, Then and Now* (New York: Free Press, 2007), 12–13. Kugel asks: "But did these interpreters actually believe their own

and president of his synagogue, who cites this story to explain why, despite his devotion to Jewish tradition, he cannot believe in God. What sort of God would make a demand like that? Our friend cannot find a way to understand this story except as a description of a brutal God who demands we do evil just because he says so. And, indeed, the story does raise disturbing questions.

Some distressing stories can be explained relatively easily. Just because a biblical character, even a revered one, does something, does not make it right. Everything about the Jephthah story indicates he has made a rash vow. As Robert Alter observes, "The Midrash Yanhuma shrewdly notes that the first creature out of the house could have been a dog or a pig, animals unfit for sacrifice."[18] The story of Jephthah begins with his expulsion from his house because his mother was a prostitute, and now the return to his house, which he envisages will be a triumphant celebration, results in "the destruction of the house in the extended sense of the term" since, "besides her, he had neither son nor daughter" (Judg. 11:34).

The rest of the tale is dedicated to raising our sympathy for the sacrificed child, who is willing to die but begs two months to mourn her maidenhood. Neither the father, nor daughter, nor even the narrator can speak of the horrible act of child sacrifice directly: "He did to her as he had vowed" is how the narrator puts it. So horrible is her fate that, ever since, "it became a fixed practice in Israel that each year the daughters of

---

interpretations? Didn't they know they were playing fast and loose with the text's real meaning? This is always a difficult question" (13).

18. Robert Alter, *The Hebrew Bible: A Translation and Commentary: Volume 2, Prophets* (New York: Norton, 2019), 124. The Bible passages in this paragraph and the next one are taken from this volume.

Israel would go to lament the daughter of Jephthah the Gile-adite four days in the year" (Judg. 11:40). Far from setting up Jephthah as a model to imitate, the tale stresses the danger of open-ended vows made by human beings, who cannot know the future.

We may appreciate the point that Jephthah's vow was terribly wrong by contrasting it with the Greek story of Agamemnon's vow to sacrifice his daughter Iphigenia so that the gods will allow the Greek fleet to sail for Troy. The Greeks were continu-ally returning to the Homeric stories that were their founding texts, examining their implications, and filling in gaps in their stories, and Greek tragedy was one way they did so. Loosely speaking, it played the role of Midrash. The Greek story is tragic precisely because the sacrifice, however heart-rending, was nec-essary. Agamemnon has made no rash promise, as Jephthah did, but finds himself in a situation, created by the gods, that leaves him no choice.

Like Jephthah's daughter, Iphigenia recognizes the injustice of her fate. In *Iphigenia in Aulis*, Euripides has her lament:

> If I had the tongue of Orpheus
> So that I could charm with song the stones to
> Leap and follow me, or if my words could
> Quite beguile anyone I wished—I'd use
> My magic now. But only with tears can I
> Make arguments and here I offer them. O Father,
> My body is a suppliant's, tight clinging
> To your knees. Do not take away this life
> Of mine before its dying time.[19]

---

19. Euripides, *Iphigenia in Aulis*, *The Complete Greek Tragedies*, vol. 7 (Euripides 3), ed. David Grene and Richmond Lattimore (New York: Modern Library), 176.

But, unlike the biblical story, Iphigenia (as Euripides portrays her) comes to recognize that her sacrifice is a noble deed necessary to her people:

> I shall die—I am resolved—
> And having fixed my mind I want to die
> Well and gloriously . . . All Greece turns
> Her eyes to me, to me only, great Greece
> In her might—for through me is the sailing
> Of the fleet, through me the sack and overthrow
> Of Troy. Because of me, never more will
> Barbarians wrong and ravish Greek women.[20]

In the biblical story, by contrast, the military victory has already been won. Nothing redeems the death. It is utterly pointless, and Jephthah's vow is revealed as a terrible mistake.

The Bible also makes clear that David, though favored by God, is no paragon of moral rectitude. Calvin, indeed, cites the moral failings of biblical sages as proof that salvation does not depend on good works.[21] Neither are Abraham, Joseph, and other sages cardboard saints. Indeed, one of the reasons the Hebrew Bible is such a compendium of wisdom is that it does not oversimplify either human beings or moral questions. Recall that two of the greatest challenges to any belief that God's world makes sense in terms of human concepts of justice and meaning— the books of Job and Ecclesiastes—occur in the Bible itself. The Sunday school version of the Bible is not the Bible.

The Bible is always posing difficult questions. The history of its interpretation is a compendium of possible answers. For

---

20. Euripides, *Iphigenia in Aulis*, 186–87.

21. See John Calvin, *Institutes of the Christian Religion*, ed. John T. McNeill (Philadelphia: Westminster, 1960), 937–38.

later readers in a given tradition, earlier interpretations seem to be present, or at least implicit, in the text itself. For Jews, rabbinic readings came to be simply what the text meant, and both Jews and Christians "recall" incidents in the Bible that are not literally there.[22] That is the point of the old schoolboy joke that the ancient Greeks did not know the most important thing about themselves: that they were *ancient* Greeks. Over the centuries we have discovered what Bakhtin calls great "semantic values" in antiquity, "values of which the Greeks were in fact unaware, although they themselves created them."[23]

Different traditions thus come to detect different incidents and meanings in the same set of words. And, as the weight of interpretation grows, some readers, who find the mountain of readings apparently contradicting the text's plain meaning implausible, try to strip away tradition, or the part of tradition they do not accept, and go back to the text itself. Karaite Judaism and various forms of Protestantism regarded themselves as recapturing what had been made obscure.

For different reasons, the more recent interpreters who read the Bible as literature—some seeing it as no different than other human masterpieces, others as divinely inspired—also focus on the text itself, since that is how literary interpretation works. Midrash, the decrees of Church councils, or the works of theologians play the role of influential criticism that is worth considering, but not part of the Biblical text itself.

The recognition that the Bible does not necessarily commend what its central figures do does not resolve all questions.

22. See Kugel, *How to Read the Bible*, 13.

23. Mikhail Bakhtin, "Response to a Question from the *Novyi mir* Editorial Staff," in *Speech Genres and Other Late Essays*, ed. Caryl Emerson and Michael Holquist, trans. Vern McGee (Austin: University of Texas Press, 1986), 6.

Some moral commands—against homosexuality, for instance—
strike almost all of us today as wrong. Others, like the countless
apparently arbitrary prohibitions in Leviticus, seem ridiculous.
Why should we not be able to mix two kinds of fabric, and what
sense does it make that we can eat one kind of locust whereas
to eat another is an "abomination"? And how are we to come to
terms with stories like the binding of Isaac, where Abraham's
willingness to sacrifice Isaac is praised?

We think it is fair to say, first, that there is no single authoritative answer to these questions. Both Jews and Christians have
struggled with these problems for centuries. Second, they confront every contemporary Jewish and Christian believer. While
we offer our own speculations on these issues, we are neither
rabbis nor professional theologians and don't pretend to have
definitive solutions. No trichina of "intelligence and will" has
infected us (at least, we hope not). Rather, we bring to bear our
own training—one of us as an economist, the other as a specialist in Russian literature and thought—in hopes of creating a
dialogue about these questions, a dialogue about our dialogue,
today, with the Bible's eternal truths.

7   The Relevance of the Timeless

Sacred texts remain relevant precisely because we *can't* make
them mean whatever we choose. If we could, we would already
know what they have to say and would have nothing to learn
from them. And that is true not only of divinely inspired works,
but of those that occupy other kinds of special status. If one
could make the Constitution mean whatever one wanted it to
mean, it would not be a constitution at all. The whole point of
a Bill of Rights, for instance, is to preclude authorities from
doing what they would like to do. The First Amendment would

guarantee nothing if authorities could reinterpret it at will. On paper, the "Stalin Constitution" of 1936 was the most liberal in the world, but in practice the rights it guaranteed were subject to the principle that they could not preclude what socialism— the Party—demanded.

Great literature, too, is capable of offering wisdom only if it can say things we do not already know and believe. Like the Bible, the classics offer insights that, on the one hand, can participate in contemporary dialogues and, on the other, reflect a perspective not already present among our contemporaries. That is one reason it is profoundly mistaken to reject the very idea of a canon of classic works.[24] In Russia, the tradition of great literature has enjoyed a quasi-sacred status—someone who criticizes Pushkin might be accused of "blasphemy"—and the great works of the past have been mined to tell later generations how to live their lives. Some foreign classics, especially those that influenced the greatest Russian authors, were read in the same way.

Dostoevsky, Shakespeare, and the Bible somehow manage to say something pertinent today and yet speak with a voice outside normal discourse. And not only for Russians, but, to a greater or lesser extent, to all who acknowledge great literature as something extraordinary. That is one reason we turn to it: because today's whispered gossip and impassioned shouting are insufficient, all the more so in the case of the Bible if one regards it as divinely inspired. The voice of the Bible is both intelligible and unfamiliar, pertinent but not already present.

For this reason, Alter argues, it is a mistake to translate the Bible into relentlessly colloquial English. Its language needs to

24. By contrast, it is not at all mistaken to call for a revision of the canon, a process essential to its existence *as* a canon. We discuss this point in detail in chapter 6.

speak to us in the present but from outside the present. "All the modern translators," Alter writes, "have shown a deaf ear to diction, acting as though the only important considerations in rendering a literary text were lexical values and grammatical structures, while the English terms chosen could be promiscuously borrowed from boardroom or bedroom or scholar's word hoard, with little regard to the tonality and connotation the words carried with them from their native linguistic habitat."[25] The language of the Bible, he explains, differed from the vernacular and "in its own time was stylized, dignified, and readily identified by its audience as a language of literature, in certain ways distinct from the language of quotidian reality."[26] While formal, it is still "plainspoken." For all these reasons, Alter concludes, the right direction for the translator "was hit upon by the King James Version," which employs a "language that is stylized yet simple and direct, free from the overtones of contemporary colloquial usage but with a certain timeless homespun quality."[27]

The King James Bible, like the original Hebrew as Alter reads and translates it, is intelligible to us and yet somehow strange, requiring some effort. That strangeness is not just a product of the fact that the King James Bible is four hundred years old, since it was deliberately archaized from the start. Both of our time and an earlier epoch, "with a certain timeless homespun quality," it speaks to us without being just another one of us.[28] The Gettysburg Address, whose diction carries a biblical aura,

25. Robert Alter, "To the Reader," in *Genesis: Translation and Commentary* (New York: Norton, 1996), xxii.

26. Alter, "To the Reader," xxv.

27. Alter, xxv.

28. See Robert Alter, *Pen of Iron: American Prose and the King James Bible* (Princeton, NJ: Princeton University Press, 2010).

has much the same quality, as does Martin Luther King Jr.'s "I Have a Dream" speech. So do many liturgical texts. Those who render such texts into colloquial English destroy their ability to speak from outside our time. They take an ancient clock and paste a modern Hollywood face on it. It is like rewording Hamlet's soliloquy: "Living or croaking, that's on my mind."

The amazing thing about the Hebrew Scriptures is how relevant they are today despite their origin in another world with very different concerns. We all respond to the verse about beating swords into ploughshares and spears into pruning hooks even though most of us are urban, and no one uses ancient agricultural implements. There is no need to update the verse by substituting modern tools. Would we gain or would we lose if we made it say "retrofit tanks into tractors"? The biblical images are remote yet comprehensible, and it is precisely this combination of the familiar with the archaic, of todayness with timelessness, that makes such passages meaningful. Society has changed in unimaginable ways, we reflect, but some truths seem eternal.

Or do they? Though many biblical pronouncements seem timeless, others appear to belong to a day long past: no one needs detailed instructions on how many cubits of this or that material must be used in building the temple. Still others are hard to classify one way or the other—or, perhaps, are eternal, but not directly so. How can one tell the difference between that which is eternal and that which is not? Or perhaps one should ask: How can one find the eternal element in what does not at first glance seem so?

Many people who notice that the Bible's vision and ethical tenets do not fit today's standards decide to reject it altogether. Others, of course, do the same with the Constitution and the works of great poets and novelists. In the early days of the Russian

Revolution, many recommended that the new society reject entirely literature written by those aristocrats Pushkin and Tolstoy and by all writers, Russian or foreign, compromised by prerevolutionary values. In his frequently cited poem "It's Too Early to Rejoice" (*Radovat'sia rano*), Vladimir Mayakovsky called for putting Raphael and Rastrelli against the wall: "And why is Pushkin not attacked? And other classics?"[29] Given the status enjoyed by the Russian classics, this recommendation was the equivalent of calling for the destruction of the great Orthodox cathedrals and monasteries, which, to a considerable extent, did indeed take place. Thankfully, Mayakovsky's view did not prevail, as the Bolsheviks decided to preserve the riches of Russian literature and teach them in the schools—suitably reinterpreted in Marxist-Leninist terms, of course. A recent scholar of Soviet history has argued that a key factor in the ultimate collapse of Russian Communism was precisely the Russian classics, which everyone knew and whose fundamental values were radically at odds with those of Bolshevism.[30]

Some have gone further than the Bolsheviks. The Khmer Rouge made a point of executing anyone who could read. In 212 BCE Chinese emperor Qin Shi Huang, who adhered to the newly triumphant school of legalism, ordered the burning of all other books. Anyone who discussed them, or used them to criticize the present, was to be executed. To make sure that all memory of nonlegalist works would disappear, 460 Confucian scholars were buried alive. This incident—known as "the burning of books and burying of scholars"—may stand as an ex-

29. Vladimir Mayakovskii, *Izbrannye proizvedeniia*, vol. 1, ed. V. Pertsov and V. Zemskov (Moscow–Leningrad: Sovetskii pisatel', 1963), 250.

30. Yuri Slezkine, *The House of Government: A Saga of the Russian Revolution* (Princeton, NJ: Princeton University Press, 2017).

treme example of one way to deal with past wisdom that does not accord with present beliefs.[31]

In *The Decline and Fall of the Roman Empire*, Gibbon tells the story of the Arabian chief Amrou, who tries unsuccessfully to convince the caliph Omar to spare that wonder of the world, the royal library of Alexandria. "The well-known answer of Omar," Gibbon reports, "was inspired by the ignorance of a fanatic: 'If these writings of the Greeks agree with the book of God [Koran], they are useless and need not be preserved; if they disagree, they are pernicious and ought to be destroyed.'" So numerous were the volumes of paper and parchment, which were sent to four thousand locales to be burnt, "that six months were barely sufficient for the consumption of this precious fuel."[32]

Today, of course, people who reject past wisdom do not go so far. But they may find the existence of sacred or canonical texts threatening. Some may be banished from the canon, others preserved but taught as examples of past prejudice. Though motivated by high ethical concerns, people who think this way demonstrate a supreme confidence that, just as contemporary physics is better than Aristotle's and Galileo's, so present moral understanding is necessarily better than what can be found in Shakespeare and the Bible. If such teachings agree with modern science and mores, they are needless, and, if they disagree, they are pernicious. To accept biblical ethics, in their view, is like preferring creationism to Darwinism.

31. See "Memorial on the Burning of Books," in *Sources of the Chinese Tradition*, vol. 1, ed. Wm. Theodore de Bary and Irene Bloom (New York: Columbia University Press, 1999), 209–10.

32. Edward Gibbon, *The History of the Decline and Fall of the Roman Empire*, ed. J. B. Bury (New York: Heritage, 1946), 1821.

Thinking this way entails regarding the views of one's own moment in time ("Wisdom since Tuesday," as someone we know has called it) as the only authority. People who accept the authority of the present this way seem to forget that other people—or themselves in the recent past—were just as certain of other views as they are of theirs: those fools regarded their wisdom as the be-all and end-all, whereas ours really is. Since these discrepant views cannot all be right, it would seem that certainty of one's beliefs regarding questions that have concerned cultures and brilliant people around the world for millennia, is not a very good indication that one's beliefs are correct. As the English saying has it, self-praise is no recommendation.

Compassion and Holiness

However confident one may be that it is now 10:57, or 11:03, and not 11, as the town clock says, and however certain that all other people's watches who tell a different time are wrong, one might be wise to imagine how one's own confidence appears to others just as confident of something else. In his *Essay on Criticism*, Alexander Pope observed, "'Tis with our judgments as our watches. None / Go just alike, yet each believes his own."[33] That is why one needs a town clock, even if—or just because—it does not accord with each individual watch.

Some who are disturbed by the distance of Scripture from our own beliefs and values still try to preserve it. They may retain an attachment to traditional ritual, or to the celebration of holidays, or to a sense of belonging to a community, and so they

33. Alexander Pope, "An Essay on Criticism," in *Selected Poetry and Prose*, ed. William K. Wimsatt Jr. (New York: Holt, Rinehart & Winston, 1965), 63 (lines 9–10).

find a way to retain Scripture, while allowing it to make no un-
wanted demands. Some Jews surely think this way. They may
say the Shema, and fast on Yom Kippur, while denying the existence of God: "Hear O Israel, the God Who does not exist is
One." Rabbi Abraham Joshua Heschel once remarked that before he came to America he could not have imagined it possible
to be an atheist rabbi.

From such a perspective, liturgy is rewritten and the Bible
retranslated to accord with our tastes. We repent for sins not
imagined five years ago. The language of the Bible is dumbed
down. Instead of "Am I my brother's keeper," how about "Who
says his affairs are any of my concern?" The language is adjusted,
and the thought explained, so that everyone can understand it,
which is absurd because even in ages when few people were
literate, the King James Bible spoke to them. Is anybody really
confused by the word "thou"? Is "love your enemy" clearer than
"love thine enemy"?

Something else is involved here: the desire to make sure no
one is disturbed by something unfamiliar, something unlike
oneself, or some demand that might be uncomfortable. That
impulse is not new, as Pope notes:

> Then unbelieving Priests reformed the nation,
> And taught more pleasant methods of salvation:
> Where Heaven's free subjects might their rights dispute,
> Lest God himself should seem too absolute.[34]

Refer to God as a sort of figure of speech. This is a God who
reads the *New York Times*, listens to NPR, and thinks just as we
do. But who needs this God?

---

34. Pope, "Essay on Criticism," 78 (lines 546–49).

If one takes neither of these routes, and accepts scriptural authority, one has still not solved all problems. Just as Scripture uses parables that one would be mistaken to take literally, so its commandments and stories seem to require interpretation. Some ethical demands and values really do seem eternal, but others do not, and some do, but only after an appropriate understanding that makes their deeper meaning apparent. Even fundamentalists have to consider verses that are not self-interpreting. Not all fundamentalists agree on all points, after all.

We begin with the easy ones. Who could argue against honoring our parents, refraining from murder, telling the truth, and showing compassion to the most vulnerable? If so, aren't these needless platitudes? Actually, no. To begin with, not all cultures accept these values (Nietzsche explicitly rejected the value Jews and Christians place on compassion. He was, to use his own term, "the Antichrist," calling for a revaluation of these very values. For different reasons, so did both the Nazis and the Soviets. Lenin and Trotsky regarded an ethic of compassion and the sanctity of human life as despicable precisely because it was the heritage of religion. We do not accept the bourgeois idea of the "sanctity of human life," Trotsky sneered.[35] Lenin was positively revolted by the ethics of compassion.

As for honoring one's father and mother, Marx and Engels famously called for "the abolition of the family. . . . the bourgeois family will vanish as a matter of course when its complement [prostitution] vanishes, and both will vanish with the vanishing of capital"—a line that echoes Plato's call for the end of marriage and the raising of children in common and that has

---

35. For a justification of this position, see Leon Trotsky, *Terrorism and Communism: A Reply to Karl Kautsky* (Ann Arbor: University of Michigan Press, 1963).

inspired numerous communal experiments.[36] Stalin did everything he could to root out such values. Every schoolchild had
to learn the story of the boy Pavlik Morozov, who was celebrated for turning in his parents for holding anti-Soviet attitudes. In the early days of the Soviet Union, plans were afoot to
abolish the family altogether.[37]

To be sure, as one reader of this manuscript noted, we read
in Luke 14:26: "If any man come unto me, and hate not his
father, and mother, and wife, and children, and brethren, and
sisters, yea, and his own life, he cannot be my disciple." Whether
this be an example of what Albert Schweitzer called "interim
ethics"—ethics that applies only to times right before the end
of the world—or for some other reason, no lasting Christian
society has prescribed hatred of one's own parents or children.
It is perhaps the supreme irony of history that only the mili-
tantly atheist Soviets seem to have taken this idea seriously!

Even if we set aside such ideologies, there have been and still
are cultures that, while not rejecting compassion, do not give it
the priority we tend to give it. If we take an anthropological or
historical perspective, we recognize that other cultures, or other
parts of our own culture, think of moral questions differently
from the way we do. Taking this fact seriously can help us grasp
why some fundamental biblical values are not just universal
platitudes. Why not kill a few people—or even a few million—
if doing so benefits humanity as a whole?

36. Karl Marx and Friedrich Engels, "Manifesto of the Communist Party," in *Basic
Writings on Politics and Philosophy*, ed. Lewis S. Feuer (Garden City, NY: Anchor,
1959), 24.

37. See Yuri Druzhnikov, *Informer 101: The Myth of Pavlik Morozov* (New York:
Transaction, 1997).

Once we recognize that some core biblical values are not mere truisms, we can more readily see ourselves as others with different values see us. We can also gain self-knowledge when we take seriously the fact that some other core biblical values are indeed different from ours. By "core" values we mean those without which the Bible would no longer resemble itself. Compassion is one essential value we accept.[38] A core value that gives many people pause is the Bible's insistence on holiness and the divine as something apart from and above ourselves.

Some cultural anthropologists have stressed that the values most secular people take for granted—to the point where they cannot believe that anyone but a villain or an idiot could think differently—are decidedly weird. Not just weird in the sense of extremely atypical of humanity as a whole, but also—taking WEIRD as an acronym—Western, Educated, Industrialized, Rich, and Democratic.[39] WEIRD people often reduce ethics to John Stuart Mill's principle of harm—that the only legitimate use of force is to restrain people from doing harm to others.[40] This principle is linked to a notion of autonomy: the individual is the fundamental unit about which moral questions

38. In his classic study *An Essay on the Development of Christian Doctrine*, John Henry Newman, while arguing that the Christian idea is by its nature one that develops, cautions that one must distinguish between true developments and corruptions, the former being true to its "essential idea" and the latter contrary to it: "When we speak of its developing, we consider it to be fulfilling, not belying, its destiny." John Henry Neuman, *An Essay on the Development of Christian Doctrine* (London: Aeterna, 2014), 49–50.

39. Jonathan Haidt, *The Righteous Mind: Why Good People Are Divided by Politics and Religion* (New York: Pantheon, 2012).

40. Mill writes, "That principle is, that the sole end for which mankind are warranted, individually or collectively in interfering with the liberty of action of any of their number, is self-protection. That the only purpose for which power can be rightfully exercised over any member of a civilized community, against his will, is to pre-

are asked. Life is about securing the happiness of individuals. Other cultures find such a view repellent. It reduces life, they say, to an amusement park. In 1992 Lee Kuan Yew famously observed that "what Asians value may not be what Americans or Europeans value. Westerners value the freedoms and liberties of the individual."[41] In many societies the fundamental unit transcends and outlives the individual, whether the unit is the family, the nation, or some other. With its emphasis on Israel as a people, the Bible shares this perspective. God's covenant was not with Abraham personally, but with the people descended from him for all generations.

The Bible also presumes the value of the sacred. To owe one's greatest loyalty to anything of this world is idol worship, the first and perhaps worst sin. To owe one's first allegiance to oneself is to make an idol of oneself. Much of Judaism, from the Sabbath to dietary laws, presumes a radical difference between the sacred and the profane. It presumes that something not of this world can make demands on us.

A person who wishes to be a Jew or Christian must confront both the values we share with the Bible, which to a considerable extent our culture inherited from the Bible, and those we do not. We need to expand our horizon. But what happens when doing so runs counter to our core values today? The Bible's disturbing passages, some of which we cited above, raise just this question.

---

vent harm to others. His own good, either physical or moral, is not a sufficient warrant." John Stuart Mill, *On Liberty* (Buffalo: Prometheus, 1986), 16.

41. Speech by Lee Kuan Yew, Senior Minister of Singapore, Create 21 Asahi Forum November 20, 1992, Tokyo, https://www.nas.gov.sg/archivesonline/data/pdfdoc/lky19921120.pdf, paragraph 36.

Equivalents

When can we adjust the clock, and when should we refrain from doing so?

One time-honored way to handle disturbing passages is to *allegorize* them so that their meanings are entirely transformed. If the text says something you don't like, make it say something else. As James Kugel has observed, "The practice of allegorizing seems to stem from the central part that the poetry of Homer came to play in Greek education." Since, for Greeks, Homer was "*the* text and constituted the average person's road to literature and high culture," its scenes of moral turpitude eventually proved disturbing and had to be thought away by making them mean something else. Jews and Christians followed this approach as well. Allegory had the power to turn what appeared to be just a historical event, like Abraham's departure from his home, into an allegory of the soul's journey to God. As Kugel observes, "Allegorizing turned everything in the Bible that was particular and historical into something more general and immediately applicable."[42]

These readings were, of course, often strained, and it is obvious that, pushed far enough, allegory can make anything mean anything else. One can always call those who don't want to allegorize away the text's evident meaning unsophisticated literalists. This sort of thinking is a reverse fundamentalism, since it treats *present* values and knowledge as inerrant. Not surprisingly, the fundamentalists rejected it. Indeed, their tendency to go in the direction of the opposite extreme of literalism, was a reaction to such interpretive methods.

42. Kugel, *How to Read the Bible*, 18–19.

One could imagine someone adept at allegory saying that the story of the woman cut into twelve parts was really just a way of referring to Israel's twelve tribes: "Only naïve people think it is about cutting up a real person." The advantage of this method is that, with a little practice, it can always be made to work. But, precisely for that reason, it does not really convince. Unless one can show that the text itself *invites* an allegory, the devising of one must be an imposition. It seems like what it is: a jerry-rigged construction. Stalin's chief of secret police Nikolai Yezhov is supposed to have said, "You find the man, I'll find the crime." Allegory allows the interpreter to say the reverse: "You find the crime, I'll find the exculpation."

Arbitrary allegorization, like changing the text itself, makes it impossible for a story to challenge us. We do not engage it in conversation; we make sure it says what we would say. It becomes a ventriloquization of ourselves. Can it really be that we must either accept the unacceptable or worship our own beliefs? Are there no better approaches than these for dealing with a disturbing passage? For most believers, this question is likely to be of supreme importance. We believe there are alternatives. For example, sometimes what is needed is a sort of *translation*. To grasp the text's original meaning, one has to find rough equivalents in our own very different world.

Every commandment and every story presumes a context and a psychology. The whole point of a story can be lost when context changes. We can appreciate this when we reflect that it is true with great literary works as well as with the Bible. To understand the moral quandaries of Jane Austen's heroines, one has to grasp the world in which they live, with all its social norms and understandings of human behavior. We ask: Given a world where women did not have and perhaps did not even envision the same options they have today, where everyone was a believing Protestant, where to engage in "trade" might be considered a demeaning activity for a gentleman, where human intentions were understood according to early nineteenth-century concepts, and many similar assumptions, what would be the ethical choice for the heroine to make? We do not suggest that Elizabeth Bennet should have entered medical school. Such a judgment would be as naïve as saying that if only Russian divorce laws had been as enlightened as ours, Anna Karenina would have had no problems.

Timeless ethical norms are *always* applied at a particular time. They never operate in abstract space, but in a particular context. To understand the behavior these norms demand or preclude, one must grasp the available options of their moment and social context, with all the consequences those options entail. To do so, it may be helpful to ask: What would be the analogue—equivalent dilemma—in our own time?

Take our friend's reaction to the story of the binding of Isaac. Of course, in a secular age, and for people who do not believe in the divine, Abraham's inner torment makes no sense. You want me to sacrifice my son for what reason? The story presumes a belief in God as real, as real as the sun and the moon that He made. Abraham does not doubt His existence for a minute. Neither does he doubt God's utter rightness. The story is not told to test those assumptions; it has meaning only within them. What is tested is not God's goodness, let alone his existence, but Abraham's ultimate loyalty.

One needs to consider: What would be the equivalent dilemma today? Suppose that, to preserve your child's life, you had to do something absolutely vile: say, commit in public a vicious racist act? Or engage in a terrible slander, or spread a disease, or swear allegiance to an evil regime that somehow possessed the only cure for your child's illness? To grasp what is

going on in the story of Abraham you must imagine yourself in
a situation where you are compelled to choose between your
greatest love and your greatest moral commitment. Only then
can you see why the story is timeless and grasp the weight of
each detail.

We need to do that with the great works of any culture very
different from our own—for example, when we read Greek
tragedies. The plot of Sophocles's *Antigone* depends on Antigone's belief in the supreme importance of making sure that her
brother Polyneices is properly buried, even though doing so
entails breaking the law, another moral evil in her own eyes. She
must be ready to sacrifice her own life and risk the life of her
innocent sister Ismene, who may be—and is—condemned as
her accomplice. Antigone explains: "Friend shall I lie with him
[Polyneices, in the grave], yes friend with friend, /when I have
dared the crime of piety."[43] The phrase "crime of piety" captures her dilemma: she finds herself in a situation where piety
itself is immoral, where whatever she does she must do wrong.

To see things this way one must suspend one's own ways of
thinking and imagine those of Antigone and her world. From a
modern perspective, Polyneices is dead anyway, so while it is
nice to show respect, it is not all that important.[44] But to think
this way is to refuse to understand the play. King Creon speaks
of the importance of law, even for those closest to him: "And he
who counts another greater friend / than his own fatherland, I

---

43. Sophocles, "Antigone," in *Sophocles I*, ed. David Grene, trans. Elizabeth
Wyckoff (Chicago: University of Chicago Press, 1954), 161.

44. But, even today, local burial practices can be at odds with bureaucratic pro-
tocols. For a fascinating example, see Jonah Lipton, "'Black' and 'White' Death: Buri-
als in a Time of Ebola in Freetown, Sierra Leone," *Journal of the Royal Anthropological
Institute* 23, no. 24 (2017): 801–19.

put him nowhere." In response, Antigone contrasts the law with justice:

> Nor did I think your orders were so strong
> that you, a mortal man, could over-run
> the gods' unwritten and unfailing laws.[45]

But, if the law and one's sense of justice conflict, how can one be sure that one perceives things correctly? Even though burial does not matter for us as much as it did for the ancient Greeks, that question is still pertinent,

Greek tragedy poses dilemmas similar to the Bible's: the conflict of love with ultimate values, of life with piety, of the human with the divine, of family love with the law, which can make goodness itself a crime. Both Sophocles's tragedy and the binding of Isaac create a situation where two ultimate loyalties conflict. Of course, the Bible story and the Greek play also have notable differences, and when we appreciate them, we can more readily grasp what makes the biblical view distinct.

Attempts to accommodate a sacred text to a later context occur within Judaism's sacred writings. As one commentator has noticed, "Midrash arose as an attempt to keep a sense of continuity between the ancient traditions of the Bible and the new world of Hellenistic Judaism."[46] After the destruction of the Temple in 70 CE, for instance, new legal questions arose, such as "How should we deal with the loss of [Temple] sacrifice? How can we expiate sin without the sin offering?"[47] One famous Midrashic passage offers an answer appropriate for the

45. Sophocles, "Antigone," 174.

46. Barry W. Holtz, "Midrash," in *Back to the Sources: Reading the Classic Jewish Texts*, ed. Barry W. Holtz (New York: Summit, 1984), 181.

47. Holtz, "Midrash," 181.

new context that the Bible does not explicitly address: "The Temple and its sacrifices do not alone expiate our sins, rather we have an equivalent way of making atonement and that is through deeds of human kindness."[48] Or consider the rabbis' famous interpretation of the "eye for an eye" passage (Exod. 21:24) as a more general statement of proportional punishment involving monetary compensation.[49]

Under the influence of Greek thought, the rabbis discovered the idea of the soul in the Bible. Thus we have the passage in *Leviticus Rabbah*, glossing Psalm 103, which expands on the idea that, as God fills the universe, the soul fills the body: "Let the soul which carries the body come and praise the Holy One, blessed be He, who carries the Universe. The soul outlasts the body, and the Holy One, blessed be He, outlives the world; let the soul which outlasts the body come and praise the Holy One, blessed be He, who outlives His Universe."[50] It is likely that the idea of the afterlife was also borrowed from the Greeks "and then through the process of interpretation—Midrash— grafted back onto the Bible."[51]

Crucially, the rabbis did not regard themselves as adding to the Bible, let alone improving on its dated ideas with superior modern ones. Rather, they were "*uncovering* what was already there."[52] The Torah contained all wisdom because its author was God, who foresaw the need for new interpretations and so included them in the Torah itself. The text could not be forced to mean what it did not contain, but it could be probed for

48. Cited in Holtz, 181.
49. Holtz, 182.
50. As cited in Holtz, 182.
51. Holtz, 183.
52. Holtz, 185.

meanings it really did contain even if they had not yet been discovered. The tradition was reverent and conservative without being completely rigid.

How Scripture Reads

What's more, the process of accommodating earlier texts to current needs takes place within the Hebrew Bible itself. When we speak of "the Bible," we are speaking of books written over many centuries in different contexts.[53] "Whatever is the case with regard to the Pentateuch," Kugel explains, "no one denies that the rest of the Bible comes from different authors—it is, and always has been, a collection of texts, a kind of literary miscellany. In fact, the word 'Bible' itself indicates as much: our English terms comes from what was originally a Greek plural, *ta biblia* (the books)—this is how the Greek-speaking Jews of Alexandria in ancient times referred to Judaism's sacred history."[54]

If so, how can we speak of what Scripture or "the Bible" says? Books composed by various people in different eras are bound to differ, and so, skeptics have argued, those who cite the Bible as authoritative err not only because the Bible is often wrong, but also because there is no single "Bible" at all. That skeptical argument precludes the very possibility of learning from the Bible and so destroys any faith based on it. It is also naïve. No one doubts that *The Iliad* or *Beowulf* were composed by count-

---

53. For a recent study of this process of composition, see John Barton, *A History of the Bible: The Story of the Word's Most Influential Book* (New York: Viking, 2019). For an illuminating review of this important work, see Robert Alter, "Inerrant or Oblique?" *Jewish Review of Books*, Spring 2020, 9–11.

54. Kugel, *How to Read the Bible*, 6.

less bards over many centuries, but interpreters still understand them as meaningful wholes.[55] That, we take it, is the point of the old joke that *The Iliad* was not written by Homer but by another Greek of the same name. It is entirely possible to speak of how Homer designed the poem even if we know there was no Homer. For that matter, England has no written constitution, just a series of documents and traditions going back at least to the Magna Carta in 1215, but arguments about the constitution's meaning, which presume it has a meaning, continue to rage.

A crucial event, as Kugel explains, occurred when a corpus of diverse writings became Scripture. This transformation involved the canonization not only of certain texts but also of certain ways of reading them under the influence of what Kugel calls "the wisdom mentality" that was "in its ascendancy after the return from the Babylonian exile." Like the wisdom writings themselves—Proverbs, Job, Ecclesiastes—"*all* of Israel's ancient library now became a series of eternally valid lessons, the wisdom of the ages." Scripture became a meaningful whole and history became not just a record of events but also "instruction, and the people whose lives it charted there acquired a *representative* character."[56]

The scholarly tradition that came to be called "the higher criticism," which teased out different strains of authorship, turned books into patchworks by different hands, detected apparent contradictions, and insisted that the meaning of biblical

55. So were many other "primary" epics—like the Finnish *Kalevala* and the Kyrgyz *Manas*—as C. S. Lewis famously called them in opposition to "secondary" epics, like Virgil's *Aeneid* and Milton's *Paradise Lost*. See C. S. Lewis, *A Preface to Paradise Lost* (London: Oxford University Press, 1961).

56. Kugel, *How to Read the Bible*, 671.

texts was what they meant when they were written, came to describe as anachronistic and unscientific interpretations making psalms, prophetic writings, and historical narratives relevant to the time of each reader. But this sort of "anachronism" is no later imposition, since it occurs in the Bible itself. Indeed, it is essential to making the Bible the Bible. Whoever included the Song of Songs in the canon already interpreted this love song as an allegory of God and Israel. As Kugel argues, the very fact that this book is in the Bible testifies that "by that stage in the development of the Biblical canon, all sorts of texts were being interpreted in a way quite out of keeping with their apparent meaning." Bible stories became universally applicable tales of moral instruction already in the late biblical period.[57]

Thus it is not a modern idea to interpret prophetic writings "as bits of timeless ethical instructions, or evidence of the divine plan for history."[58] By the same token, "in the Psalter is evidence of the emergence of a new kind of psalm that had no connection with the original psalms' use in temple worship" and that instead seems designed to be read in private. This sort of psalm suggests that ones composed earlier were now read differently, so that the "offerings" to God were now "offerings of the lips and of the heart." The reverberations of such a shift were enormous: "Properly interpreted, the reading and study of *any* part of Scripture could become a kind of offering."[59]

Reading the Bible for wisdom by taking its stories and poetry as referring to timeless moral truths is essential to reading the Bible *as Scripture*, to making its many books composed at different times into a meaningful whole. "It was this way of read-

57. Kugel, 670–71.
58. Kugel, 671.
59. Kugel, 670.

ing, as much as the texts themselves," Kugel concludes, "that Jews and Christians canonized as the Bible."[60] If so, then the process of deriving relevant truths today is in the spirit of the Bible and its early interpreters. How we can do that without making the text just a reflection of our own complacent beliefs is the real question, which we continue to explore below.

The Difference That Science Makes

Many differences between our world and the world of the Bible derive from our acceptance of the scientific worldview. One fundamental tenet of that view, as we currently understand it, is the inapplicability of moral questions to natural phenomena. One does not ask whether the second law of thermodynamics is ethical or unethical. We sense that "the law" and the laws of nature are two entirely different sorts of things.

To be sure, Newton himself saw the world in religious terms and regarded the laws he discovered as revealing the mind of God. It was common in the seventeenth and eighteenth centuries to imagine that God gave us two books: the Bible and nature.[61] The study of each was a pious activity, and both activities constituted a reverent way to understand the divine intelligence. But, for the past two centuries at least, the scientific

60. Kugel, 671.

61. Thus the well-known observation by Sir Thomas Browne (1605–1682): "There are two Books from whence I collect my Divinity, besides that written one of God, another of His servant Nature, that universal and publick Manuscript, that lies expans'd unto the Eyes of all: those that never saw Him in the one, have discovered Him in the other." As cited in Basil Willey, *The Seventeenth-Century Background: Studies in the Thought of the Age in Relation to Poetry and Religion* (Garden City, NY: Doubleday Anchor, 1953), 58.

worldview has largely banned questions of ethics, meaning, and purpose.[62]

If moral categories apply to the natural world, then it follows that we must apply the same sort of thinking to both. In her celebrated study "The Abominations of Leviticus," the anthropologist Mary Douglas contends that countless ad hoc attempts to explain each dietary law were bound to fail, since there are an infinite number of such explanations, and none can "explain" more than a few prohibitions.[63] Whatever reason we may dream up for the prohibition against eating pork or shellfish probably does not explain why, as we mentioned above, it is permissible to eat one kind of locust but not another. The power of Douglas's argument lies in her discovery of the explanation in the text itself. She enters the worldview of Deuteronomy and Leviticus, which base their prohibitions on a classification of animals. Douglas quotes several such passages. We read in Leviticus, chapter 11:

> These are the living things which you may eat among all the beasts that are on the earth. Whatever parts the hoof and is cloven-footed and chews the cud, among the animals you may eat. Nevertheless among those that chew the cud or part the hoof, you shall not eat these: The camel, because it chews the cud but does not part the hoof, is unclean to you. And

62. To be sure, Catholics endeavored to accept the Darwinian explanation of human origins by treating the account in Genesis as allegorical, and evolution as the method God chose to create humanity, an interpretation that makes the evolutionary process purposeful and goal-directed. To argue this way is to accept evolution as a historical fact while putting at a distance the scientific worldview that precludes questions of meaning and purpose.

63. See Mary Douglas, "The Abominations of Leviticus," in *Purity and Danger: An Analysis of Concepts of Pollution and Taboo* (London: Routledge & Kegan Paul, 1966), 51–71.

the rock badger, because it chews the cud but does not part
the hoof, is unclean to you. . . . And the swine, because it
parts the hoof and is cloven-footed but does not chew the
cud, is unclean to you.[64]   *? eh ?*

Numerous cultures offer a classification of animals and treat
those that fall between categories, or that do not behave as an
animal of that sort should according to the culture's classificatory logic, as either taboo or sacred. In Africa, the platypus, as
a mammal that lays eggs, is often either worshipped or shunned.
To grasp a given taboo, one must not supply reasons derived
from our own culture, but understand the classificatory logic
actually used.   *demands*

In the Bible, this logic derives from the divine order, and
holiness demands that one *separate*—the root meaning of the
Hebrew word for "holy"—the orderly from the confused, the
paradigm from the hybrid, and the clean from the unclean. As
Douglas paraphrases the biblical text, "Holiness requires that
individuals should conform to the class to which they belong.
And holiness requires that different classes of things shall not
be confused" in order to "preserve the order of creation."[65]

What is holy conforms fully to its class. Cattle and other livestock have cloven hoofs and chew the cud; therefore, to exhibit
either characteristic without the other—the camel chews the
cud but does not part the hoof, the pig parts the hoof but does
not chew the cud—is to fall between categories and to be impure. That is the explanation, period. Nothing is said about the
pig's dirtiness or the many allegorical interpretations of the
camel or other forbidden animals.

64. Cited by Douglas, "Abominations of Leviticus," 52, from Leviticus 11:2–7.
65. Douglas, 67–68.

By the same token, animals on land, sea, and air each have their own proper form of locomotion, and one is allowed to eat only those that move properly for their element. In the water scaly fish swim with fins, and so only those can be eaten. On land animals hop, jump, or walk. The reason one can eat one kind of locust but not others is given in the text: the edible type hops, while the others just "swarm." Dietary laws—and other rules of Leviticus— "would have been taken as signs which at every turn inspired meditation on the oneness, purity, and completeness of God. . . . Observance of the dietary rules would thus have been a meaningful part of the great liturgical act of recognition and worship which culminated in the sacrifice in the Temple."[66]

This whole way of thinking is foreign to us. The scientific worldview does not divide animals into "clean" and "abominable." They are all equally products of evolution. We may decline to eat certain creatures for health reasons, but that is an entirely different sort of consideration. To be sure, it has become common for people to create their own dietary laws—the kashruts of our times—by applying moral categories to nature, as vegans and others may do. In groceries in our neighboring town of Skokie, Illinois, some foods are labeled kosher and others organic. Some people revere Earth or "Gaia." Today's examples of rejecting some foods in favor of others can serve as a first step to grasping the Bible's way of looking at things.

If we look at the world in the modern way, which treats nature in one set of terms and morality in quite another, Biblical commands are bound to seem strange, arbitrary, or abhorrent. What is more, we do not classify the world the way Leviticus does. For us "livestock" is no more a natural category—it depends on human use—than "weed." And we do not classify

66. Douglas, 73.

insects according to whether their locomotion is proper for their element. Could it not be that the biblical abhorrence of homosexuality derives from this kind of thinking? Such relations may easily be felt to be "unnatural," to compromise a natural order, and thus to be unholy. If so, then it is also clear how one can be a believer and yet not share this abhorrence. One can accept the core idea of holiness but reject either the particular classification system or the whole idea of nature containing the unnatural. In so doing, one preserves the idea of holiness as separation as it applies to human categories, but is not required to apply it when doing so entails a biblical classification of nature. One may observe the separation of the Sabbath from the rest of the week, but not maintain the separation of foods, or regard some sexual practices as "unnatural." Or one can keep kosher but not regard homosexuality as a sin. Once the prohibitions depend on a classification of nature we no longer accept, then the extension becomes a matter of choice.

There are cultures that regard identical twins as unnatural and taboo. Personal identity should be unique, so such twinning is dangerous, something essentially wrong. If such a culture should come to accept a scientific understanding of twinning, it might still maintain a distinction between the pure and impure—say, in ways of burial—but abandon the taboo against twins. In much the same way, Jews could retain a distinction between the holy and the unholy without classifying homosexuality as unholy.

How Old Is the World?

Core values must always be applied in a particular context. Each biblical story tells how that happens. To understand these stories, one must enter their world. We have seen that since our world is so different, one may choose to translate into our own context. That translation will never be perfect, since there are often no exact equivalents.

As with translations of literary works from one language to another, one often has to choose among multiple possibilities. The grammar of a source language may force the speaker to specify gender or tense, or to indicate whether the information conveyed was acquired directly or by report, while the grammar of the target language may not. Should the translator supply that information by adding words ("the *female* doctor said X, *which she learned from another*")? Such decisions depend on an understanding of the point of the translated passage and, beyond that, of the entire work. Translation therefore cannot be done by formula, but only case by case. Fundamentalist translators, who claim the superiority of being absolutely literal, make poor choices. Unformalizable judgment is required.[67] The same is true with the sort of cultural translation of biblical passages we have in mind. One has to develop sensitivity on a case-by-case basis. There are no certain answers, and judgments are always open to revision in light of new evidence and experience.

In some cases, translation itself may not be the best option. Sometimes what we need is a *double vision*, the ability to see in two different ways at the same time without choosing one or the other, or forcing a compromise between them. As F. Scott Fitzgerald observes, "The test of a first-rate intelligence is the ability to hold two opposed ideas in mind at the same time, and

---

67. On this sort of fundamentalist translating, see Gary Saul Morson, "The Pevearsion of Russian Literature," in *Commentary* 130, no. 1 (July–August 2010): 92–98.

still retain the ability to function."[68] In a famous letter John Keats wrote, "At once it struck me, what quality went to form a Man of Achievement, especially in Literature, and which Shakespeare possessed so enormously—I mean *Negative Capability*, that is, when man is capable of being in uncertainties, mysteries, doubts, without any irritable reaching after fact and reason."[69] Of, we may add, without insisting that one perspective is right in all circumstances.   *author* ←

How old is the world? When Jews welcomed in the Hebrew year 5781 this past fall, should they have felt confused about when the world was created, or even embarrassed to maintain an obviously unscientific chronology? From a scientific perspective, we know that the earth was formed around five billion years ago. The geological layers under our feet, and the fossils that are millions of years old, make the biblical chronology absurd. And yet we also say it is 5,781 years old.

If we are concerned with questions about life's meaning, or about the significance of our actions, it makes a big difference which perspective we adopt. Looked at from the perspective of five billion years—let alone the much longer time since the Big Bang—all of human history is but an instant. The ratio of human history to the age of the earth is about the same as that of one second to a year. It would seem that there is no point in asking about the significance of our actions, since they have no significance. As for meaning—well, as we have seen, the scientific perspective precludes questions of meaning altogether.

68. As cited from "The Crack-Up," in *The Yale Book of Quotations*, ed. Fred R. Shapiro (New Haven, CT: Yale University Press, 2006), 273.

69. As cited from a letter to George and Thomas Keats, December 21, 1817, in *Complete Poems and Selected Letters of John Keats* (New York: Modern Library, 2001), 595.

Contemplating life from a scientific point of view, numerous thinkers have experienced emotions ranging from terror to despair. "The eternal silence of these infinite spaces terrifies me," wrote Pascal, and he might have felt the same about infinite ages.[70] After the death of his brother, Konstantin Levin, the autobiographical hero of Tolstoy's *Anna Karenina* cannot banish terrifying questions about the meaning of life and death. He tries to answer these questions with the scientific "new convictions" that have replaced his old religious beliefs, but he finds that they go nowhere:

> The organism, its decay, the indestructability of matter, the law of the conservation of energy, evolution, were the words that usurped the place of his old belief. These words and the ideas associated with them were very useful for intellectual purposes. But for life they yielded nothing, and Levin felt suddenly like a man who has changed his warm fur coat for a muslin garment, and, going for the first time into the frost, is immediately convinced, not by reason but by his whole nature, that he is as good as naked, and that he must perish miserably.[71]

Levin comes to realize that, by their very nature, scientific concepts cannot address questions of meaning. The conservation of energy does not "mean" anything, in the sense that Levin has in mind. In the whole arsenal of his convictions, "he was unable to find anything at all like an answer." The scientific vision does not give a wrong or inadequate answer: it gives no answer,

---

70. As cited in *The Oxford Dictionary of Quotations*, 6th ed., ed. Elizabeth Knowles (Oxford: Oxford University Press, 2004), 587.

71. Leo Tolstoy, *Anna Karenina*, trans. Constance Garnett, rev. ed. by Leonard J. Kent and Nina Berberova (New York: Modern Library, 2000), 888.

nothing even "like an answer." Levin finds himself "in the position of a man seeking food in a toy shop or at a gunsmith's."[72] He experiences—as Tolstoy himself experienced—"fearful moments of horror" and existential dread that almost drive him to suicide.[73] A happy husband and father, a man in perfect health and with no material needs, Levin (and Tolstoy) "hid a rope so that he might not be tempted to hang himself, and was afraid to go out [hunting] with his gun for fear of shooting himself."[74]

The problem, Levin realizes, is not with current scientific theories, in which case he might hope that future ones will serve his purpose. No matter what progress science makes, it will merely be able to supply more details to a hopeless picture: "In infinite time, in infinite matter, in infinite space is formed a bubble-organism, that bubble lasts a while and bursts, and that bubble is I."[75] More knowledge about the physics of bubbles will not help.

Levin at last does find meaning through a complete change of perspective. Instead of looking for a theory to justify life, instead of reasoning from abstractions down, he learns to think (as case reasoning does) from experience up. How that happens, and the specific difference it makes, is less important than the change itself. Levin learns to look at scientific questions one way, and questions of meaning in another. Levin does not reject science, but he no longer asks it to address questions that by its very nature it excludes. Tolstoy's greatest admirer, the philosopher Ludwig Wittgenstein, drew the same conclusion. As Alan

72. Tolstoy, *Anna Karenina*, 888.

73. Tolstoy, 891.

74. Tolstoy, 892. For Tolstoy's account of how he experienced this existential dread, see "A Confession," in *A Confession, The Gospel in Brief, and What I Believe*, trans. Aylmer Maude (London: Oxford University Press, 1971), 1–84.

75. Tolstoy, 893.

Janik and Stephen Toulmin have pointed out, the last section of Wittgenstein's *Tractatus Logico-Philosophicus* follows Levin's meditations so closely it might almost be taken as a philosopher's paraphrase of the novelist's vision.[76] The modern idea of the laws of nature, Wittgenstein explains, "tries to make it look as if *everything* were explained," but it necessarily leaves questions of sense, meaning, and ethics untouched.[77] Science explains the world, but "the sense of the world must lie outside the world. In the world everything is as it is, and everything happens as it does happen; *in* it no value exists—and if it did exist, it would have no value. If there is any value that does have value, it must lie outside the whole sphere of what happens and is the case. . . . It must lie outside the world."[78]

The root fallacy, as both Levin and Wittgenstein come to understand, is the demand that one way of thinking, one grand system, address *all* questions. When people try to address ethical questions in evolutionary terms—for instance, by explaining that altruism arose because it ensured group survival, or maximized the chance of one's genes being passed on—they are committing this fallacy. This is not to address ethical questions, but to bypass them. We don't need sociobiology to tell us that people evolved to be capable of both kindness and cruelty, self-sacrifice and egoism—that's obvious, because we see those qualities all the time. But what we actually do says nothing about what we should do. Nor does this way of thinking bring us a step closer to the *meaning* of what we do.

76. See Alan Janik and Stephen Toulmin, *Wittgenstein's Vienna* (New York: Simon & Schuster, 1973).

77. Ludwig Wittgenstein, *Tractatus Logico-Philosophicus*, trans. D. F. Pears and B. F. McGuinness (London: Routledge & Kegan Paul, 1977), 70.

78. Wittgenstein, *Tractatus Logico-Philosophicus*, 71.

Russian has two words for "why," one meaning "from what cause" (*pochemu*) and the other "for what purpose" (*zachem*). Aristotle's physics addressed both questions. Modern science can address only the causal why. In Wittgenstein's view, neither science nor philosophy is a sort of supertheory to be applied outside its appropriate realm. Take any theory outside its proper context, its proper "language game," and it yields nonsense. Then "language goes on holiday," as Wittgenstein memorably put it. With scientific disciplines, "problems are solved (difficulties eliminated), not a *single* problem. There is not *a* philosophical method, though there are indeed methods, like different therapies."[79]

When Levin realizes that he must think about astronomy with one set of tools, and about meaning with another, he finds himself lying on his back gazing up at the high, cloudless sky. He muses: "Do I not know that that is infinite space, and that it is not a rounded vault?" And yet, where everyday life is concerned, "in spite of my knowing about infinite space, I am incontestably right when I see a firm blue vault, far more right than when I strain my eyes to see beyond it."[80] And with this insight, Levin realizes that he has found faith.

So, if asked how old the world is, our reply is: Are we doing geology or something else? A biological explanation of how Homo sapiens arrived at their ethics is one thing, and the question of what is right or wrong is quite another. It is as foolish to demand that science answer questions of meaning as it is to rely on the Bible for an understanding of geology. In fact, it is more foolish, because the Bible answers many scientific questions

79. Ludwig Wittgenstein, *Philosophical Investigations*, 3rd ed., trans G. E. M. Anscombe (New York: Macmillan, 1968), 51e, paragraph 133.

80. Tolstoy, *Anna Karenina*, 903.

incorrectly, whereas science cannot begin to address questions of meaning at all.

The world is billions of years old and it is also 5,781 years old—not an average of the two, and not one or the other, but both depending on what question we are asking. With each question we ask, in each case, we must first decide which perspective to adopt.

Propositions and Prayer

Atheists often presume that religion consists of a series of propositions about the world. Then they examine those propositions and weigh them against evidence (if not against their own prejudices). That is the approach taken by David Hume. His famous essay "Of Miracles," dear to the heart of philosophic unbelievers, first argues against the existence of miracles, then extends the argument to prophecies, and finally concludes that since the Christian religion depends on belief in miracles, it "cannot be believed by any reasonable person."[81] It is obvious that the same argument extends to Judaism and to other religions.

The real miracle, Hume suggests, is that there are any intelligent believers at all. With delicate but pointed irony, he concludes that any believer must be "conscious of a continued miracle in his own person, which subverts all the principles of his understanding and gives him a determination to believe what is most contrary to custom and experience."[82] By "miracle in his own person," Hume means something like a determined,

81. David Hume, "Of Miracles," in *An Enquiry Concerning Human Understanding*, ed. Anthony Flew (La Salle, IL: Open Court, 1991), 143–66.

82. Hume, "Of Miracles," 166.

irrational insistence on accepting absurdities in the face of all argument and evidence. However, as Hume has already argued, this sort of miracle is not a miracle at all, but another example of what we see so often: people being swayed by enthusiasm, vanity, the prospect of advantage, "the passion of surprise and wonder," and many other agreeable emotions.[83] "If the spirit of religion join itself to the love of wonder," Hume explains, "there is an end of common sense."[84]

There is a certain sort of argument, writes Hume, "which must at least *silence* the most arrogant bigotry and superstition. . . . I flatter myself that I have discovered an argument of like nature, which if just, will, with the wise and learned, be an everlasting check to all kinds of superstitious delusion and consequently will be useful so long as the world endures."[85] In its essentials, the argument is a straightforward one. A wise person proportions belief to evidence. If someone asserts something that happens all the time, like snow in Norway, one does not require much evidence to believe it. Sometimes the fact that the person has no reason to lie is enough. But if what is claimed is truly marvelous, something one has never seen or heard of, then the evidence must be much stronger. If based on human testimony, that testimony had better be from numerous people who have had no opportunity to confer, no reason to assert a falsehood, no track record of believing in absurdities, and, even after questioning, are free from contradiction or other suspicious behavior. Even then, one might be cautious, especially if the marvel is gratifying. How much stronger must the evidence

83. Hume, 150.
84. Hume, 151.
85. Hume, 144.

be supporting a miracle—that is, an actual violation of the laws of nature?

Presumably, the evidence would have to be amazingly powerful. But, for Hume, the miracles of the Bible rest on the testimony of remote witnesses belonging to an ignorant and gullible people. Which is more probable, Hume asks, that the laws of nature have been violated, or that these witnesses were deceived or deceiving? And if the miracles cannot be believed, what are we to say of the veracity of the book in which they repeatedly appear?

Hume's argument rests entirely on the view of the Bible as a set of propositions. Some of these are what we would today call scientific. These can no longer be believed. Others are historical, and even these often include accounts of miracles, like the splitting of the Red Sea or the stopping of the sun at Jericho. Why, then, Hume and his followers ask, should we give any credence to the Bible's commandments, especially when they run against our own wisdom? Why allow one's behavior to be guided by a book which is a tissue of absurdities?

But the Bible does not have to be regarded as a series of propositions. As Wittgenstein observes, "Propositions can express nothing that is higher," and the Bible is all about what is "higher."[86] Let us imagine that religion is about the sense of the world as a whole: "We feel that when all *possible* scientific questions have been answered, the problems of life remain completely untouched."[87] It is not that the person of faith knows some fact that the unbeliever does not. Rather, the person of faith lives in "an altogether different world. . . . The world of the happy man is a different one from that of the unhappy man."

86. Wittgenstein, *Tractatus Logico-Philosophicus*, 71.
87. Wittgenstein, 73.

When one finds faith—Wittgenstein seems to have Levin in mind—"[the world] must, so to speak, wax and wane as a whole."[88]

Wittgenstein also loved Dostoevsky, and there is a passage in Dostoevsky's great novel of faith *The Idiot* that enunciates a similar view. The novel's hero, Prince Myshkin, recounts experiences pertaining to belief and disbelief. While listening to the ideas of a learned atheist, Myshkin explains, "One thing struck me: that he seemed not to be talking about that [faith] at all, the whole time; and it struck me just because whenever I have met unbelievers before, or read their books, it always seemed to me that they were speaking and writing in their books about something quite different, although it seemed to be about that on the surface."[89] Myshkin tried to convey this thought, but could not express himself clearly enough for the atheist to understand.

The next day, Myshkin continues, he encountered a mother with a six-week-old baby who had just smiled at her for the first time. The mother kept crossing herself with great devotion, and when Myshkin asked why, she answered, "God has just such gladness every time he sees from heaven that a sinner is praying to Him with all his heart, as a mother has when she sees the first smile on her baby's face." Myshkin discerns in "this deep, subtle and truly religious thought" the very essence of faith, "the whole conception of God as our Father and of God's gladness in man, like a father in his own child."[90]

This simple peasant woman understood faith the way the atheist did not. She offered no arguments; she enunciated no

---

88. Wittgenstein, 72.

89. Fyodor Dostoevsky, *The Idiot*, trans. Constance Garnett (New York: Modern Library, 1962), 207.

90. Dostoevsky, *Idiot*, 208.

theological doctrines, scientific propositions, or historical facts. What she expressed was a sense of the world as a whole, one in which people matter, in which their goodness and gladness, their love and care, are what the world itself is all about. The difference between her and the learned atheist is not one of factual knowledge or abstract reasoning. As Wittgenstein would say, she lives in a wholly different world. Myshkin concludes, "The essence of religious feeling does not come under any sort of reasoning or atheism, and has nothing to do with any crimes or misdemeanors. There is something else here, and there will always be something else—something that the atheists will forever slur over; they will always be talking of something else."[91]

When Levin's wife, Kitty, is in labor, and he hears her screams for hours in the next room, he enters a strange spiritual state unlike any he has experienced before. Even though he is an unbeliever, he finds himself praying. Later, when he reflects on this moment, he does not know what to do with it: "At the moment of praying he believed. But that moment had passed and he could not make his state of mind at that moment fit into the rest of his life."[92] Levin cannot dismiss his act of praying as a mere effect of terror, like a nightmare, hallucination, or groundless fear of the dark as in childhood, because he truly believed when praying. What's more, that moment of prayer remains precious to him and to treat it as mere weakness would be to desecrate it. On the other hand, Levin cannot reject everything else he believes. He does not know what to do with this contradiction.

Even after he finds faith, another moment when he finds himself praying mystifies him. When he learns that his wife and

91. Dostoevsky, 208–9.
92. Tolstoy, *Anna Karenina*, 889.

child are out in the woods as a storm rages, and he sees a tree hit by lightning fall, he prays, "My God! My God! Not on them."[93] He immediately recognizes that it makes no sense to pray this way, since he is asking not that something should not happen, but that it did not happen: "And though he thought at once how senseless was his prayer that they should not have been killed by the oak that had fallen now, he repeated it, knowing that he could do nothing better than utter this senseless prayer."[94]

What is going on here? Tolstoy's point, we think, is that these prayers, though they may take the grammatical form of a petition, are not petitions. They are not even deliberate actions, since Levin doesn't decide to pray; he just finds himself praying. The prayers are, rather, reminders to himself of his sense that he lives in a world of meaning. He can of course dismiss that reminder as illogical or unscientific, but he can also acknowledge it and make the world it evokes his own. He can repeat the senseless prayer, as he does.

To be sure, not all prayer is of this kind. There are numerous types. Levin's is only one kind among many that prompt us to examine our sense of the world. It does not solve the question of faith once and for all.

Here as elsewhere, there are many other cases of a different kind to consider. Like Levin, we must learn to be "capable of being in uncertainties, mysteries, doubts, without any irritable reaching" for an all-encompassing system. It is not a top-down chain of reasoning we need, but a series of cases and reminders about our complex experiences, about the multifarious world, and about the endless mystery of questions of faith.

93. Tolstoy, 917.
94. Tolstoy, *Anna Karenina*, 917.

The Great Dialogue

Let us return to the question of how to read Scripture so that it can be meaningful today without reducing it to a mere paraphrase of what we already know and believe. To Bakhtin, this "question of meaning," as he called it, was central. A believer arrested by the Bolsheviks for his activities in the underground Russian Orthodox Church, he recognized its importance. He appreciated that it applies not only to Scripture but also to the canon of Russian literature, which, even for secular Russians, functioned as a sort of quasi-Scripture. Perhaps the best way to understand Russians' reverence for their literature is to compare the tradition to that of the ancient Hebrews when it was still possible to add books to the canon. The question of meaning that Bakhtin addressed applies to both sorts of sacred, or quasi-sacred, writing.

Bakhtin rejected two influential (and still influential) views. On the one hand, he denied that a work's meaning lies wholly in the text, or in the author's intention, as understood at the time of composition. On the other, he rejected the opposite view, that a work means whatever readers can make it mean. The first, absolutist alternative permits works to mean one and only one thing, while the second, relativist alternative licenses them to mean anything according to one's needs and desires. Taken to their logical conclusion, both are fundamentalist, one positive and the other negative. Or, as Bakhtin would say, both are monologic. But real understanding for Bakhtin, as we discussed in chapter 2, is dialogic.

Both fundamentalisms ignore the concept of *potential*. When a great author creates a work, she senses when it is rich with potential meanings she cannot identify. She intends it to contain such meanings—"intentional potentials"—because she knows by experience as a reader that their presence is what makes a work truly great.[95] If she could not sense such potentials, she would not be a great author in the first place. Without them, she knows, her work would not be a true masterpiece. As she creates, this sense of richness in potential guides her as much as her desire to express specific meanings; her full intention includes both. The great author knows the difference between simply saying what she "means to say" and creating a work that contains "semantic treasures."[96]

If the interpreter limits himself only to meanings the author (or original audience) "intended" or had in mind, he in fact misses a crucial part of the author's intention. In doing so, he "encloses" the work "within the epoch" of its creation.[97] This form of reading makes it impossible to understand all the richness of the work. As Bakhtin memorably observes, "We can say that neither Shakespeare himself nor his contemporaries knew that 'great Shakespeare' whom we know now. There is no possibility of squeezing our Shakespeare into the Elizabethan epoch," and, we may surmise, Shakespeare, an experienced reader, knew (or hoped) as much.[98] Shakespeare drew on the riches of the English language, the wisdom inherent in the genres he chose for his works, and the lines of development inherent in the ideas his characters express to create the "semantic treasures" he sensed, and we still sense, as greater than any critic's paraphrase, however insightful. He "took advantage of and included in his works immense treasures of potential meaning

95. M. M. Bakhtin, "Discourse in the Novel," in *The Dialogic Imagination: Four Essays*, ed. Michael Holquist, trans. Caryl Emerson and Michael Holquist (Austin: University of Texas Press, 1981), 421.

96. Bakhtin, "Response to a Question," 5.

97. Bakhtin, 4.

98. Bakhtin, 4.

that could not be fully revealed or recognized in his epoch" or, for that matter, in any single epoch.[99]

Enclosing the work within its epoch makes its later life seem like a sort of "paradox" or, indeed, a series of anachronistic errors.[100] And minor works do indeed die with their epoch and lose nothing by being enclosed within it. "To put it somewhat simplistically and crudely," Bakhtin observes, "if the significance of any work is reduced, for example, to its role in the struggle against serfdom (as is often done in our secondary schools), it will lose all of its significance when serfdom and its remnants no longer exist in our life."[101] If Shakespeare were a mediocre author, his history plays would have nothing to teach us except about how English history was perceived in his time. In fact, they and other great works "break through the boundaries of their own time, they live for centuries, that is, in *great time* and frequently (with great works, always) their lives are more intense and fuller than are their lives within their own time."[102]

By entering into dialogue with Shakespeare's works, readers of subsequent epochs can discover some of these potential meanings. Their own experience of the time and culture in which they live creates a new dialogic standpoint and allows them to activate potential meanings as they read. In a true dialogue, both sides are active; consequently, each readership enters into a different dialogue and, if the work is rich enough, finds new richness in it. One test that a work is not as great as it once seemed is that, after a while, its potentials have been ex-

99. Bakhtin, 5.
100. Bakhtin, 4.
101. Bakhtin, 4.
102. Bakhtin, 4.

hausted. That is why authors that a given generation regards as great—think of Carl Sandburg, John Steinbeck, or Thomas Wolfe—become much less revered over time. Where are some of the Nobel laureates of yesteryear?[103] "The test of time" is a test of openness to dialogue. In short, "semantic phenomena can exist in concealed form, potentially, and be revealed only in semantic and cultural contexts of subsequent epochs that are favorable for such disclosure."[104] Good readers can liberate the author from the captivity of his epoch, and good literary criticism does exactly that.

But what good criticism does not do, and must not do, is to enclose the author in *our* epoch. Bakhtin calls this way of reading—in America today, the legacy of reader reception theory—"modernization and distortion," and he regards it as even worse than enclosure within the author's epoch. For to limit the work to the time of its composition at least teaches us something about that time, but modernizing and distorting it make it nothing but an echo of what we already know.

Both enclosure in the epoch and modernization preclude dialogue and the activation of potentials. There is all the difference in the world between forcing our meaning on a text and discovering the potentials actually in it. True "creative understanding," as Bakhtin calls it, creates the dialogue that shows something that was really there, and that the author sensed, in potential, all along.[105] It respects the author's intention more fully than the form of reading that limits the work's meaning to

103. Who now reads Nobel laureates Rudolph Christoph Eucken (1908), Paul Johann Ludwig Heyse (1910), Henrik Pontoppidan and Karl Adolph Gjellerup (1917), or Carl Friedrich Spitteler (1919)? Among those who did not win the prize were Leo Tolstoy, Anton Chekhov, James Joyce, Franz Kafka, and Jorge Luis Borges.

104. Bakhtin, "Response to a Question," 5.

105. Bakhtin, 7.

what the author knew he was expressing—because it acknowledges both parts of authorial intention.

Even if one does not regard it as divinely inspired, the Bible demands this sort of respectful dialogic reading, because it is the greatest work of Western literature. If one takes it to be not entirely the work of human hands and minds, it demands it all the more. Then the dialogue is with the divine.

? what

Adjusting the Clock

Let us return to the rabbi's parable of the clock. Like so many wisdom tales, just when one thinks it has ended, it adds one more complication. The clock has been mounted out of reach so it cannot be altered, and yet, every once in a while, a workman climbs up a ladder and adjusts the clock, which, over a long period, has inevitably lost time. While those adjustments are rare, they are critical.

Truth might not be relative, but what we take to be truth is certainly not inviolable. Neither positive fundamentalism nor negative fundamentalism will do. It is important that changes in liturgy and ethical tenets be rare so that they do not become just echoes of our own shifting beliefs. If religion is to be meaningful, one needs to enter into dialogue with it, not just nod in agreement at our own wisdom. Otherwise, one is praying to oneself.[106]

106. By the same token, if the Constitution can readily be made to mean what current opinion wants it to mean, and if rights can be expanded or contracted to accord with opinion polls or the preferences of the educated, then there might as well be no Constitution or Bill of Rights at all. On the other hand, if it cannot accommodate anything that has happened since it is written, the Constitution becomes inapplicable to so many current circumstances that it again loses its purpose. For

For much the same reason, an authoritative translation of the Bible or the liturgy, even if it changes, must not change too frequently. There is all the difference in the world between correcting a translated passage either because a more accurate text has been discovered or because scholarship has revealed a better interpretation of a word—like correcting a clock that has lost time—and amending it because tastes have changed. Morson was brought up in the Reform tradition when the prayers were in elevated language ("And thou shalt love the Lord thy God"). Years later he encountered a modernized, more colloquial, version of the liturgy, which necessarily cut him off from his early education. And, years after that, he encountered another version and then yet another, with changes made to render the language more "accessible." The problem with these newer versions lies not only in their colloquialisms, but also in the very frequency of the changes. One cannot help sensing that no version is likely to last more than a few years, and that the text one reads is, like all its predecessors, on a suspended sentence. It is not worth committing to memory, as sacred words should be. It is this year's eternity. The very idea of a lasting tradition disappears.

The significance of a prayer is greater than its content. As Kugel observes, "Someone rhythmically chanting 'Hari Krishna' may, in some technical sense, be speaking words, but these phonemes are clearly only a kind of vehicle. So too for formulaic prayers and hymns, repeated week after week or day after day."[107] Their function is to make the contact between the human and the divine, and they cannot do that if they change

---

more on this topic, we recommend Emily Bazelon's insightful article "The Originalists," *New York Times Magazine*, March 1, 2020, 26–33, 46–47.

107. Kugel, *How to Read the Bible*, 688.

frequently at human whim. One may change the clock, one may even adjust the calendar as Europe did when the Gregorian calendar was first introduced in 1582 and then gradually adopted by different countries over the centuries (by Denmark in 1700, by England in 1752, by Russia in 1918). But one does not change the calendar every decade. If someone suggested we abandon it for a ten-day week, and then a decade later replace twelve months with ten, and then a decade after that abandon months altogether, we might say that something is wrong. By the same token, countries that change their constitution at the whim of any powerful leader who wishes to extend his term may be said to have no real constitution at all. A constitution differs from laws precisely because it is more permanent and governs other changes.

If changes come slowly, then they last. They reflect not the enthusiasm or irritations of a moment, but a long process of consideration and reconsideration. Some of what does not change in sacred texts will run counter to our taste, but that is why they can speak to us from somewhere beyond our tiny island of the present moment. And some of what does not change will remain mysterious.

There is nothing wrong with contemplating the mysterious. "He hath made everything beautiful in its time," we read in Ecclesiastes, "so that no man can find out the work that God maketh from the beginning to the end" (Eccles. 3:11). But what we cannot find we can keep looking for and, case after case, grow wiser in the process.

6

Literature

HOW TO RUIN IT AND WHY YOU SHOULDN'T

Alibis for Reading

We doubt that readers are surprised that, in a book on the rise of fundamentalism, we would have a chapter on religion. After all, as we discussed at length in chapter 2, that very term originated in treatises on faith. Economists have been weaned on "market fundamentalism" long before its coinage two decades ago, so it is understandable that we would have an economics chapter as well. And, with the rise of extremes in politics, you ignore political fundamentalism at your own risk.

But fundamentalism in literature? Do we include that topic simply because Morson happens to be a literary scholar and Schapiro happens to love reading fiction? How many of us really care about who is winning the "culture wars," whose battles have lasted for decades?

We do. And if you made it this far in the book, you will know why. Great literature, let us count the ways we love you.

In chapter 2 we looked to Fyodor Dostoevsky's *The Possessed* and to Leo Tolstoy's *War and Peace* to illustrate the fundamentalist's hostility to principled skepticism and reasoned moderation of thought. We turned next to Daniel Defoe's *Moll Flanders* as an example of case-based reasoning and then to Tolstoy's *Anna Karenina* to represent how to grapple with a moral dilemma. George Eliot's *Middlemarch* illustrates how ethical quandaries require wisdom gained through experience rather than an overriding abstract theory, as do *War and Peace* and *Anna Karenina*. Why rely so heavily on the classics of realism? Because the realist novel shows far better than any argument why the great fundamentalist systems cannot begin to comprehend the complexities of life.

In chapter 3, on politics, Arthur Koestler's *Darkness at Noon* illustrated how fanatics may eventually be done in by the very fanaticism they support. Then it was back to *Anna Karenina* to examine not just what people believe, but how they believe it. For Tolstoy and other great novelists, "belief" is a single word for many different states of mind. Self-deception and cognitive bias of many kinds are at work, and to arrive at beliefs authentically is difficult indeed. From Jane Austen on, self-deception has been a defining theme of the genre. Pride and prejudice shape our perceptions.

Two highly influential literary utopias—Edward Bellamy's *Looking Backward* and William Morris's *News from Nowhere*, the first an American dream enthusiastic about technology, the second a British one that idealizes the middle ages—exemplify a point of view the exact opposite of that conveyed by realist novels. Utopias see the world as radically simpler than it seems, realist novels as decidedly more complex. The two genres are philosophical opposites, and each polemicizes with the other. From the perspective of Bellamy and Morris, all denials that simple solutions could solve all social problems reflect a desire to defend the terrible status quo; for Eliot and Dostoevsky, denials of complexity bespeak an impoverished view of life and threaten to create a world far worse than the one they would replace.

Utopians are especially inclined to think that the truth is clearly visible and totally perspicuous, while *Middlemarch* and Turgenev's *Fathers and Children* dramatize how personal egos shape our view of facts. As the title of Turgenev's classic suggests, each generation views the world differently and is inclined to dismiss earlier, or later, visions as benighted. We argued earlier that *The Possessed*, often regarded as the greatest political novel ever written, was the only nineteenth-century work, literary or nonliterary, to predict in amazing detail the phenomenon we have come to call "totalitarianism." The idea that great writers merely create nice stories to illustrate the ideas of philosophers could not be more mistaken.

Laurence Sterne's *Tristram Shandy* famously satirizes the tendency of intellectuals to ignore obvious counterevidence in their rush to embrace an overriding system. The more preposterous the claims they make, the more ingenious they become in disposing of objections. Dostoevsky's *Notes from Underground* takes on influential systems—utilitarianism, laws of progress, materialisms and determinisms of various sorts—with arguments and dramatized irrationalities that were to shape Existentialism and several other modern movements. Again, the philosophers lagged behind him. Freud acknowledged as much when he recognized that *The Brothers Karamazov*, which he regarded as one of the three great literary works ever written, expressed an understanding of human psychology equaled nowhere else.

In chapter 4, on economics, Anton Chekhov's *Uncle Vanya* and *The Cherry Orchard* demonstrate the folly of chances missed, and other forms of waste. *The Brothers Karamazov* illustrates the shallowness of well-intentioned forms of materialism and atheism, and the social nostrums that often accompany them. A passage in *Anna Karenina* shows why the moral imperative to help the less fortunate is not enough to determine what form of help would do more good than harm. Dickens's *Bleak House* offers a moving parable about the dire consequences of imagining that it is possible to ignore the plight of the poor.

And, in chapter 5, our discussion of religion, a famous passage in Lewis Carroll's *Through the Looking Glass*—everyone's favorite source of nonsensical reasoning—points to how ridiculous it is to adopt standards to suit one's own shifting preferences. Dostoevsky's *Crime and Punishment* again shows that no one is shallower than those who regard all religious belief as shallow, while illustrating, as novels of ideas often do, that individual certainty is a poor test of truthfulness.[1] The Hebrew Bible arrives at this point by a quite different route, while displaying the deep interiority of the human soul. The very strangeness of the heroine's plight (from a modern perspective) in Sophocles's *Antigone* shows how literature can help us understand cultures very different from our own, and yet, for all its difference, the play offers insights into a dilemma still with us, because it is part of the human condition—namely, the conflict of love and morality with law.

Death, and the fear of it, will also always define human life, and there is, perhaps, no one who probed these questions more deeply than the author often called "the poet of death," Tolstoy. In some of the most famous passages in world literature, Levin,

---

1. The forms of simplistic atheism Dostoevsky had in mind are still very much with us. For a recent discussion of them, written by an atheist, see John Gray, *Seven Types of Atheism* (New York: Penguin, 2018).

the hero of *Anna Karenina*, suffers from, and finds a way to come to terms with, existential dread. Russian literature prides itself on forthright consideration of the eternal, "accursed questions," especially whether we should have faith at all, as we show with readings of Dostoevsky's *The Idiot* and *Anna Karenina*.

That is a lot of literature! To be sure, we relied as well on nonfiction works. But, for us, nothing teaches more about the human world than the best of fiction.[2] When you read a great novel and identify with its characters, you sense from within what it is like to be someone else. You see the world from the perspective of a different social class, gender, religion, sexual orientation, moral understanding, or many other categories that define and differentiate human life. You experience how cultural norms and individual psychology shape each other. By living a character's life vicariously, you not only feel some of what she feels, but also reflect on those feelings, consider the nature of the actions to which they lead, and, with practice, acquire the wisdom to appreciate actual people in all their complexity.

Understanding real people is critical in politics and in economics, as in any other discipline. If you don't understand what motivates human beings, how can you possibly predict how they will act or know what will benefit them? Sure, you can simply assume that individuals act rationally and in their own self-interest and presume that one's own standards of rationality and self-interest are shared by all people at all times. But, as we discussed in chapter 4, even the founder of modern economics,

---

2. That is a central theme of our recent book: Gary Saul Morson and Morton Schapiro, *Cents and Sensibility: What Economics Can Learn from the Humanities* (Princeton, NJ: Princeton University Press, 2017). Some of the arguments there are summarized, and developed, in the pages below.

Adam Smith, considered and rejected the idea that people always act rationally and in their own self-interest. One needs a subtle appreciation for the countless shades of human emotion, an ability to grasp how the world feels to other people, and an appreciation of particulars—in short, the sort of sensitivity that was dramatized a half century after Smith's moral treatise, by Jane Austen and her successors.

That is why, in examining various fundamentalisms, we have turned time and again to literature for arguments and examples showing where fundamentalisms fall short. A fundamentalist might naturally ask: Why not make one's argument directly? Isn't it some sort of trick to rely on the rhetorical power of great stories rather than logical argument and scientific examination of evidence?

In our view, literature, and especially the great realist novels, not only offer counterarguments. More important, they exemplify a way of thinking contrary to fundamentalisms and offer an alternative to them. To sense that way of thinking from within and allow it to shape one's perception of the world is to acquire an appreciation of human complexity beyond the reach of systems.

Great literature resists reduction to propositions. One can, of course, paraphrase Tolstoy's and Eliot's thought, and such "transcriptions," as Bakhtin calls them, can serve as satisfactory starting points for (and recollections of) the experience of reading their novels.[3] At its best, that is what good literary

---

3. On Bakhtin's use of this term, which occurs in several of his works from different periods, see Gary Saul Morson and Caryl Emerson, *Mikhail Bakhtin: Creation of a Prosaics* (Stanford, CA: Stanford University Press, 1990), 56, 59, 176–7,7 183, 281–83, 307, 366; and Morson and Emerson, "Introduction: Rethinking Bakhtin," in

criticism does. But it is not that experience itself. As in Wittgenstein's famous metaphor of the ladder, a wise reader will use the transcriptions of good literary criticism "as steps—to climb up beyond them. (He must, so to speak, throw away the ladder after he has climbed up it.)"[4]

It is easy enough to summarize works in a sentence. First impressions can be deceptive (*Pride and Prejudice*). War is chaos, and peace is baffling (*War and Peace*). There is no perfect crime, and no theory that can justify murder (*Crime and Punishment*). Vulgarity is the worst sin (*Madame Bovary*). In the pursuit of success we neglect the goodness around us (*Great Expectations*). Life cannot be caught in a paraphrase, even this one (all of William James).

These paraphrases are not inaccurate, just woefully inadequate, as even the best paraphrase would be. Only mediocre works illustrate a single, clearly formulated idea. Those are the works that, our students report, many high school English teachers (and some of their university counterparts) tend to favor, because such works are easily teachable. Even when they teach more complex works—like Harper Lee's ever-popular *To Kill a Mockingbird*—some treat them as if they were no more than didactic parables. But if a book can be reduced to its message, why not just memorize the message?[5]

Great novels cannot be transcribed adequately, not only because they convey a highly complex vision, but also, as we

---

Morson and Emerson, eds., *Rethinking Bakhtin: Extensions and Challenges* (Evanston, IL: Northwestern University Press, 1989), 1–30.

4. Ludwig Wittgenstein, *Tractatus Logico-Philosophicus*, trans. D. F. Pears and B. F. McGuiness (London: Routledge & Kegan Paul, 1977), 74 (paragraph 6.54).

5. We discuss this question at length in chapter 6 of *Cents and Sensibility*.

shall see, because the experience of reading them is essential to their wisdom. Much as no paraphrase can substitute for the experience of taking a violin lesson, so no summary can take the place of truly engaging with *Anna Karenina* and *Middlemarch*. There is no alibi for actually reading them. Unfortunately, recent forms of "negative fundamentalism" in literary studies have offered such alibis, as if it were a gain to bypass the slow process of attentive reading.

But if literature is so valuable, why is the study of it, and of the humanities more broadly, in decline? University enrollments and majors in these fields continue to plummet, and their professors feel besieged.[6] And that was *before* the global pandemic hit! We fear that massive unemployment and the enhanced prestige of the STEM fields will strike another blow against studying and teaching the humanities.

6. See, for example, Colleen Flaherty, "Withering Humanities Jobs," *Inside Higher Ed*, November 21, 2017, https://www.insidehighered.com/news/2017/11/21/full-time-jobs-english-and-languages-reach-new-low-mla-report-finds. Moreover, even when faculty positions in the humanities are available, the long-standing trend continues of having non-tenure-track positions growing more rapidly than tenure-track ones, with contingent faculty often working under less than ideal conditions. See Scott Jaschik, "The Shrinking Humanities Market," *Inside Higher Ed*, August 28, 2017, https://www.insidehighered.com/news/2017/08/28/more-humanities-phds-are-awarded-job-openings-are-disappearing; and Colleen Flaherty, "GAO Report on Non-Tenure-Track Faculty," *Inside Higher Ed*, November 21, 2017, https://www.insidehighered.com/quicktakes/2017/11/21/gao-report-non-tenure-track-faculty. Kevin Carey ("The Bleak Job Landscape of Adjunctopia for Ph.D.s," *New York Times*, March 6, 2020, https://www.nytimes.com/2020/03/05/upshot/academic-job-crisis-phd.html) summarizes the situation well: "The humanities labor market is in crisis. Higher education industry trade publications are full of essays by young Ph.D.s who despair of ever finding a steady job. Phrases like 'unfolding catastrophe' and 'extinction event' are common. The number of new jobs for English professors has fallen every year since 2012, by a total of 33 percent."

Literature Lost[7]

Oddly enough, professors of literature themselves seem to have lost faith in its importance. The idea that great literature is a repository of wisdom has become positively quaint, while the assumption that it contains moral lessons to be found nowhere else seems politically suspect. Indeed, the very concept of "great literature" has turned into something of an embarrassment. It is associated with hopeless traditionalists who regard literary value as an objective reality, rather than a play of ever-changing power interests. They cling to a belief that there is something special about art or, to use the term coined by the Russian Formalists, that there is such a thing as "literariness" at all.[8]

If there is no such thing as great literature, why should students take courses in it? One anticipates that some chemists and social scientists may not appreciate aesthetic masterpieces, but, if even literature professors deny that such masterpieces exist, it is hardly surprising that students don't bother to study them. For decades, in short, professional careers in literary studies have been made by adopting ideas destructive to the discipline itself, a dynamic worth the attention of sociologists of knowledge. Negative fundamentalism reigns.[9]

---

7. We borrow this phrase from John M. Ellis, *Literature Lost: Social Agendas and the Corruption of the Humanities* (New Haven, CT: Yale University Press, 1997).

8. See Boris M. Èjxenbaum, "The Theory of the Formal Method," in *Readings in Russian Poetics: Formalist and Structuralist Views*, ed. Ladislav Matejka and Krystyna Pomorska (Cambridge, MA: MIT Press, 1971), 3–37.

9. For more on how humanists sow the seeds of their own destruction, while failing to articulate a compelling defense of their usefulness, see Charlie Tyson, "The Rise of Reassurance Lit," *Chronicle of Higher Education*, February 28, 2020, https://www.chronicle.com/article/the-rise-of-reassurance-lit/; Karen E. Spierling, "The Humanities Must Go on the Offensive," *Chronicle of Higher Education*, December 8, 2019, https://www.chronicle.com/article/the-humanities-must-go-on-the-offensive/;

Mikhail Bulgakov's novel *The Master and Margarita*—often considered the greatest Russian novel of the twentieth century—opens with the devil, who in the guise of a foreign professor visits officially atheist Soviet Russia, intruding on a conversation between an editor, Berlioz, and a poet, Bezdomny. Bezdomny, it appears, has written a poem insulting Jesus, which might seem to accord with official ideology, but, as Berlioz explains, does not. For the poem presumes that Jesus actually existed, whereas, according to the official view, he was a myth constructed after the fact. The devil finds this denial amusing, because he actually witnessed Jesus's interview with Pontius Pilate, which he describes in detail. The devil is still more delighted when Berlioz and Bezdomny also deny the existence of God and, at last, the devil himself. "Well, now, this is really getting interesting,' cried the professor, shaking with laughter. 'What is it with you? Whatever comes up you say doesn't exist!'"[10] In much the same spirit of negation, modern "theory and criticism" has, for decades, favored a rhetoric of denial. Arguably, the discipline's defining move has been assertions of nonexistence. As the Russian revolutionary Michael Bakunin

---

Eric Adler, "When Humanists Undermine the Humanities," *Chronicle Review*, May 14, 2017, https://www.chronicle.com/article/when-humanists-undermine-the-humanities/; Timothy Brennan, "The Digital-Humanities Bust," *Chronicle Review*, October 20, 2017, https://www.chronicle.com/article/The-Digital-Humanities-Bust/241424; and Scott Jaschik, "Hoax with Multiple Targets," *Inside Higher Ed*, May 22, 2017, https://www.insidehighered.com/news/2017/05/22/faux-scholarly-article-sets-criticism-gender-studies-and-open-access-publishing. Not that changing student tastes are completely blameless for problems in the humanities: see Colleen Flaherty, "Liberal Arts Students Are Getting Less Artsy," *Inside Higher Ed*, February 21, 2017. https://www.insidehighered.com/news/2017/02/21/liberal-arts-students-fears-about-job-market-upon-graduation-are-increasingly.

10. Mikhail Bulgakov, *The Master and Margarita*, trans. Diana Burgin and Katherine Tiernan O'Connor (New York: Random House, 1995), 35.

famously proclaimed, "The will to destroy is also a creative will."[11]

A few examples might clarify what we mean. When Barbara Herrnstein Smith published her celebrated study *Contingencies of Value: Alternative Perspectives for Critical Theory* in 1988, her denial of objective literary value was still somewhat shocking. "All value," she contends, "is radically contingent, being neither a fixed attribute, an inherent quality, or an objective property of things, but rather an effect of multiple, continuously changing, and continuously interacting variables or, to put this another way, the products of the dynamics of a system, specifically an *economic* system."[12] She means "economic" literally, even if her usage of the term has little to do with mainstream economics as a discipline. Much as the market value of some good or service depends not on its intrinsic nature but on the contingent factors that create demand, so, she explains, the value of a literary work has nothing to do with its supposed intrinsic qualities. In fact, there is no such thing as intrinsic aesthetic value.

The value of *Moby-Dick*, she explains, is not fundamentally different from the price of a copy of *Moby-Dick*. The work and its copy belong to different economic systems and are traded on different marketplaces, but the value of one is determined much the same way as the price of the other. "Like its price in the marketplace," she writes, "the value of an entity to an individual

11. Michael Bakunin, "The Reaction in Germany," in *Bakunin on Anarchy*, ed. Sam Dolgoff (New York: Random House, 1971), 57, translation amended. Written in German, the original reads: "Die Lust zur Zerstörung ist auch eine schaffende Lust." The best study of Bakunin's thought is Aileen Kelly, *Mikhail Bakunin: A Study in the Psychology and Politics of Utopianism* (New Haven, CT: Yale University Press, 1987).

12. Barbara Herrnstein Smith, *Contingencies of Value: Alternative Perspectives for Critical Theory* (Cambridge, MA: Harvard University Press, 1988), 30.

subject is *also* the product of the dynamics of an economic system, specifically, the personal economy constituted by the subject's needs, interests, and resources—biological, psychological, material, experiential, and so forth. Like any other economy, moreover, this too is a continually fluctuating or shifting system."[13] What's more, the two economies are interdependent, since our personal environment includes the market economy and the market economy "is composed, in part, of the diverse personal economies of individual producers, distributors, consumers."[14] The mention of "producers, distributors, and consumers" is of course meant to demystify any view of art as something special. Indeed, there is really no such thing as "art." Smith makes sure to tell us that when she speaks of "works of art" she does not mean that there are such things, but is referring merely to "that which is *called* 'art' in the indicated discourse(s)."[15]

And how about the self whose needs and interests the "work of art" satisfies? Smith cautions that when she speaks of the self's interests she does not mean to suggest that there is such a thing as "self" (the quotation marks are hers): "It must be emphasized that any particular subject's 'self'—or that in behalf of which he or she may be said to act with 'self-interest'—is also variable, being multiply and differently configurable in terms of different roles, relationships, and, in effect, identities (citizen, parent, woman, property owner, teacher, terrestrial organism, moral being, etc.) in relation to which different needs acquire priority . . . under different conditions."[16] "And so forth," "etc.":

13. Smith, *Contingencies of Value*, 30–31.
14. Smith, 31.
15. Smith, 34.
16. Smith, 31.

Smith resorts to lists like these—we might call this "the rhetoric of etcetera"—to suggest that whatever can take so many
forms, or be influenced by so many factors, surely cannot be
said to exist in itself.

Since everything "may be said" to play different roles in different "discourse(s)," it is hard to see why this reasoning singles
out the nonexistence of art, literature, value, or the self. "Society," "money," "science," and "law" also play different roles in
different discourses. So, for that matter, do stars, including our
very own sun. And, indeed, criticism and theory love to describe something previously taken as real as a mere phantom,
simply "called" what it is held to be. There is no value, just evaluation, and no art apart from what is called art. "Whatever comes
up you say doesn't exist!" This way of thinking was pioneered
by those who denied the existence of authors. But, if there are
no authors, where did the works of Sophocles, Shakespeare,
and Sterne come from?

More than half a century ago, the New Critics denied that
the author's intention, rather than the text taken on its own,
determines the meaning of a work (the "intentional fallacy" argument). But the strategy known as "the death of the author"
goes a lot further; the very concept of authorship is called into
question. In his classic essay "The Death of the Author,"[17] Roland Barthes reveals it to be an emptiness: "The author is never
more than the instance writing, just as *I* is nothing other than
the instance saying *I*: language knows a 'subject' not a 'person,'
and this subject, empty outside of the very enunciation which
defines it, suffices to make language 'hold together,' suffices,

17. Roland Barthes, "The Death of the Author," trans. Stephen Heath, in *The
Norton Anthology of Theory and Criticism*, 2nd ed., ed. Vincent B. Leitch (New York:
Norton, 2011), 1322–26.

that is to say, to exhaust it."[18] By the same token, Barthes explains, the hand of the writer "cut off from any voice, borne by a pure gesture of inscription (and not of expression), traces a field without origin—or which, at least, has no other origin than language itself, language which ceaselessly calls into question all origins."[19]

Barthes means that it is not the author who creates a text but "language." There is no author who, as has always been assumed, is the progenitor of the text and so exists before it, "in the same relation of antecedence to his work as a father to his child."[20] Quite the contrary, the modern author is a mere "scriptor . . . born simultaneously with the text . . . in no way equipped with a being preceding or exceeding the writing."[21] It should be no surprise that this scriptor does nothing more than assemble "a tissue of quotations from the innumerable centres of culture" and so is "never original."[22] Having replaced the author, the scriptor "no longer bears within him passions, humors, feelings, repressions, but rather this immense dictionary from which he draws a writing that can know no halt . . . the book itself is only a tissue of signs, an imitation that is lost, infinitely deferred."[23] As a result, meaningfulness, too, disappears, as "writing ceaselessly posits meaning ceaselessly to evaporate it, carrying out a systematic exemption of meaning."[24]

18. Barthes, "Death of the Author," 1323.

19. Barthes, 1324.

20. Barthes, 1324.

21. Barthes, 1324.

22. Barthes, 1324.

23. Barthes, 1325.

24. Barthes, 1325. No less influential than Barthes's essay is Michel Foucault's "What Is an Author?" Foucault observes, "It is obviously insufficient to repeat empty slogans: the author has disappeared, God and man died a common death. Rather,

As it became increasingly desirable to infuse criticism with "historical" (which usually means political) content, the writer's scriptoriness rendered her a mere recording tool for ideologies deployed by social forces. Fast forward to the development of "cultural studies" as a field, and we find the same rhetoric of denial. The widely used *Norton Anthology of Theory and Criticism* explains a key tenet of this new field: "Literary texts, like other artworks, are neither more nor less important than any other cultural artifact or practice. Keeping the emphasis on how cultural meanings are produced, circulated, and consumed, the investigator will focus on art or literature insofar as such works connect with broader social factors, not because they possess some intrinsic interest or special aesthetic values."[25]

Art contains no "aesthetic values." Neither does it exhibit any "intrinsic interest" making it more important than "any other cultural artifact or practice." Artifact, practice, production, circulation, consumption: the language here, as in Smith's book, demystifies literature and art (or "literature" and "art") by reducing

---

we should examine the empty space left by the author's disappearance; we should attentively observe . . . the reapportionment of this void; we should await the fluid functions released by this disappearance." In this view, we need to speak not of "the author" but of "the author-function" in given social conditions. Foucault concludes, "We can easily imagine a culture where discourse would circulate without any need for an author. Discourses, whatever their status, form or value. . . . would unfold in a pervasive anonymity. No longer the tiresome questions: 'Who is the real author?' 'Have we proof of his authenticity and originality?' 'What has he revealed of his most profound self in his language?' New questions will be heard: 'What are the modes of existence of this discourse?' 'Where does it come from; how is it circulated; who controls it?' 'What placements are determined for possible subjects?' 'Who can fulfill these diverse functions of the subject?' Behind all these questions, we would hear little more of the murder of indifference: 'What matter who's speaking?'" Michel Foucault, "What Is an Author?," in *The Norton Anthology of Theory and Criticism*, 2nd ed., ed. Vincent B. Leitch (New York: Norton, 2010), 1479, 1489–90.

25. "Dick Hebdige," *Norton Anthology*, 2478.

them to mere commodities. This is the economics not of economists, but of literary critics. Only non-existence exists. As Milton wrote of "darkness visible," we keep stumbling on nothingness palpable.

The political implications of this way of thinking become clear when applied to key democratic concepts. In a well-known essay, Stanley Fish did not call for free speech to be limited (as he was misunderstood to say). Rather, he denied that it existed at all. "There's No Such Thing as Free Speech, and It's a Good Thing, Too" deems free speech a "conceptual impossibility."[26] Fish arrives at this curious conclusion by using the all-or-nothing reasoning characteristic of fundamentalisms. Speech cannot be entirely free, he reasons, since it always excludes some speech felt to be particularly dangerous, such as "fighting words" or incitement to riot. Whoever sets the limits is already imposing a set of values, and so whatever form First Amendment formulas may "have at the present moment will favor some interests more than others."[27] There can be no neutrality. It will not do to classify some speech as action, and so not protected, since "everything we say impinges on the world in ways indistinguishable from the effects of physical action."[28] Only speech that is pure noise and mattered to no one could be free, and then it would hardly be speech at all.

To a critic who argued that an open mind is not the same thing as an empty one, Fish replies—no surprise—that "in my analysis . . . they *are* the same."[29] To be truly open, a mind

26. Stanley Fish, "There's No Such Thing as Free Speech, and It's a Good Thing, Too," in *There's No Such Thing as Free Speech, and It's a Good Thing, Too* (New York: Oxford University Press, 1994), 115.

27. Fish, "There's No Such Thing," 114.

28. Fish, 114.

29. Fish, 117.

would have to have no framework at all, and then it couldn't think anything intelligible; it would be not a mind but "a sieve."[30] By this logic, we suppose, it makes no sense to ask for an unbiased judge, since a truly unbiased judge couldn't think at all. (Though he has no formal legal training, Fish has taught at several prestigious law schools.) If some benighted liberal soul should object that such reasoning creates a slippery slope leading to ever more serious restrictions on free speech, Fish counsels us to reply: "Some form of speech is always restricted, else there could be no meaningful assertion; we have always and already slid down the slippery slope; someone is always going to be restricted next, and it is your job to make sure that the someone is not you."[31]

Fish argues that we should judge restrictions on a case by case basis, but he means something quite different from case-based reasoning as we have described it. The way Fish would judge cases is by asking, Whose ox is gored? "So long as free speech principles have been fashioned by your enemy . . . contest their relevance to the issue at hand; but if you manage to refashion them in line with your purposes, urge them with a vengeance."[32] In short, "'Free speech' is just the name we give to verbal behavior that serves the substantive agendas we wish to advance."[33] It is, like aesthetic value, art, literature, authorship, and self, just a "name": "Free speech, in short, is not an independent value but a political prize."[34]

30. Fish, 117.
31. Fish, 111.
32. Fish, 114.
33. Fish, 102.
34. Fish, 102.

Curiously, Fish, the negative fundamentalist, arrives at the same conclusion as Lenin, the positive fundamentalist. For Lenin, too, free speech was just a name, much as democratic institutions were to be defended when they help your side and abolished as soon as you are in power. For those not mystified by what Fish calls "liberal epistemology" and what Lenin called "liberal moralizing vomit," everything reduces to what Lenin famously called "Who Whom?"—that is, who can dominate whom, and who can destroy opponents and potential opponents.

But isn't there a difference between Stalinist Russia, where the slightest mistake in verbal behavior could earn one a twenty-five-year sentence of hard labor in the frozen far north, and, let us say, America or Britain today? For someone who thinks in all-or-nothing terms, and for whom there is no middle ground, the difference is absent or, at most, insignificant.

In a climactic scene in *War and Peace*, Prince Andrei, who is certain that the meaning of life lies in glory, heroically charges the French but is suddenly bludgeoned on the head. Finding himself on his back, he looks up at the sky. Literally and figuratively, he has changed his point of view. Instead of knowing everything, he now realizes he knows nothing. "There is nothing certain, nothing except the nothingness of everything comprehensible to me," he thinks.[35] "Yes! All is vanity, all is delusion, except those infinite heavens. There is nothing but that. And even that does not exist."[36] Andrei and his friend Pierre oscillate between these two extreme perspectives until they learn to seek wisdom neither in certainty nor in denial, but in the prosaic world of lights and shadows.

35. Leo Tolstoy, *War and Peace*, trans. Ann Dunnigan (New York: Signet, 1968), 359.
36. Tolstoy, *War and Peace*, 344.

The Need for Stories

It is therefore plain that it is not of necessity that everything is
or takes place; but in some instances there are real alternatives.

—ARISTOTLE, "ON INTERPRETATION"[37]

As literary critics have denied the aesthetic, some social scientists have, for a quite different reason, rejected narrative. Some two decades ago, when Morson spent a year at the Center for Advanced Studies in the Behavioral Sciences in Palo Alto, he was struck by one social scientist's impatience with narrative explanation. When a discipline achieves scientific status, this scholar observed, it has no need for stories inasmuch as equations and timeless laws account for facts. The less story, the more science. To be sure, a true science may still use narratives to *illustrate* a concept, but not to *explain* anything.

Of course, this understanding of science would exclude historical sciences, like geology and evolutionary biology. But the point nevertheless raises interesting questions. Are there domains where narrative explanation is not just a makeshift tool for prescientific days, but essential to the domain itself? If so, what makes it essential?

When one does physics, one does not "take a history" the way physicians do. Mathematicians prove theorems by deduction, not by watching to see how things work out. Since the 1950s, economists have tried to do with ever fewer stories, a process that, we argue in *Cents and Sensibility*, has gone too far, a view endorsed in Robert Schiller's recent call for a "narrative

37. Aristotle, "On Interpretation," in *The Basic Works of Aristotle*, ed. Richard McKeon (New York: Random House, 1941), 48.

economics."[38] For much the same reason, doctoral programs
in economics that once required courses in the history of economic thought now rarely do so. Once a discipline has attained,
or claims to have attained, scientific status, its history is of no
more relevance than the history of chemistry might be to a
chemist.

By contrast, historians cannot avoid telling stories, and novels *are* stories. There is no doing without them. There is such a
thing as *narrativeness*, which may be defined as the need for
narrative. Narrativeness comes in degrees.[39] No one would tell
a story to explain the orbit of Mars. Equations on their own
allow us to trace the planet's path. Physics of this sort displays
zero narrativeness. Novels have maximal narrativeness. Other
disciplines, like evolutionary biology or historical linguistics,
lie somewhere between physics and novels.

Narrative traces a sequence accounting for why something
happened, not why it had to happen. If the result were given in
advance by some law, one could just state the law. What happens on one occasion may not happen on another. Narratives
dwell in an indeterministic world. They do not promise certainty. For this reason, the great fundamentalisms claiming certainty typically aspire to overcome narrativeness. A good sign
of a pseudoscience is a theory purporting to replace narratives
with laws. The historical materialism developed by Marx and
Engels replaces the old view of history as contingent events

38. Robert Shiller, "Narrative Economics" (presidential address to the American
Economic Association), *American Economic Review* 107, no. 4 (April 2017): 967–
1004. See also Shiller, *Narrative Economics: How Stories Go Viral and Drive Major
Economic Events* (Princeton, NJ: Princeton University Press, 2019).

39. On narrativeness, see Gary Saul Morson, "Narrativeness," in *Prosaics and
Other Provocations: Empathy, Open Time, and the Novel* (Boston: Academic Studies
Press, 2013), 33–49; and Morson and Schapiro, *Cents and Sensibility*, 39, 169.

with a science that demonstrates their inevitability. With this new science, Engels explained in *Socialism: Utopian and Scientific*, "it was seen that *all* past history . . . was the history of class struggle," and so it became possible "to present the capitalist method of production in its historical connection and its inevitableness during a particular historical period, and, therefore, also, to present its inevitable downfall."[40] In this famous book, words like "inevitable" and "necessary" and various synonyms occur frequently enough to create a sense of rhetorical inevitability. It is just this ability to trace events to "inevitable" laws that makes the socialism of Marx and Engels, unlike its many predecessors, "scientific." + S Top

Narrative is required when laws cannot explain everything. And that happens when events can be contingent in Aristotle's sense of the term: "They can either be or not be; [such] events also therefore may either take place or not take place."[41] Whatever happened, something else might have. As William James puts the point, there are more possibilities than actualities.[42] To understand a historical event or a personal choice one must sense the other possibilities, the "might-have-beens."[43]

In a world governed by laws, suspense is an illusion. It pertains not to the events, but to our insufficient knowledge of them. If we knew enough, everything would be predictable and

40. Friedrich Engels, "Socialism: Utopian and Scientific," in Karl Marx and Friedrich Engels, *Basic Writing on Politics and Philosophy*, ed. Lewis S. Feuer (Garden City, NY: Doubleday, 1959), 88–89.

41. Aristotle, "On Interpretation," 47.

42. See William James, *"The Dilemma of Determinism," "The Will to Believe," and "Human Immortality"* (New York: Dover, 1956), 145–83.

43. On narrative and "might-have-beens," see Gary Saul Morson, *Narrative and Freedom: The Shadows of Time* (New Haven, CT: Yale University Press, 1994); and Morson, *Prosaics and Other Provocations*, 33–124.

foreseeable and so, as Dostoevsky's underground man observes, "there would be no more incidents or adventures in the world," since adventures entail risk and uncertainty.[44] To know what will happen in a world of contingency, you have to wait and see. If one reads the history of the Hundred Years' War, or a detective story, one can always skip to the last page to find out the outcome. But at a live sports event or the stock exchange there is no equivalent. Suspense pertains to events; the world itself is suspenseful. In short, there is narrativeness when the present moment is not the automatic derivative of earlier moments, but has real weight. The moment is truly momentous. In this sense, the present moment has "presentness," and this "presentness" of the moment is what creates narrativeness.

Narrative comes in kinds or, as we usually say, genres. As Bakhtin explains, stories of different genres describe events in different ways.[45] In ancient Greek romances, for instance, people suffer the vicissitudes of fate, but do not have any control over what happens. They can choose only how to endure their suffering, with folly or wisdom. The plot does not change them; it tests them. And they pass the test. The hero and heroine suffer countless adventures, yet at the end of the story they

44. Fyodor Dostoevsky, *"Notes from Underground" and "The Grand Inquisitor,"* ed. Ralph E. Matlaw (New York: Dutton, 1960), 22.

45. See Mikhail Bakhtin, "Forms of Time and of the Chronotope in the Novel," in *The Dialogic Imagination: Four Essays,* ed. Michael Holquist, trans. Caryl Emerson and Michael Holquist (Austin: University of Texas Press, 1981), 84–258; M. M. Bakhtin, "The *Bildungsroman* and Its Significance in the History of Realism (Toward a Historical Typology of the Novel)," in *Speech Genres and Other Late Essays,* ed. Caryl Emerson and Michael Holquist, trans. Vern McGee (Austin: University of Texas Press, 1986), 10–59; and Gary Saul Morson and Caryl Emerson, *Mikhail Bakhtin: Creation of a Prosaics* (Stanford, CA: Stanford University Press, 1990), 271–305, 366–432.

are the same people as at the beginning. As Bakhtin likes to say, in such genres time forges nothing new.

In the realist novel, by contrast, people do have initiative, they make real choices, and they change, bit by bit, as a result both of what happens to them and of the choices they make. By the end of the story, they are no longer the same people as when it started. "In writing *Phineas Finn*," observes Anthony Trollope, "I had constantly before me the necessity of progression in character,—of marking the changes in men and women which would naturally be produced by the lapse of years."[46] Since people keep changing, Trollope kept tracing a hero's and heroine's development in sequels forming a series of novels: "I was continually asking myself how this woman would act when this or that event had passed over her head, or how that man would carry himself when his youth had become manhood, or his manhood declined to old age . . . I got round me a circle of persons as to whom I knew not only their present characters, but how those characters were to be affected by years and circumstances."[47]

One could easily transpose the adventures in a Greek romance, and in some variants they occur in different sequence. But one could not rearrange the events of a realist novel, because the hero and heroine change and so might not respond in the same way to a given occurrence had it happened sooner or later. Dorothea Brooke learns from experience to make wiser choices. In many novels, the whole point is to describe such learning. We may say that time in the novel is untransposable and irreversible. By the same token, in ancient romances the

46. Anthony Trollope, *An Autobiography* (Newcastle upon Tyne: Cambridge Scholars, 2008), 159.

47. Trollope, *Autobiography*, 159–60.

social world is mere background and has no effect on events, which is why the same stories have been told in different cultures with a mere change of names. But one could not set *Middlemarch* in Russia, where Dorothea's Protestant sensibility would make no sense, and where one could find no equivalent to Mayor Vincy or contractor Caleb Garth. The opportunities open to women, the ideas in the air, the attitudes to work and class, which all play a shaping role in realist novels, differ from country to country.

They also differ from period to period in the same culture. Ancient romances can be hard to date because their action could have taken place at almost any time, but one could not set *Middlemarch* a decade earlier or later, since the story focuses on events leading to the reform bill of 1832. Turgenev was so concerned to situate manners, forms of speech, and moral norms at a precise historical moment that it is sometimes impossible to shift the plot by even a few months, which is why the concluding words of *Fathers and Children*—"August 1861"—are not an extraneous statement of when the author finished writing, but an intrinsic part of the book. Time and social history are essential to novels; therefore, we can go to them to learn what people were like in a given period. That is the whole point of historical novels, and historians have read Turgenev's fictions as if they were ethnographical treatises.

As Nobel laureate in chemistry Ilya Prigogine would say, time and culture are not mere parameters, but operators.[48] In realist novels, individuals and society actively shape each other, which is why people differ from age to age and personalities are unique. The ancient romance and the realist novel are but two

---

48. Ilya Prigogine, *From Being to Becoming: Time and Complexity in the Physical Sciences* (San Francisco: W. H. Freeman, 1980); and Prigogine and Isabelle Stengers, *Order Out of Chaos: Man's New Dialogue with Nature* (Toronto: Bantam, 1984).

of many narrative genres, each of which conveys, in the very way it tells a story, an understanding of how events happen and what a human being is. The history of narrative genres is a history of how people perceived the shape of their lives. Or, to put the point differently, literature makes *discoveries* about human action and social change that philosophers and theorists struggle to "transcribe."

For yet another reason, then, it is a mistake to think, as historians sometimes do, that writers compose nice stories to illustrate the ideas of philosophers. Historians have typically maintained that nineteenth-century thinkers were the first to appreciate historical development in a strong sense, but in Bakhtin's view they were transcribing discoveries made by novelists in the previous century. Fielding, Richardson and, especially, Goethe had already represented lives and cultures in their "historical multitemporality" and ongoing development. "This process of preparing for the disclosure of historical time took place more rapidly, completely, and profoundly in *literary creativity*" than in the works of other thinkers.[49]

Historians err because they are not used to reading literature this way. It is to literary masterpieces and genres we may turn to trace the human understanding of how lives develop. Once one appreciates narrativeness and the many ways stories can be shaped, great literature reveals much more than is contained in any paraphrase or philosophical transcription.

World Literature

Classic literature conveys, as nothing else can, how people unlike ourselves have seen the world. As one immerses oneself in *The Iliad* and *The Aeneid*, one senses what it is like to acknowledge

---

49. Bakhtin, "*Bildungsroman* and Its Significance," 26.

heroism and glory as the highest values. If you want to understand the values and assumptions shaping life in eleventh-century Japan or eighteenth-century China, you could do no better than to enter the world of *The Tale of Genji* or *The Story of the Stone*. In making yourself the "implied reader" presupposed by these works, you learn much more than facts about the world they depict; you also learn how those facts were experienced. As one shares characters' concerns and the author's evaluations, one expands one's repertoire of human possibilities. As this process becomes a habit, you come to live your daily life with a consciousness of the otherness of others.

It is easy to forget that other cultures and periods understood life differently. Each was just as certain as we are that its vision was the only correct one and measured others against it. Unless one overcomes this cultural self-centeredness, one is likely to assume without reflection that the values shared by those among whom one lives are the only ones possible for decent people. The way one's culture—or even social class—views life will seem like the way life just is. Ambrose Bierce defined "egotist" as "a person of low taste, more interested in himself than in me," and what is true of individuals is often true of groups as well.[50] We live on a little island of space and time, and literature is, perhaps, the best way to see beyond it.

A curriculum in world literature would, in addition to the Western canon with which we are familiar, expose students to the masterpieces of other civilizations. To the classic novels of Japan and China, one might add the Indian *Bhagavad-Gita* and the Persian *Shahnameh*. A negative fundamentalist would see little point in doing so. Only those who believe that there is such a thing as great literature can add the great literature of

---

50. Ambrose Bierce, *The Devil's Dictionary* (Garden City, NY: Doubleday, n.d.), 52.

other civilizations. The rhetoric of nonexistence locks one into one's own little world.

In recommending expanding the canon in this way, we have in mind something different from what is often done in the name of "postcolonialism": assigning texts from other traditions showing the harm that Westerners do. That is rather like the old joke about the egotist who tells a friend: "That's enough about me, let's talk about you. What do you think of me?" There is something insufferably condescending in the implication that other cultures first had something important to say as a result of their encounter with our own.

Equivalent Centers of Self

We have argued that literature, and especially novels, allow us to understand the individuality of other individuals. Great novels are designed to make their particular way of experiencing the world palpable. They are lessons in binocular vision and in empathy. By identifying with other people for hour after hour, novels offer practice in empathy available nowhere else. Philosophers and theologians can urge us to acquire the skills empathy requires, but they do not, like novels, offer actual practice in doing so.

"We are all born in moral stupidity, taking the world as an udder to feed our supreme self," observes George Eliot in a chapter of *Middlemarch* describing how newly married Dorothea unwittingly hurts her husband by not seeing his life from his own point of view.[51] She wants to help him, but she understands his situation as she would experience it, not as he experiences it. To use Adam Smith's distinction, she has put herself in

51. George Eliot, *Middlemarch* (New York: Modern Library, 1984), 205.

his position, but not in his person and character.[52] Her help turns out to be exactly what would wound him the most. Eliot continues: "Dorothea had early begun to emerge from that stupidity, but yet it had been easier to her to imagine how she would devote herself to Mr. Casaubon . . . than to conceive with that distinctness which is no longer reflection but feeling—an idea wrought back to the directness of sense, like the solidity of objects—that he had an equivalent center of self, whence the light and shadows must always fall with a certain difference."[53] Here George Eliot voices the moral not only of *Middlemarch*, but also of the genre to which it belongs. Realist novels allow us to see how and why light and shadow are never the same for any two people. It is not enough to realize abstractly that each person has a self like our own. They want us to experience that equivalent center of self "with that distinctness which is no longer reflection but feeling." That idea must seem tangible, like the solidity of objects.

In *The Theory of Moral Sentiments*, Adam Smith argues that when we make moral judgments, we do so by imagining the position of the other person so we can determine which actions would be appropriate. To do so, "we enter, as it were into his body and become in some measure the same person, and

---

52. Smith argues that care for others is not just another form of selfishness. Those who think it is believe that, when we sympathize with another (say, for the loss of a son), we are simply imaging what we would feel like in such circumstances and so are being entirely selfish. On the contrary, says Smith, when I enter your grief "I do not consider what I, a person of such a character and profession, should suffer, if I had a son." Rather, "I not only change circumstances with you, but I change persons and characters. My grief, therefore, is entirely upon your account, and not in the least upon my own." Adam Smith, *Theory of Moral Sentiments*, ed. D. D. Raphael and A. L. Macfie (Indianapolis: Liberty, 1982), 317.

53. Eliot, *Middlemarch*, 205.

thence form some idea of his sensations." "Some idea" is as good as we can do because we must deduce that person's "sensations" from external signs. In the world as we experience it, "we have no immediate experience of what other men feel."[54] Our sense of others and our capacity for moral judgment would be so much richer if we could experience another person from within! And we can, through great novels. That was the extraordinary achievement of the genre, which, beginning with Jane Austen, found ways to allow us to do what we cannot do in real life.

Those ways were needed so novels could show us the uniqueness of each person. This interest in individuality explains why the title of so many novels is the name of a person: Anna Karenina, Jane Eyre, David Copperfield, Effi Briest, Phineas Finn, Madame Bovary, Père Goriot, and others. As we have seen, realist novels also exemplify a casuistical approach to ethics, which requires a deep understanding of a situation's particulars and how they are perceived. There could be no better way to explore the otherness of others and to understand a situation as others perceive it than to coexperience their thoughts and feelings.

Stream of consciousness is obviously one way to do this, but the real invention that made the realist novel possible, and can be said to define it as a genre, is the technique known as "free indirect discourse," or "double voicing." Although earlier novelists had used this technique in some passages, Jane Austen appears to be the first to have made it the basis of an entire novel. With this technique, the novelist combines two (or more) perspectives in a single passage. Narrated in the third person, it conveys the character's sequence of feelings and thoughts from within. Grammatically, the narration belongs to the author, but semantically it belongs primarily to the character. We sense two

---

54. Smith, *Theory of Moral Sentiments*, 9.

points of view at once, the character's and the author's, which is why Bakhtin preferred the term "double-voicing." In *Pride and Prejudice* and, especially, in *Emma*, the reader easily mistakes third-person description as the author's testimony only to discover later that the author has been narrating through the heroine's limited perspective. And so the reader makes the same mistakes as the heroine and learns, in the process, how easy it is to succumb to "pride and prejudice." Most novelists make the interaction of perspectives readily apparent so that the perception of double-voicing is immediately clear.

It would take us too far afield to explore double-voicing in detail, and so a couple of examples (one of which we explored in *Cents and Sensibility*) will have to do. On her train ride back to Petersburg, Anna Karenina lays down the English novel she has been reading to think about her intense flirtation with Vronsky, and

she suddenly felt that *he* ought to be ashamed, and that she was ashamed of the same thing. But what had he to be ashamed of? "What have I to be ashamed of?" she asked herself in injured surprise. She laid down the book and sank against the back of the chair, tightly gripping the paper cutter in both hands. There was nothing. She went over all her Moscow recollections. All were good, pleasant. She remembered the ball, remembered Vronsky and his face of slavish adoration, remembered her conduct with him: there was nothing shameful. And for all that, at the same point in her memories, the feeling of shame was intensified, as though some inner voice, just at the point when she thought of Vronsky, were saying to her, "Warm, very warm, hot."[55]

55. Leo Tolstoy, *Anna Karenina*, trans. Constance Garnett, rev. ed. by Leonard J. Kent and Nina Berberova (New York: Modern Library, 1965), 107.

Although this passage is narrated largely in the third person, we sense the sequence of thoughts, choice of words, and tone of voice as Anna's. It is immediately clear we are tracing her thoughts from within when we read "*he* ought to be ashamed" rather than "Vronsky ought to be ashamed." Speaking to ourselves, we do not have to specify to whom a pronoun refers as we would to another. This must be inner speech.

We eavesdrop on Anna's increasingly strained attempts to convince herself that she did nothing "shameful," but her feeling of shame, and the constant repetition of the word in her thoughts, suggest otherwise. "There was nothing"; "all were good, pleasant"; and, again, "there was nothing shameful": these reassurances are how she justifies herself to her conscience as if before an accuser. The more she tries to banish her feeling of shame, the more strongly it reasserts itself. The passage continues: "'Well, what is it?' she said to herself resolutely, shifting her seat in the lounge. . . . 'Am I afraid to look it straight in the face? Why, what is it? Can it be that between me and this officer boy there exist, or can exist, any other relations than such as are common with every acquaintance?' She laughed contemptuously, but was now definitely unable to follow what she was reading."[56]

We see here what first-person narration would omit. To begin with, the author is able to comment on what Anna is doing but not consciously choosing to do and so couldn't comment on, like switching her position or becoming unable to follow what she is reading. Her inner speech would also not register her tone of injured surprise, which would therefore not appear in first-person narration. Most important, we hear, in addition to her voice, the author's implicit ironic commentary on Anna's self-refuting attempts at self-exculpation. What at first looks

56. Tolstoy, *Anna Karenina*, 107.

like a simple third-person passage turns into a dialogue of voices and perspectives.

Sometimes the author can also suggest the perspective of someone not present, what he or she would have said if able to overhear an inner dialogue as we do. In that way, a third perspective is added, and so double-voicing becomes, in effect, triple- or even multiple-voicing. At the beginning of the novel, Anna's brother Stepan Arkadyevich (Stiva), whom his wife Dolly has caught in infidelity, confides in himself about the difficult, and to him surprising, situation:

> Stepan Arkadyevich was a truthful man with himself. He was incapable of deceiving himself and persuading himself that he repented of his conduct. He could not at this date feel repentant that he, a handsome, woman-prone man of thirty-four, was not in love with his wife, the mother of five living and two dead children, and only a year younger than himself. All he was sorry about was that he had not succeeded in hiding it better from his wife. But he felt the seriousness of his position and was sorry for his wife, his children, and himself. Possibly he might have managed to conceal his sins better from his wife if he had anticipated the effect on her should she discover them. He had never clearly thought out the subject but . . . he had even supposed that she, a worn-out woman no longer young or good-looking, and in no way remarkable or interesting, merely a good mother, ought from a sense of fairness to take an indulgent view. It had turned out quite the other way.[57]

It is not the author but Stiva, the perpetually unfaithful husband, who calls himself a "truthful man"—truthful because he

57. Tolstoy, *Anna Karenina*, 5–6.

does not lie to himself and pretend to repent of his conduct! This is the sort of truthfulness that every conscious perpetrator of fraud and deceit could claim, and we detect the narrator's irony at an adulterer praising himself for his honesty because he doesn't repent. When we overhear how Stiva justifies his behavior as completely natural, and almost inevitable, for someone in his position, we detect in the paraphrase of his thought the author's irony at excusing a choice repeatedly made as the workings of necessity. Stiva regrets how his wife and children—and he himself, of course—have been harmed by his wife's discovery of his infidelity (not the infidelity itself), and so he does reproach himself for not concealing it better.

We then hear Stiva imagining—for the first time!—his wife's perspective, an omission he regards not as a moral shortcoming but as a simple blunder. His self-indulgence reaches a comic apogee when he supposes that out of "a sense of fairness" his wife would see his infidelities in the correct way—that is, from his point of view. The snap of the last sentence—"It had turned out quite the other way"—derives from the difference between his evident surprise at her failure at "fairness," on the one hand, and her easily foreseeable reaction, on the other. Its humor marks the radical difference between Stiva's perspective and the narrator's, both audible in the final sentence.

Implicitly, we are asked to consider not only how the discovery of her husband's infidelity makes Dolly feel, but also her reaction if she could overhear, as we do, Stiva's inner dialogue about it. Far from seeing the justice of his perspective, she would feel much worse as she learned that he regards her as "a worn-out woman no longer young or good-looking, and in no way remarkable or interesting, merely a good mother." We can also guess at how she would react to the casual mention of "two dead children," whom she cannot think of without unbearable pain. Dolly is implicitly present throughout this passage, her potential reaction registered along with those of Stiva and the narrator.

In this way, the author turns inner speech into a conversation. Novels record not only dialogues that do happen, but also those that might happen. As Bakhtin likes to say, they "draw dotted lines" so that points of view that in life may never even encounter each other can argue, and so that readers can hear how each perspective might sound to the others. By doing so, not only individual people but also the classes, generations, and professions that have shaped their understanding can enter into a great symposium. And so novels achieve special sociological, as well as psychological, insight. Readers, in turn, can sense not only the individuality of other people, but also the world view of classes different from their own. Instead of seeing the world through the eyes of a single ideology, as it appears to fundamentalisms positive and negative, readers appreciate it in all its spectacular complexity. Systems of whatever sort seem ludicrous. Doctrine yields to dialogue. "There is no general doctrine," observes George Eliot in *Middlemarch*, "which is not capable of eating out our morality if unchecked by the deep- seated habit of direct fellow feeling with individual fellow men."[58] And there is perhaps no better way for a student to acquire that habit than attentive reading of novels like *Middlemarch*.

Novels are made from dialogue and foster it. They can serve as an antidote to fundamentalism—if only humanistic fundamentalists would stop depreciating their value.

58. Eliot, *Middlemarch*, 591.

7

A Path Forward

CARL VON CLAUSEWITZ, the Western world's most famous theorist of war, is usually quoted as saying, "War is the continuation of politics by other means."[1] We are entering an era when politics seems to be conducted as war by other means. And not just war, but the "absolute form of war" as Clausewitz described it: "In the absolute form of war . . . there is only one thing that counts: *final victory*. Until then, nothing is decided, nothing won, and nothing lost."[2] The point is not just to defeat but to annihilate the enemy. In Lenin's philosophy, indeed, to refrain from annihilating an enemy when it is in one's power to do so is criminal.

In a democracy, parties alternate power and sometimes share power. No victory, and no defeat, is final. Different interests are balanced and rebalanced, events that no one could have

---

1. Clausewitz's text actually reads: "We maintain, on the contrary, that war is simply a continuation of politics, with the addition of other means." The statement is often misread as a callous justification of violence (it's just another form of politics), but Clausewitz was making an entirely different point. War is always fought for some political objectives, and so one needs to formulate strategy accordingly. See Carl von Clausewitz, *On War*, ed. and trans. Michael Howard and Peter Paret (Princeton, NJ: Princeton University Press, 1984), 605.

2. Clausewitz, *On War*, 582.

foreseen continually raise new questions and reshape old ones, and each side learns from the other, often appropriating some of its policies. As utopia is the dream of the impossible, "politics," as British politician R. A. Butler has observed, "is the art of the possible."[3]

Fundamentalist thinking is utopian, if not apocalyptic. One knows the truth, and those who disagree are ignorant, evil, or insane. All goodness belongs to one's own camp. Normal democratic politics involves what is now derisively called "bipartisanship." Given his long career, Joe Biden, as one periodical notes, can seem "like a figure from another age—which he is. His was an era when politicians from both parties got along personally and sometimes worked together to compromise. . . . He was [even] friends with his longtime Republican colleague John McCain."[4] The change from "another age" is telling: it is no longer acceptable to get along with, let alone work "together to compromise" with, someone from the other party. In the same spirit, *Jacobin* magazine complained that Biden, who "had spent virtually his entire adult life" in the Senate, "was one of the most outspoken proponents of its culture of chummy deal-making."[5] No one would have accused the Jacobins of that! But what is the alternative to deal-making? Whether or not one likes Biden or the particular deals he made, one either works with those who disagree or tries to annihilate them. The latter is fundamentalist politics, and it is the major threat we face.

3. *The Macmillan Dictionary of Quotations*, ed. John Dainith et al. (Foster City, CA: Chartwell, 2000), 433.

4. Henry Cheadle, "Of Course Joe Biden Supported a Republican in a $200K Speech," *Vice*, January 23, 2019, https://www.vice.com/en_us/article/yw8zy7/of -course-joe-biden-supported-a-republican-in-a-dollar200k-speech.

5. Branko Marcetic, "Joe Biden Has a Long History of Giving Republicans Exactly What They Want," *Jacobin*, February 29, 2020, https://jacobinmag.com/2020 /02/joe-biden-history-republicans-tax-cuts-barack-obama-yesterdays-man/.

It is also part of a wave of new fundamentalist thinking. In addition to political fundamentalism, economic fundamentalism is at least as powerful as ever. Religion also suffers as the world divides itself between those quick to remake holy texts in their own image and those who treat them as idols to which one must bend the knee but that one cannot question. A negative fundamentalism has overtaken the humanities. Given our belief—expressed not just in chapter 6 but throughout the book—that literature elucidates these divisions in a unique way, we care deeply about how it is read and taught. Although some doubt that the debate over the canon matters, and others remain unaware that the very existence of great literature is in question, it troubles us immensely. So far as we are concerned, the debate is anything but "academic."[6]

These new fundamentalisms, in politics, economics, religion, and literature, have common attributes and may demand common responses. It is therefore important to explore the connections among these areas and to arrive at thoughtful ways to adjudicate among differing viewpoints. We are persuaded that the habits of thinking and feeling we can acquire from great literary masterpieces, and especially great realist novels, can help us exchange the temptations of putative certainty for the attentive listening learned in true dialogue.

How the New Fundamentalisms Are Connected

Let's recall for a moment some ways in which fundamentalism (as we use the term) transcends its original meaning in religion. The Christian fundamentalists who coined the term believed

---

6. How we hate the use of the word "academic" as a pejorative! For us, "academic" signifies the impartial analysis of facts, and the pursuit of knowledge that enlivens our lives. It is troubling that in the popular vernacular "academic" denotes irrelevance.

that every word of the Bible is divinely inspired, must be taken literally whenever possible, and is perspicuous in its meaning. To argue with the text is to argue with God. Unlike other forms of devoutness, this fundamentalism leads not only to strict observance of all commandments taken at face value, but also to fears of dialogic engagement as, at best, impious.

In economics, market fundamentalists also worship certain laws—in this case, those of the free market. The revelation supposedly proclaimed by Adam Smith over two centuries ago—which, as we argue in chapter 4, is actually not what Smith said—becomes quasi-sacred. Market solutions are accepted not just as superior "on the whole and for the most part," but categorically, on an a priori basis. Just as abiding by the Lord's word leads to salvation, so abiding by unfettered competition leads to optimality. In the first case it is the devil tempting you toward skepticism; in the second the lure of benefits without costs leads sinners away from economic redemption. The road to socialism is paved with good intentions. Fundamentalist socialists are sure that the answer is always government control, as if human nature did not apply to bureaucrats. What these two opposing economic fundamentalisms share is the certainty that the law is known and unfailing, and that any deviation must, by the very nature of things, be erroneous or sinful.

Fundamentalist thinking is not limited to any camp. It exists on the right and on the left. To paraphrase H. L. Mencken, toss an egg out of a passenger train and you are sure to hit a fundamentalist of some sort.[7] In various parts of the Western world—

7. Mencken's widely quoted comment reads: "Heave an egg out a Pullman window and you will hit a Fundamentalist almost anywhere in the United States today." As cited in George M. Marsden, *Fundamentalism and American Culture: The Shaping of Twentieth-Century Evangelism, 1870–1925* (Oxford: Oxford University Press, 1980), 188. Marsden also quotes Mencken's other well-known insult: "Christendom may be

including not only Europe and the United States, but also Latin America and Russia—there have arisen far-right political fundamentalists that seek salvation in the purity and the sanctity of origins. Like Luther, they despise the traditions and current institutions that have obscured what was once so plain. Also like Luther's, this kind of thinking at its worst leads to, or tolerates, a new anti-Semitism, among other horrors. It may also feed the desire to ward off all external influences. Among literary scholars or the educated general public, we know of no one who still believes in a rigid, unchanging canon of texts to which we must simply bow down or at which we must silently gape in astonishment, but so long as there is no coherent alternative to the complete denial of great literature and intrinsic aesthetic value, the possibility is there—all the more so because negative fundamentalism reigns. Nationalist fundamentalism has led in some places to an angry nativism and an impatience with democratic processes. No less unbending at times is a fundamentalist view of markets, sacred texts, or cultural heritage. Even in places where these ways of thinking are still undetectable, the increasing power of fundamentalist mental habits in the West (and elsewhere) makes them more likely.

At the heart of any fundamentalism, as we define it, is a disdain for learning from evidence. Truth is already known, given, and clear. If you know from the outset that a government-mandated minimum wage, or that any restriction on free trade, must be mistaken, why bother to explore the historical record? If you are certain you know exactly what the Bible means, and that that meaning is apparent on the surface, why peer into the depths?

---

defined briefly as that part of the world in which, if any man stands up in public and solemnly swears that he is a Christian, all his auditors will laugh" (3).

Karl Popper and his successors famously argued that a meaningful claim must in principle be falsifiable, and that standard is presumed throughout this book. Just as a scientist verifies hypotheses by subjecting them to experiments where they might fail, so those interested in better policies will not just tolerate opposing viewpoints and inconvenient facts; they will also seek them out. But tests imply doubt. One does not test what is certain, just as one does not conduct experiments to verify the binomial theorem. In human affairs, mathematical certainty is a chimera. As John Stuart Mill famously observed, "He who knows only his own side of the case knows little of that . . . if he is equally unable to refute the reasons on the opposite side, if he does not so much as know what they are, he has no grounds for preferring either opinion."[8] But, as we discuss in chapter 3 and elsewhere, no fundamentalist thinks like Mill.

Fundamentalism exists on the left as well. Throughout the Western world, we have witnessed groups that, in denouncing the politics of hate, practice it. Some have actually revived Marxist ideas that not so long ago were pronounced forever, consigned to what Trotsky called "the dustbin of history." Others are less clear about what they support than about what they wish to destroy, which can be a clear sign that they are motivated more by hatred than by empathy. Bakunin notwithstanding, the will to destroy, by itself, is not a creative will.

Sometimes proposals are simply incoherent: replacing "no free lunch" with "everyone eats all the time" is not merely unrealistic, it is dangerous. Those who advance such suggestions typically demand a level of government intervention that history

---

8. John Stuart Mill, *On Liberty* (Amherst, NY: Prometheus, 1986), 43. The essay was originally published in 1859.

shows to be a disaster. At other times, when real fundamentalist thinking predominates, proposals are all *too* coherent. Doctrinaire socialism gains in appeal, to the astonishment of Russians or Chinese who suffered under central planning or the cultural revolutions that accompanied it. But history doesn't seem to matter when you just know that utopia is around the corner.

In religion, the fundamentalism of the left transforms liturgy and sacred texts into an Etch-a-Sketch to be reinscribed at will. Durable truths? How naïve. Here, as in literary studies, fundamentalism may take a negative form, with blanket denial replacing categorical assertion. Meaning is what we want it to be, truth changes with social needs, and moral precepts must be updated frequently. There is no art, only "what is called art," and no truths but the ones that currently appeal to us.

Neither changing everything nor changing nothing, neither revolution nor its opposite, strikes us as a productive response to today's challenges. If the world is actually teetering on a precipice, as extremists tell us, the rise of fundamentalisms isn't going to help. If it is not, fundamentalism may well place us on one. Whether or not fundamentalism has arisen as a result of crises real or perceived, it tends to create the world it fears. It is a self-fulfilling apocalypse.

Return to Dialogue

So how does one best judge between opposing views? The logic of fundamentalism acknowledges no middle ground and regards all compromise as cowardice, if not treason. Recall the words heard by John of Patmos in the book of Revelation: "I know thy works, that thou art neither cold nor hot: I would thou wert cold or hot. But because thou art lukewarm, and neither cold nor hot, I will spue thee out of my mouth" (Rev. 3:15–16).

When politics is seen apocalyptically, a society lurches toward civil war. Democracy thrives neither in Siberia nor in the inferno, but in the lukewarm. It is temperate. In a democratic society, politics is not about purity but about adjudicating among multiple overlapping and conflicting interests. But no one split the difference at Armageddon.

We offer no comprehensive theory promising a surefire remedy. On the contrary, the first step must be to forswear the temptations of theoretical panaceas. Recall Kant's famous line, which we quoted in the conclusion to chapter 1: "From the crooked timber of humanity no straight thing was ever made." In human affairs, there are always unintended consequences and, as Isaiah Berlin notes, "we cannot legislate for the unknown consequences of consequences of consequences."[9] To be sure, Berlin continues, Marxists (and others who think this way) assure us that in the world they would create, free of oppression and intellectual distortions, problems will generate their own solutions, but this, Berlin dryly observes, "seems to me a piece of metaphysical optimism for which there is no evidence in historical experience."[10] Alas, those in the grip of a theory—like those in Dostoevsky's *The Possessed*—don't look to historical experience. The whole appeal of such theories, and of the fundamentalist mindset, is that the messiness of mere history is transcended.

What, then, is the alternative? Like Berlin, we must recognize that "the first public obligation is to avoid the extremes of suffering" generated by extreme solutions and to recognize that

9. Isaiah Berlin, "The Crooked Timber of Humanity," in *The Crooked Timber of Humanity: Chapters in the History of Ideas*, ed. Henry Hardy (New York: Knopf, 1991), 14.

10. Berlin, "Crooked Timber of Humanity," 15.

whatever measures we may adopt, in ordinary situations or critical ones, "we must always be aware, never forget, that we may be mistaken, that certainty about the effect of such measures invariably leads to avoidable suffering of the innocent."[11] For this reason, "we must engage in tradeoffs—rules, values, and principles must yield to each other in various degrees in specific situations."[12] One of the themes of this book is to be wary of anyone who proposes solutions without enumerating the costs. In the real world, but not in the thinking of fundamentalists, there are always trade-offs. In politics, as well as economics, we live in a world where there is no gain without loss, and where to choose one thing means forgoing something else.

We should cultivate good judgment, and judgment, by definition, cannot be reduced to an algorithm. It results from experience sensitively considered and reconsidered. In ethics, this perspective suggests what Stephen Toulmin calls for: a rebirth of case-based reasoning, or casuistry in its neutral, nonpejorative sense. The great seventeenth-century rationalists, who regarded ethics as a form of theoretical rather than practical reasoning, have at last led us to a dead end. As we argue at length in chapter 2, the very fact that the word "casuistry" is now an insult—nobody would praise someone by calling him "a master casuist"—shows the success of the rationalists.[13] As Montaigne, Erasmus, and Shakespeare appreciated, life requires practical as well as theoretical reasoning. In ethics, this means that, instead of reasoning down from timeless theories, we should acquire

11. Berlin, 17.

12. Berlin, 17.

13. The great attack on casuistry, and its abuse by the Jesuits, belongs to Pascal in *The Provincial Letters*.

the skill of reasoning up from particulars. Instead of deductive theories, we need to create taxonomies, much as clinical medicine identifies syndromes. Let principles become maxims, which do not guarantee a right answer but remind us of similar cases and earlier insights to consider. By constantly reflecting on one's decisions, and understanding why some of them were mistaken, one gradually acquires sophistication in moral reasoning. But one never reaches perfection. With casuistry, and practical reasoning generally, conclusions are always tentative. Depending on what happens, one could be proven wrong. There is always room for honest disagreement. And even the wisest decisions are subject to revision.

When rationalism triumphed in philosophy, casuistry found a home in the realist novel. From Defoe onward, the novel developed its ability to present difficult moral questions. Whereas the basic impulse of the rationalist or the scientist is to abstract the essence of a situation and apply general principles to it, the novel tends to make the exact opposite move. Instead of showing the essential simplicity of things, it shows their complexity and teaches us to reason appropriately. We learn a lot by seeing how simplification distorts, and how abstraction becomes distraction. When realist novels depict someone who believes in a simplifying philosophy—say, some form of materialism, utilitarianism, anarchism, or socialism—that claims, with science on its side, to cut through to the essence of things, the plot typically demonstrates how mistaken such views are. In the novel of ideas, we examine how people embrace such philosophies for contingent psychological reasons, and we trace how simplicities lead to disaster.

The fate of democracy depends on our forswearing fundamentalist politics. We must learn again the art of reasoning together. Nothing is so disheartening as seeing political figures condemned for having friends on the other side or for imagining that, since decent people may disagree, compromising with and even learning from one's opponents is possible. There is no substitute for real dialogue. We need less shouting and more conversation. And we must keep the conversation going.[14]

Chekhov with the Final Word

We conclude this volume with a return to literature. Anton Chekhov was perhaps the greatest short story writer who ever lived, and "Enemies" (1887) is exemplary of his work.[15] In some twenty pages, only five thousand words, he explores where the lack of dialogue—and the failure to empathize—may lead.[16]

The story begins when the impecunious doctor Kirilov is suffering deep despair.[17] The doctor's only son, Andrey, a child

14. "Keep the conversation going" was a signature phrase of the late Michael André Bernstein.

15. Chekhov, of course, was also a playwright of note. One of our favorite stories is that Tolstoy, seemingly on his deathbed, assembled family and friends to say good-bye. He motioned for Chekhov to approach his bed and reportedly (according to Chekhov) whispered in his ear, "Shakespeare was a bad playwright, but you are worse." Ironically, Tolstoy survived that illness, living until the ripe old age of eighty-two, dying six years after Chekhov who passed away at the age of forty-four. Fortunately, Chekhov's plays survive as well!

16. The translation we use below is from Anton Chekhov, *The Schoolmaster and Other Stories* (New York: Ecco, 1986).

17. It is important to note that, at this time and place, doctors had little of the prestige and income typically associated with that profession. They were considered tradesmen, "plumbers of the body." Hence, the marked contrast between Kirilov's modest home and the aristocratic Abogin's, whom we will meet shortly, and in the description of the two men: Abogin "was a thick-set, sturdy-looking, fair man with a big head and large, soft features; he was elegantly dressed in the very latest fashion." On the other hand, Kirilov's "unkempt head and sunken temples, the premature greyness of his long, narrow beard through which his chin was visible, the pale grey

of six, has just died of diphtheria. His "faded and invalid wife" is unlikely to bear other children, so "Andrey was not merely the only child, but also the last child." In that room, "there was something that attracted and touched the heart, that subtle, almost elusive beauty of human sorrow which men will not for a long time learn to understand and describe, and which it seems only music can convey." The story shows that people react to sorrow differently from conventional descriptions, and Chekhov's subtlety in noticing what it really looks and feels like demonstrates why his stories are so revered.

The doorbell rings. Abogin, an aristocrat from the other side of town, has come to summon the doctor. "'My wife has been taken dangerously ill. . . . And the carriage is waiting . . .'" "As people always do who are frightened and overwhelmed, he spoke in brief, jerky sentences and uttered a great many unnecessary, irrelevant words." "Kirilov listened and said nothing, as though he did not understand Russian." His reaction to intense grief is no longer acute pain, but sheer abstraction from the unbearable present. He does not register what is said to him, and he moves as if he were not at home but in a strange place. "Excuse me, I cannot come . . . my son died . . . five minutes ago!" But Abogin persists.

"Doctor, I am not a stone, I fully understand your position . . . I feel for you," Abogin cajoles. "But I am not asking you for myself. My wife is dying." He appeals to "the love of humanity," as if such a principle must do the trick with the doctor as it would with someone of his own circle. This invocation of social virtue in the high-toned language favored by the edu-

---

hue of his skin and his careless, uncouth manners—the harshness of all this was suggestive of years of poverty, of ill fortune, of weariness with life and with men" (25).

cated irritates the doctor, who responds: "Humanity—that cuts both ways."

Abogin is entirely unaware that Kirilov and members of his class do not use language like this. Abogin means what he says, but his words seem fake, and he has no awareness that he is showing his class superiority. Chekhov observes: "Abogin was sincere, but it was remarkable that whatever he said his words sounded stilted, soulless, and inappropriately flowery, and even seemed an outrage on the atmosphere of the doctor's home and on the woman who was somewhere dying." He does not consider that the way he speaks is bound to remind the doctor of his poverty and lower social status. Still, Kirilov agrees to go.

As the carriage takes them the eight miles between their homes, "Abogin heaved a deep sigh and muttered: 'It's an agonizing state! One never loves those who are near one so much as when one is in danger of losing them.'" The doctor must be reflecting that for him that danger is over. They arrive at Abogin's fine home, adorned with the abundant luxuries of the day. Abogin runs upstairs to check on his wife, only to discover that she has faked illness to get her husband out of the way so she could run off with her lover. "'She has deceived me,' he cried, with a strong emphasis on the second syllable of the verb. 'Deceived me, gone away. She fell ill and sent me for the doctor only to run away with that clown Paptchinsky! My God!'" "Tears gushed from his eyes." "She sent me off that she might run away with a buffoon, a dull-witted clown, an Alphonse! Oh God, better she had died! I cannot bear it! I cannot bear it!" Abogin addresses his absent wife: "If you have ceased to love me and love another—so be it; but why this deceit, why this vulgar, treacherous trick?" "If she did not love me," he asks, "why did she not say so openly, honestly, especially as she knows my views on the subject?"

Here we need to elucidate what would have been obvious to Chekhov's readers. Progressive opinion had for decades maintained that should a wife fall in love with someone else, her husband should bless her new union. By concealing her departure, Abogin's wife has deprived him of the chance to play the prescribed part, as if she were not sure that he would. And so Abogin feels not only injured by her, but also insulted as his progressive credentials are implicitly questioned. For the doctor, Abogin's sense of insult for such a reason, which no one of the doctor's social class would share, comes off as still more class condescension. Reading the story today, one wonders how often well-educated people with advanced opinions needlessly and obliviously insult their social "inferiors" in much the same way.

"With tears in his eyes, trembling all over, Abogin opened his heart to the doctor with perfect sincerity." "Who knows," Chekhov asks, "if the doctor had listened to him and had sympathized with him like a friend, he might perhaps, as often happens, have reconciled himself to his trouble without protest, without doing anything needless and absurd . . . But what happened was quite different." Speaking from his own sense of insult, Kirilov does not empathize but expresses anger: "What are you telling me all this for? I have no desire to hear it!" "Abogin staggered back from Kirilov and stared at him in amazement." "How dare you say that to me!" at which point Kirilov replies: "No, how dared you, knowing of my sorrow, bring me here to listen to these vulgarities!"

Kirilov takes Abogin's lack of concern for his own grief as the disregard of a superior to a hired servant. He becomes enraged by the signs of class superiority, the displays of both wealth and progressive opinions. "Go on squeezing money out of the poor in your gentlemanly way," the doctor snarls. "Make a display of humane ideas, play (the doctor looked sideways at the violin-cello case) play the bassoon and the trombone, grow as fat as capons but don't dare to insult personal dignity!"

Abogin, who has not intended to insult the doctor, is amazed. He does not realize that this very amazement can be read as a sign that he has presumed Kirilov's feelings are not worth considering.

Things deteriorate from there, as "Abogin and the doctor stood face to face, and in their wrath continued flinging unde-served insults at each other. I believe that never in their lives, even in delirium, had they uttered so much that was unjust, cruel, and absurd."

We tend to imagine that poverty and suffering ennoble a per-son, and that the unfortunate are by nature more understanding of the sufferings of others, but that is sentimentality. Chekhov writes, "The egoism of the unhappy was conspicuous in both. The unhappy are egoistic, spiteful, unjust, cruel, and less capa-ble of understanding each other than fools. Unhappiness does not bring people together but draws them apart, and even where one would fancy people should be united by the similar-ity of their sorrow, far more injustice and cruelty is generated than in comparatively placid surroundings."

As the carriage takes Kirilov home, "the doctor thought not of his wife, nor of his son Andrey, but of Abogin and the people in the house that he had just left." Evidently the sense of insult overpowers even his grief over the loss of his son: "He con-demned Abogin and his wife and [her lover] Papchinsky and all who lived in rosy, subdued light among sweet perfumes, and all the way home he hated and despised them till his head ached."

As "a firm conviction concerning those people took shape in his mind," Kirilov's hatred is translated into political belief. The story's ending, largely unanticipated by the reader, concerns the origin of such beliefs. The most deeply held social and political convictions derive not from economic self-interest, nor from rational evaluation of alternative policies, but from condescension experienced as insult. It is a lesson well worth contemplating today.

The story concludes: "Time will pass and Kirilov's sorrow will pass, but that conviction, unjust and unworthy of the human heart, will not pass, but will remain in the doctor's mind to the grave." Long after the grief of his son's death softens, the doctor's hate-fueled political belief, "unjust and unworthy of the human heart," will—astonishingly and surprisingly—remain sharp and present.

Abogin and Kirilov both had the chance to empathize with each other. Their grief would have been eased by mutual understanding, and both would have been ennobled in the process. But they chose otherwise. The opportunity was lost. Here Chekhov's great themes—the supreme importance of empathy and the terrible consequences of waste—shape a lesson in how social and political hatred are formed. So great is Chekhov's genius, and so profound is his own understanding of human weakness, that we empathize even with their failure of empathy. We live in anything but "placid" times. This is an age when we are "less capable of understanding each other than fools."

We conclude this volume where we began. With rising fundamentalism all around us, "hate thine enemy" seems to be the catchphrase of the day. We readily accuse others of being motivated by hate, and we hate them for it. Righteous indignation abounds. People speak over each other, screaming louder and louder, but it isn't clear that anybody is listening. Today, "unhappiness does not bring people together but draws them apart." "The egoism of the unhappy" is driving what purport to be "conversations" in the media, and too often in our homes and communities.

Let's not give up hope. The better we understand the fundamentalist mindset, the more likely it is that we can banish its practitioners to the "dustbin of history," where they belong.

INDEX

Abraham, 189–90, 189n, 194, 208–9
adherents of fundamentalisms:
contempt/disdain shown by, to
nonadherents, xxvii, 30–31, 33;
monitoring of, 108; psychology of,
33–34, 82–83, 125–26; reversal of
fortunes of (becoming the enemy),
78–83. *See also* nonadherents of
fundamentalisms
Affordable Care Act, 162
Afghanistan, 16
afterlife, 211
Agamemnon, 192
agnosticism, xxv, 35, 36
Aitken, George A., 66n135
Alexandria, library of, 199
Algerian Armed Islamic Group, 16
Ali, Tariq, 20
allegory, 206–7, 216
all-or-nothing mentality: about
climate change, 146–56; about free
speech, 254–55; about politics,
256; about science, 90–100; Soviet
thought characterized by, 77, 94,
105, 106–7. *See also* compromise;
extremism; us vs. them mentality
Almond, Gabriel A. See *Strong
Religion*
Al Qaeda, 16
Alter, Robert, 190, 195–96

alternatives to fundamentalism:
casuistry as instance of, 57–65;
dialogue as chief among, 70–74,
279–83; encounters with, 7–8;
Erasmus-Luther exchange as
instance of, 51–56; features of, xxv,
10–11; fundamentalist attacks on,
xxv; ignorance of, 10; novels as
instance of, 65–73, 244
animals, religious classification of,
216–18
anthropology, 86–87
Antigone, 209–10
anti-Semitism, 277
apocalyptic thinking: attraction of,
1–2; evidence when subjected to, 5;
in politics, 280; presentism implicit
in, 2–3; religion as basis for, 2–3, 35;
successful predictions and, 3–4;
theories underlying, 5. *See also*
revolutionism
Appleby, R. Scott. See *Strong Religion*
argument. *See* criticism; dialogue;
disagreement
argumentum ad lapidem, 38
Aristophanes, *The Clouds*, 118
Aristotle: on ethics, 58–62; on
necessity and contingency, 257, 259;
on purpose, 225; on reasoning, 11,
43, 58–62

Armenia, 170

Armstrong, Karen, 16–17, 21, 26

atheists, 10, 29, 36, 114, 201, 203, 226, 229–30, 242, 242n, 248

Auden, W. H., 144

Austen, Jane, 10, 113, 207, 240, 244, 267; *Emma*, 268; *Pride and Prejudice*, 71–72, 245, 268

autonomy, 204–5

Avenarius, Richard, 106

Bacon, Francis, 26, 27, 40, 92

Bakhtin, Mikhail, 7–8, 70–73, 193, 232–35, 244, 260–61, 263, 268, 272

Bakunin, Michael, 248–49, 278

Barthes, Roland, "The Death of the Author," 251–53

Bazelon, Emily, 48n

Becker, Gary, 24, 31, 45, 131

Bellamy, Edward, *Looking Backward, 2000–1887*, 27, 110, 240

Bentham, Jeremy, 23, 24, 57

Berger, Peter, 21n26, 36

Berkeley, Bishop, 40–41

Berlin, Isaiah, 22, 280

Bhagavad-Gita, 264

Bible: authorship of, 13–14, 51, 193, 212–15, 236; canonization of, 213–15; core values of, 204; dialogic approach to, 236; inerrancy of, 13–14, 43, 212, 275–76; interpretation of, 13–15, 43–44, 52–53, 82n, 192–94, 202, 206–15, 232; language use in, 226–28; meaning of/belief in, 14, 212–15, 228, 232, 236; moral questionability of stories in, 189–94, 197, 202–12; moral wisdom sought in, 214–15; relevance of, 197, 200–201; sacredness/holiness as value in, 204–5, 217–19; science in relation to,
26; translations of, 52, 195–97, 201, 237

Biden, Joe, 274

Bierce, Ambrose, 20, 264

Bill of Rights, 194–95, 236n

Black Death, 4

Blake, William, 42–43

Blanchard, Charles, 46

Bolsheviks, 11, 34–35, 77, 79, 198, 232

Boot, Max, 141

Boswell, James, 40–41

Brexit, 141

Breyer, Stephen, 48n

Bryan, William Jennings, 15

Bukharin, Nikolai, 79

Bulgakov, Mikhail, 120; *The Master and Margarita*, 248

Bush, George H. W., 123

Butler, R. A., 274

Buttigieg, Pete, 81

calendar, 238

Calvin, John, 128, 192

capitalism, 6, 136

carbon emissions, 145–56

Carlyle, Thomas, 165

Carroll, Lewis, *Through the Looking-Glass*, 182, 242

Case, Shirley Jackson, 14

casuistry (case-based reasoning), 58–70, 74, 255, 281–82, 281n13. *See also* practical reasoning

categorical thinking, 6–7

Catholicism, 19, 43

central planning. *See* command economies

certainty: criticism in relation to, 103–9; dangers resulting from strong commitment to, xxvii, 35–36, 38–39, 85–86, 89; disconfirming evidence vs., 32–33; as fundamentalist characteristic, xxiv, 7, 22–35, 85–86, 90; hatred linked to, 126–27; morality and, xxvii, 34–35; novels as antidote to worldview based on, 73, 114; opinion in relation to, 85; popular misunderstanding of, 7, 90; psychological appeal of, 125–26; science in relation to, 90–92; simplification linked to, 24–25. *See also* complexity and uncertainty; truth

Charisma (magazine), 81

Chaucer, Geoffrey, 185

Chechnya, 16

Chekhov, Anton, 138–39, 283, 283n15; *The Cherry Orchard*, 139, 241–42; "Enemies," 283–88; *Uncle Vanya*, 138–39, 241–42

Chicherin, Georgy, 106

Christian fundamentalism: certainty as feature of, 8, 14, 31; inerrancy of scripture in, 13–14, 43, 275–76; nonreligious fundamentalisms compared to, 28; in politics, 81–82; scientific claims made by, 26–27, 31–32; truth as perspicuous in, 39, 43–44, 46

Clausewitz, Carl von, 273

climate change, 95–96, 145–56

Clinton, Hillary, 124n, 128

clock parable, 181–82, 200, 236

Club of Rome, 94

Coase theorem, 130n1

"Come, let us reason together," 77

command economies: failures of, 132, 135–36, 158, 167–75, 279; Soviet Union as, 135, 167–74

Common Sense philosophy, 26, 40–41

Communist Party, 33–34. *See also* Marxism-Leninism; Soviet Union

compassion, 138, 202–4. *See also* empathy; sympathy

complexity and uncertainty: decision making in situations of, 7; dialogue as tool suited for, 56; domains characterized by, 59; economic life characterized by, 174–75; fear of, 54, 115, 125, 280; negative capability and, 221; the novel's worldview based on, 10, 66, 68–69, 110–14, 116, 207–8, 240–41, 243–44, 261–72, 282; opinion—not dogmatism—suited for, 85, 100–101; practical—not theoretical—reasoning suited for, 59, 175; religious faith as response to, 231; satire's worldview based on, 116; science—in contrast to pseudoscience—characterized by, 95

complicity, 81–83

compromise: democracy characterized by, xxiv, 64, 274, 280; hostility toward, xxiv, xxv, 7, 77, 105. *See also* all-or-nothing mentality

Comte, Auguste, 23–24, 86, 89

Condorcet, Marquis de, 25, 57

confirmation/disconfirmation, 5, 32, 53, 120

Confucianism, 131, 198

Conquest, Robert, 172

Conrad, Joseph, 10

conservativism: criticism of, during World War I, 14–15

constitutions, 194–95, 213, 238. *See also* U.S. Constitution

Corbyn, Jeremy, 158

COVID-19 pandemic, xxv–xxvi, 2, 3–4, 30, 96–100, 175, 246

criticism: certainty in relation to, 103–9; as feature of dialogue, 55–56;

criticism (*continued*)
  function of, in fundamentalist
    worldview, 104–5; necessity of,
    100–103; others' experiences as
    source of, 74, 100–103, 278; refine-
    ment of thought by means of, 74,
    84–85, 100–103. *See also* dialogue;
    disagreement; higher criticism, of
    the Bible; perspective-taking
"crooked timber of humanity" (Kant),
  11, 280
Crusades, 19
Cuban Missile Crisis, 3
Cultural Revolution, 115
cultural studies, 253
culture: dialogic perspective on, 74;
  literature as lens on, 263–65; moral
  differences in, 202–5
culture wars, 239

Dagestan, 16
danger, attributed when fundamentalist claims are not embraced, 3, 5,
  98–100
Daniel, 188
Darwinism/evolution, 15, 27, 45, 49,
  88, 92–93, 216n62, 224
David, 192
Davies, William, 141
death, 242–43
death of the author, 251–53
deconstruction, 9
Defoe, Daniel, 65–66, 282; *Moll
  Flanders*, 66, 240
democracy: characteristic features of,
  xxiv, xxv, xxvi, 77, 273–74; compromise as feature of, xxiv, 64, 274, 280;
  dialogic thinking as feature of, 74,
  76–77, 84–85, 282–83; disagreement
  as feature of, 76, 84; fundamental-

ism in tension with, 84–89; multi-
  vocal nature of, 122; opinion as
  basis of, 84; threats to, xxiv, xxvi,
  4, 74, 83, 124, 277, 280, 282–83
democratic centralism, 79
Democrats: attitudes of, 75–76, 80–81;
  and climate change, 153; Republicans' views of, 75–76, 140
Descartes, René, 42, 44, 57, 60
dialectical materialism, 28–29,
  32–34, 42, 106, 258. *See also*
  Marxism-Leninism
dialogue: as basis of alternative to
  fundamentalism, 70–74, 279–83;
  benefits of, 55; conflicting concep-
  tions of, 54–56; culture and society
  seen in perspective of, 74; decline
  of, xxv; democracy based on, 74,
  76–77, 84–85, 282–83; facts' role in,
  xxvi; features of, 55–56; meaning
  attained through, 232–36; the novel
  form and, 70–73, 111, 272; opinion as
  basis of, 55–56; religious/spiritual,
  236; requirements for, xxvii; significance of, xxv, xxvii; threats to,
  xxvii. *See also* criticism
Diamond, Jared, 24
Dickens, Charles: *Bleak House*,
  156–57, 242; *Great Expectations*,
  245
dictionaries, 182–86
Diderot, Denis, 111
disagreement: as feature of democracy, 76, 84; nonexistent in utopias,
  110; not countenanced by fundamentalist outlooks, 79, 89, 98–100.
  See also criticism
disciplinary fallacy, 183–84
disconfirmation. *See* confirmation/
  disconfirmation

divisiveness and polarization: contemporary manifestations of, 5; extremism as cause of, 5–6, 64–65; group-based, 128n93; human attraction to, xxiii; social and political effects of, xxiii–xxiv

Dixon, A. C., 13, 26–27

"dog whistle," 109

Dostoevsky, Fyodor, 4, 10, 195, 240–41; *The Brothers Karamazov*, 114, 125–27, 148, 241–42; *Crime and Punishment*, 187–88, 242, 245; *The Idiot*, 229, 243; *Notes from Underground*, 119–20, 241, 260; *The Possessed*, 37, 114–16, 240–41, 280

"dotted lines," 272

double vision (thought), 220–21

double voicing, 267–72

doubt, 33, 36, 125–26. *See also* skepticism

Douglas, Mary, 215–17

Dryden, John, 185

Dukakis, Michael, 123

"dustbin of history" (Trotsky), 6, 278, 289

earth, age of, 221, 225–26

Ecclesiastes, book of, 192, 213, 238

economics: choice as fundamental in, 136–39; consensus and middle grounds in, 159–62, 176; of contemporary social issues, 145–65; disciplinary fallacy in, 183–84; and efficiency, 138–39, 147, 154–55, 161, 167, 172; fairness in, 132, 132n, 165–67; government's role in, 129–30, 134–36, 165–66; human behavior explained by principles of, 24, 131, 134–37, 149, 178–79, 243–44; humanism and, 134–39,

165–67, 180; literary value from perspective of, 249–50; practical reasoning in, 131, 175, 179–80; predictions concerning, 94; and scarcity, 137–39, 145, 151, 156; scientific claims made by, 258; Soviet experiment in, 167–74; trade-offs in, 136–37, 137n, 139–40, 145–49, 160, 281. *See also* command economies; market fundamentalism

Ehrlich, Paul, 94–95

Einstein, Albert, 91

elections, xxiv, 89

Eliot, George, 10, 240–41; *Middlemarch*, 67–69, 112–13, 240–41, 262, 265–66, 272

empathy, 73, 265–67, 272, 278, 288. *See also* compassion; sympathy

"endless variety of men's minds," 38

"end of history" (Fukuyama), 136

Engels, Friedrich, 24, 28–29, 32, 47, 48–49, 88, 93, 166, 166n48, 202, 258–59; *Socialism: Utopian and Scientific*, 259

"engineers of human souls" (Stalin), 11

epistemology. *See* knowledge/epistemology

Erasmus, Desiderius, 22, 51–57, 74, 281

ethics. *See* morality

eugenics, 27, 92

Euripides, 45; *Iphigenia in Aulis*, 192

evidence, fundamentalism's treatment of, 5, 9, 20, 32–33, 49, 109

evil, ascribed to nonadherents of fundamentalism, 23, 34, 64, 77, 83, 86, 104, 105, 109, 121, 127

evolution. *See* Darwinism/evolution

Existentialism, 241

experience. *See* perception/experience, theories of

expertise: ineffectual use of, 143, 166–68; positive use of, 99, 144, 176

externalities, 129, 129–30n

"extraneous historical forces" (Engels), 166

extremism: in economics, 140–42; epistemological, 36; polarization resulting from, 5–6, 64–65; in public opinion, 76; silos as contributing factor to, 122; status quo as target of, 140; vicious cycle of, 5, 82–83; violence resulting from, 114–15. *See also* all-or-nothing mentality

"eye for an eye," 211

Facebook, xxiii

facts: in analyses of contemporary social issues, 145–65; in contemporary information environment, 141–42; cultural or relativistic perspective on, 37; numbers regarded as, 143–45; reinterpretation of myths as, by fundamentalisms, 26, 29–30; revelation of truth behind, by fundamentalisms, 33–34; role of, in dialogue and argument, xxvi, 180; values in relation to, 29, 215, 224

faculty, university, 136–37

fairness, 132, 132n, 165–67

faith, religious, 19, 25, 212, 225, 228–31, 243

"false choices," 137, 139, 145

false consciousness, 47

falsifiability, of science, 32, 90–91, 278

family, 202–3

family resemblances, theoretical concept of, 17–18, 20

famine, 94–95

fanaticism, xv, 22, 124–25, 199, 240. *See also* ideological thinking

Farias, Bert, 81–82, 82n

Ferguson, Neil, 96–99, 97n33

Fielding, Henry, 263

Finnish Green Party, 150

First Amendment, 194–95, 254

Fish, Stanley, 254–56

Fitzgerald, F. Scott, 220

Flaubert, Gustave, *Madame Bovary*, 245

Floyd, George, xxv

Foucault, Michel, "What Is an Author?," 252–53n24

fox vs. hedgehog analogy, 22–23, 44, 52, 58

fracking, 150, 155

free indirect discourse. *See* double voicing

Freemasonry, 38

free speech, 1–2, 56, 254–55

free trade, 160–61

French Revolution, 82

Freud, Sigmund, 23, 24, 47, 48, 51, 87–88, 241

Freudianism, 28, 29, 32, 48

Fukuyama, Francis, 136

fundamentalism: binary worldview of, xxiv–xxv, 9, 35, 36–38, 77, 105; categorical thinking and certainty as characteristics of, xxiv, 6–7, 22–35, 85–86, 90, 277; coining of the word, 15; conception and evolution of, 12–15; contempt/disdain for nonadherents as feature of, xxvii, 30–31, 33, 104–7; dangers of, 4; democracy in tension with, 84–89; domains of thought affected by, xxiv–xxv, 4, 8, 275–79; economic (*see* market-based *in this entry*); epistemological, 23; everyday manifestations of, 7–8; evidence as handled by, 5, 9,

20, 32–33, 49, 109; features of, xxiv–xxv, 12–13, 15, 22–35, 39–51, 275–79; "hedgehogs" as example of, 22–23; of the left, 276, 278–79; in literature, 9–10, 232, 239–40, 246–47, 264, 277, 279; market-based, 6, 19, 129–38, 274; negative perceptions of, 15–16, 18–20; novels as alternative worldview to, 10, 65–73, 111–16; pacific, 21, 47; political, 5–6, 16, 19–20, 77, 120–22, 274, 277; relativism compared to, 8–9, 36–38; religion as basis for, 279; religious, 8, 13–14, 16, 206, 274; science as type of, 25–26; scientific claims made by, 23, 26–28, 30–32; in social science, 89; sympathy for difference not a feature of, 39; synthetic, 50; text/revelation as foundation of, 47–51, 194–200; utopian character of, 274; varieties of, 16–19. See also alternatives to fundamentalism; Christian fundamentalism; negative fundamentalism; positive fundamentalism

Fundamental Project (American Academy of Arts and Sciences), 17

"The Fundamentals" (pamphlet series), 13, 26–27

futuribles, 3

Galilean world view, 8

Genesis, book of, 189

Genghis Khan, 3

genres, 260–63

Germany, energy policies and use of, 149–50

Gettysburg Address, 196

Gibbon, Edward, The Decline and Fall of the Roman Empire, 2–4, 199

Glassner, Barry, 1

global pandemic. See COVID-19 pandemic

God: in Abraham story, 208; contemporary lack of belief in, 201; death of, 9; humans' knowledge of, 52–53; Islamic conception of, 19; science in relation to, 215; secular versions of, 28, 90; as source of truth, 23, 26, 43–44, 50

God substitute, 28, 90

Goethe, Johann Wolfgang von, 263

Gorbachev, Mikhail, 173

government, economic role of, 129–30, 134–36, 165–66. See also command economies

grand narratives, 4–5

Greek romance, 260–62

Greek tragedy, 44–45, 191–92, 209–10

Green New Deal, 151

Green Party (Finland), 150

green revolution, 94–95

Gresham's law, 142

"group polarization" (Sunstein), 128n93

Gupta, Sunetra, 99

Gusev, S. I., 108

Halévy, Élie, 23

Hamas, 16

harm, principle of, 204

Harvard faculty, politics of, 137n

hatred: certainty linked to, 126–27; as motivating factor, 75, 126–28, 288; in politics, 76–77, 80–81, 83, 109, 273–74, 287–88; socialization into, 122, 124

Head Start program, 159

health policy, 162

hedgehog vs. fox analogy, 22–23, 44, 52, 58

Hegel, G.W.F., 22, 28–29

"heretic in the truth" (Milton), 90, 152

Heschel, Abraham Joshua, 201

higher criticism, of the Bible, 13–15, 51, 213–14

Hill, Howard, 167–68

Hinduism, fundamentalist, 5

history: in cosmic perspective, 221; end of, 136; human control of, 166n48; narrative foundation of, 258; particularities and contingencies as subject matter of, 60, 120, 258; scientific approaches to, 24, 32, 77, 93, 258–59. *See also* dialectical materialism

"history is like foreign travel" (Descartes), 60

Hitler, Adolf, 3, 126, 128

Hobbes, Thomas, 178–79

Hoffer, Eric, *The True Believer*, 124–28, 124n

Holbach, Baron d', 57

holiness, 204–5

Holton, Gerald, 25

Homer, 206, 213; *The Iliad*, 212–13, 263–64

homosexuality, 81–82, 82n, 194, 219

Hordern, William, 15

human affairs: complexity and uncertainty of, 111, 243–44, 259–60, 280–81; dialogue as essential to progress in, 56, 100–101; fundamentalist claims of certainty about, 86–87, 92, 117, 168, 278; non-fundamentalist explanations of, 11; the novel's exploration of, 111, 280–81; practical—not theoretical—reasoning suited for, 60, 117, 175, 278, 280. *See also* human behavior

human behavior: economic explanations of, 24, 131, 134–37, 149, 178–79, 243–44; evolution of, 45; fallibility and irrationality of, 119–20, 130, 177–80, 243–44; fundamentalist claims of certainty about, 11, 23–25, 32, 86–87, 130; non-fundamentalist explanations of, 10–11; the novel's exploration of, 10, 207, 243–44, 263–64; other-directed, 179, 266–67, 266n52; sociobiological explanations of, 6, 24–25; utilitarian explanations of, 119. *See also* human affairs

humanism and the humanities: and climate change, 149–50; decline of, 246–56, 246n, 275; and economics, 134–39, 165–67, 180; Erasmus as exemplar of, 51–57; and modernity, 57–58

human nature, 11

Hume, David, 9, 40; "Of Miracles," 226–28

Huxley, Aldous, *Brave New World*, 32

Huxley, Julian, 168

idealism, 41–42

ideological thinking: dangers of, 121; Marxist criticism of, 32, 47; novels as antidote to, 73, 113–16. *See also* fanaticism

ignorance, ascribed to nonadherents of fundamentalist worldview, 23, 33–34, 86, 89, 93, 116, 274

Imperial College, London, 96–99

implied reader, 264

income inequality, 156–60

India, 16

individuality, 267

individualism, 131–32, 204–5

inerrancy: of Bible, 13–14, 43, 212, 275–76; of fundamental texts, 47–51; of Koran, 17; of Lenin's thought, 48–49; of Torah, 17

insanity, ascribed to nonadherents of fundamentalist worldview, 46, 89, 106, 274

intellectuals/intelligentsia, 90, 92, 117–20, 138, 179–80, 188, 241

"intensification of the class struggle" (Stalin), 5, 86

intentional fallacy, 251

"interim ethics" (Schweitzer), 203

International Monetary Fund, 133

"invisible hand" (Smith), 132–34

"Ionian enchantment," 25

Iphigenia, 191–92

Iran, 16

irony, 114

Isaiah, xxiii

Islam, 5, 17, 19

Jacobin (magazine), 274

James, Henry, 10

James, William, 245, 259

Janik, Alan, 223–24

Jephthah, 189–91

Jews and Judaism: anti-Semitism and, 277; biblical interpretation and moral dilemmas in, 48, 189–94, 189n, 201, 205, 210–12; Reform tradition of, 237; source text of, 50, 50n94, 212–15. *See also* Bible

Job, book of, 44, 71–72, 192, 213

John of Patmos, 279

Johnson, Lyndon, 77

Johnson, Samuel, 40–41, 158, 185–86

Jouvenel, Bertrand de, 3

Judges, book of, 189

judgment, 62, 281

Kael, Pauline, 122

Kamenev, Lev, 106

Kant, Immanuel, 11, 40, 42, 280

Karaites, 48, 193

Katsenelinboigen, Aron, 49, 168–69, 174

Keats, John, 221

Kelvin, Lord, 143

Kennedy, John F., 76–77

Keynes, John Maynard, 120

Khmer Rouge, 198

Kim Il Sung, 48

King, Martin Luther, Jr., xxvii; "I Have a Dream," 196

King James Bible, 196, 201

knowledge/epistemology: criticism as means to refining, 74, 84–85, 100–103; ethics and, 58–70; evolutionary perspective on, 45; fundamentalist approach to, 23, 120; limits of, 44–45, 53; numbers regarded as criterion of, 143; questioning of possibility of, 9, 39, 44–45; realism in, 42; relation of mind to world, 40–42, 44; silos as hindrance to, 121–22, 128n93; theoretical vs. practical reasoning, 58–70. *See also* certainty; ideological thinking; truth; wisdom

Koestler, Arthur, 33–34, 47, 82; *Darkness at Noon*, 78–80, 240

Koran, 17, 50

Kugel, James, 206, 212–15, 213, 237

laissez-faire, 132–33, 134n9, 168

language: as source of texts, rather than authors, 251–52; standards in, 182–86, 237; use and function of, in religion, 226–28, 231, 237–38

La Rochefoucauld, François de, 117

law, applications of, 60–61

Laws, Curtis Lee, 15

Lee, Harper, *To Kill a Mockingbird*, 245

Leibniz, Gottfried Wilhelm, 57

Lenin, V. I.: absolute conformity required by, 77; compassion shunned by, 202; death of, 79; domination of opponents by, 104–6, 256, 273; and free speech, 256; inerrancy of, 48–49; philosophical positions of, 29, 41–42, 93–94, 95, 106–7; violence attributable to, 121. *See also* Marxism-Leninism

Leonhard, Wolfgang, 49

"let justice be done, though the world perish," 148

Lévi-Strauss, Claude, 87

Leviticus, book of, 194, 215–18

Leviticus Rabbah, 211

liberalism, xxv

libertarianism, 131–32

Lightfoot, Lori, xxvi

The Limits of Growth (Club of Rome), 94

Lincoln, Abraham, Gettysburg Address, 196

literature: academic study of, 246–56, 246n, 275; assumptions underlying, 66, 116, 260–63; canon of, 8–10, 195, 195n, 199, 232, 247, 264–65, 275, 277; concept of, 20; cultural differences revealed by, 263–65; destruction of, 198; dialogic approach to, 232–36; experience of reading as essential to meaning of, 73, 246, 265, 267–68; fundamentalism in, 9–10, 232, 239–40, 246–47, 264, 277, 279; genres of, 260–63; meaning of, 9–10, 232–33, 244–47, 251–53; moral "equivalents" in, 207–12;

perspective-taking enabled and encouraged by, 207–12, 243–44, 264–72; politically-based theory and criticism of, 253–56; potentiality in, 232–35, 245; Russian, 195, 197–98, 232; timeless works of, 195, 197–99, 233–35. *See also* novels

Locke, John, 40

logos, 26, 29

Lucretius, 22

Luther, Martin, 48, 51–56, 74, 126–27, 128, 277

Lyotard, Jean-François, 4

Mach, Ernst, 106

Machen, J. Gresham, 27

Macron, Emmanuel, 158

Magna Carta, 213

Malinowski, Bronislaw, 23, 30, 86–87

Mao Zedong, 48, 84, 115

market fundamentalism, 129–38, 274; assumptions about human behavior underlying, 131; basic principles of, 6, 129–30, 132–34; certainty as characteristic of, 276; critique of, 133; extension of, into other domains, 131; government's role according to, 129–30, 134–36; Marxism-Leninism vs., 132; misconceptions of, 19, 134n9, 135–36; moral aspects of, 131–32; origin of concept, 130–31

Marsden, George, 13, 15, 26

Marx, Karl, 24, 32, 41, 48–49, 51, 88, 93, 104, 165, 169, 202, 258–59

Marxism-Leninism: conformity demanded by, 89; market fundamentalism vs., 132; mindset and thought patterns characteristic of, 32–34, 47–49, 89, 93–94, 105–9, 280;

objectivity in, 33–34, 78; pedagogical filter of, 198; as pseudoscience, 28; religion-like character of, 21; Socialist Workers' Party endorsement of, 140. *See also* dialectical materialism; Lenin, V. I.; Soviet Union

mass movements, 124–27

materialism, 42. *See also* dialectical materialism

Mayakovsky, Vladimir, "It's Too Early to Rejoice," 198

McCain, John, 274

McGurn, William, 134n9

meaning: of the Bible, 14, 212–15, 228; dialogue as means to, 232–36; of literature, 9–10, 232–33, 244–47, 251–53; religious/spiritual, 228–31, 236; science and, 216, 221–26, 228; tradition as source of, 46, 48, 124, 187, 192–93, 200–201, 210–13, 232, 237

measurement and numbers, as criteria of truth/importance, 143–45, 176

Medicare, 162

Mencken, H. L., 276

Menshevism, 104, 106

metanarratives, 4–5

Michelson-Morley experiment, 91

middle ground: in contemporary sociopolitical world, 64; in economics, 159–62; as target of fundamentalists, xxv, 9, 35, 36–38, 77; as target of Soviets, xxv, 36

Midrash, 39n70, 189n, 190, 193, 210–11

Mill, John Stuart, 84–85, 89, 100–101, 204, 278

millenarianism, 13

Milton, John, 84, 90, 152, 254

mind. *See* knowledge/epistemology

minimum wage, 160

"minutiae of mental make," 113

miracles, 226–28

missionary nihilism, 9

modernity, 57–58

monotheism, 19

Montaigne, Michel de, 22, 57–58, 281

morality: Adam Smith on, 178–79; Bible seen as source of, 214–15; biblical stories in tension with, 189–94, 197, 202–12; certainty and, xxvii, 34–35; cultural variation in, 202–5; "equivalents" in, 207–12, 219–20, 266–67; individualist perspective in, 131–32, 205; market fundamentalism and, 131–32; nature in relation to, 29–30; the novel's treatment of, 65–70, 66n136, 112, 282; political fundamentalist perspective on, 78–80; science in relation to, 29, 215, 221–25; standards in, 187–88; type of reasoning suitable for, 58–70, 74. *See also* casuistry; human affairs; practical reasoning

Morris, William, *News from Nowhere*, 110, 111, 240

Morson, Gary Saul, and Morton Schapiro, *Cents and Sensibility*, 134, 243, 257, 268

Muller, Jerry Z., 143

Mussolini, Benito, 84

mysteries, 231, 238

mystery, 126, 221

mythos, 26, 29

narrativeness, 258, 260, 263. *See also* stories

Nash, Diane, xxvii

nationalist fundamentalism, 277

nativism, 277

natural gas, 147–50, 155

nature, 28–30

"nature takes no leaps" (Darwin), 92

Nazis, 202

Nebuchadnezzar, 188

negative capability, 221

negative fundamentalism: all-or-nothing character of, 35–39, 64, 272; characteristics of, xxiv, 35–36; in literary studies, 9–10, 246–47, 264, 275, 277, 279; positive vs., 9, 10; in religion, 279; skepticism contrasted with, 36

neoliberalism, 136, 138, 165

New Criticism, 251

Newman, John Henry, 204n38

New Republic (magazine), 94, 146

news, 124

Newsweek (magazine), 81

Newton, Isaac, 23, 25, 26, 86, 91, 215

Nietzsche, Friedrich, 9, 15, 202

nihilism, 9

Nixon, Richard, 122

nonadherents of fundamentalisms: contempt/disdain for, xxvii, 30–31, 33, 104–7; as evil, 23, 34, 64, 77, 83, 104, 105, 109; as ignorant, 23, 33–34, 86, 89, 93, 116, 274; as insane, 46, 89, 106, 274. See also adherents of fundamentalisms

Norton Anthology of Theory and Criticism, 253

novels: alternatives to fundamentalism displayed in, 10, 65–73, 111–16; assumptions underlying, 66; complexity of world and individuals reflected in, 10, 66, 68–69, 111–14, 116, 207–8, 240–41, 243–44, 261–72, 282; dialogic character of, 70–73, 111, 272; historicity of, 262–63; moral concerns of, 65–70, 66n135, 112,

282; realist, 10, 66–73, 111–16, 240, 261–62, 266; utopian, 24, 27, 110–11, 113, 240–41. See also literature

nuclear power, 146, 150, 154

numbers. See measurement and numbers, as criteria of truth/importance

Obama, Barack, 146, 155

Obamacare, 162

objectivity, in Marxism-Leninism, 33–34, 78

Occupy Wall Street, 158

Oedipus, 29, 44

"on the whole and for the most part" (Aristotle), 59, 131, 175, 276

opinion: criticism as necessary element of, 100–101, 278; democracy based on, 84; dialogue based on, 55–56; negative views of, 54, 85; in novels, 111; positive views of, 55, 84; practical reasoning based on, 65; provisional nature of, 55, 84; in utopias, 110–11

originalism, in constitutional interpretation, 48n

Orwell, George, 119, 120; 1984, 78

Packer, J. I., 15–16, 26, 37, 43–44

pandemic. See COVID-19 pandemic

paraphrase, richness of great texts not susceptible to, 72, 232, 233, 244–46, 263

particularity: in Bible stories, 206; history's concern with, 60, 120, 258; the novel's concern with, 71, 244, 265, 267; practical reasoning's concern with, 61–63, 67, 131, 208, 219, 244, 267, 281–82

partisanship, 76, 123, 274

Pascal, Blaise, 222, 281n13

perception/experience, theories of, 40–41

perspective-taking, 207–12, 219–20, 243–44, 264–72. *See also* criticism

Peters, Tom, 143

Pierson, Arthur T., 31

Pigliucci, Massimo, 37

Plato, 9, 22, 202; *Euthyphro*, 34–35

Plekhanov, Georgi, 106–7

polarization. *See* divisiveness and polarization

politics: apocalypticism in, 280; Christian fundamentalism in, 81–82; complicity in, 81–83; contemporary context of, 64–65, 273–74, 288; domination of opponents as goal in, 273; fundamentalism in, 5–6, 16, 19–20, 77, 120–22, 274, 277; hatred in, 76–77, 80–81, 83, 109, 273–74, 287–88; literature seen through lens of, 253–56; reasoning appropriate for the domain of, 74; scientific claims made in, 86, 88, 90; trade-offs in, 281; vicious cycles of failure in, 5, 7, 82, 85–86. *See also* human affairs; partisanship

Pope, Alexander, *Essay on Criticism*, 200, 201

Popov, Vladimir, 173

Popper, Karl, 32, 278

positive fundamentalism, xxiv, 9–10, 64

postcolonialism, 265

Postman, Neil, 143–45, 176

posttruth, 141–42

potentiality, in literature, 232–35

poverty. *See* income inequality

practical reasoning: characteristics of, 59–60, 63, 65, 281–82; economics as domain for, 131, 175, 179–80; ethics as domain for, 58–70, 74, 281–82; novels as manifestation of, 65–71;

politics as domain for, 63, 74; theoretical vs., 58–70. *See also* casuistry; morality; wisdom

prayer, 188, 230–31, 237

"preemptive epistemology," 120

prejudice, 44, 46, 100, 112, 135, 186–88, 240

present: classic texts used for interpreting events in, 196, 198–99; hatred for, 125; interpretation of literature from the standpoint of, 235–36; narrativeness linked to salience of, 260–61; as only significant viewpoint, 2–3, 199–200, 206, 235–36

prices, 167–77

pride, 112, 116–17, 240

Prigogine, Ilya, 262

progressivism, 27, 92

propositions: falsifiability of scientific, 32, 90–92; geometric, 59; inappropriate uses of, 56, 226, 228, 244–45

protectionism, 160–61

Protestantism, 14, 43, 48, 193

Proust, Marcel, 2n

Proverbs, book of, 50, 213

psalms, 214

pseudoscience: and criminalization of "denialism," 95–96; examples of, 27–30, 88; and extending claims beyond proper domain, 92; market fundamentalism as, 130; and politics, 92–93; science vs., 30, 37, 90–100, 258; Social Darwinism and Marxism as, 28, 92–94; and Soviet Marxism, 93; and spectrum of certainty, 91–92; and temptation to claim certainty, 90; and understanding science as block of equally well established claims, 90–95

Ptolemaic world view, 8

public goods, 129, 129n
Puritanism, 89
Pushkin, Aleksandr, 195, 198
Pythagorean theorem, 60, 63, 86

Qin Shi Huang, 198
quantum theory, 93

radical skepticism: possibility of
    knowledge questioned by, 9, 39,
    44–45; practice as refutation of,
    40–41
rationalism, 57–60, 281–82
reader reception theory, 235
reading, wisdom gained through
    experience of, 73, 246, 265,
    267–68
realism: epistemological, 42; literary,
    10, 65–73, 111–16, 240, 261, 266
reality, experience of, 39–44
reason. See knowledge/epistemology;
    practical reasoning; rationalism;
    theoretical reasoning
Reid, Thomas, 40–41
relativism: facts from perspective of,
    37; fundamentalism compared to,
    8–9, 36–38; standards challenged
    by, 179, 181–82, 187–88, 236–37
religion: apocalyptic scenarios based
    on, 2–3; dialogic approach to,
    236; fundamentalism in, 8–9,
    13–14, 16, 206, 274, 279; Hume's
    critique of miracles and, 226–28;
    left-leaning fundamentalism in, 279;
    and meaning, 228–31, 236; moral
    tensions in, 189–94, 197, 202–12;
    science in relation to, 25–27, 215–26;
    standards in, 186–89; use and func-
    tion of language in, 226–28, 231,
    237–38

Republicans: attitudes of, 75–76, 140;
    and climate change, 153; Democrats'
    views of, 75–76
resonance, chemical theory of, 93
"retarding friction" (Eliot), 68
revelation, 50–51
Revelation, book of, 37, 279
revolutionism, 35, 79–80, 104
"rhetoric of etcetera," 250–51
Richardson, Samuel, 263
rights, 64, 236n
Riley, William B., 27
Roberts, Paul Craig, and Karen
    LaFolette, Meltdown, 168–74,
    168n50
Robespierre, 80
Russian Formalism, 247
Russian literature, 195, 197–98, 232
Russian Orthodox Church, 232
Russian Revolution, 82
Rykov, Aleksei, 106
Ryzhkov, Nikolay, 171

"sanctity of human life," 202
Sandburg, Carl, 235
Sanders, Bernie, 128, 140, 154–55
satire, 116–21, 128
Scalia, Antonin, 48n
scarce resources, 137–39, 145, 151, 156
Schapiro, Morton. See Morson, Gary
    Saul, and Morton Schapiro, Cents
    and Sensibility
Schiller, Robert, 257
Schneiderman, Eric, 95
Schweitzer, Albert, 203
science: and age of the earth, 221,
    225–26; certainty in relation to,
    90–92; COVID-19 pandemic and,
    96–100; development/progress in,
    90–92; economics modeled on,

258; extension of, into other domains, 92–96, 224–25; falsification as criterion in, 32, 90–91, 278; foundational aspects of, 91; fundamentalist claims to, 23, 26–28, 30–32; and meaning, 216, 221–26, 228; misconceptions of, 90–92, 95–96; morality in relation to, 29, 215, 221–25; political claims to status of, 86, 88, 90; progress of, versus fundamental texts of, 51; reasoning process in, 91, 99; religion in relation to, 25–27, 215–26; secular fundamentalist texts claimed as, 50–51; social science modeled on, 23–25, 86–88, 92–93, 257–58; Soviet rejections of, 49, 93–94; teaching of, 91; as type of fundamentalism, 25–26; unity of, 25; viewed superstitiously, 91–92. *See also* pseudoscience

science education, 91

"science is real," 92

Scopes Trial, 15

scripture. *See* Bible

secularization, 5

the self, 250–52, 265–72. *See also* literature

self-criticism, 109

self-deception, 113, 240

self-examination, xxvii, 204, 264

"self-fulfilling catastrophe". *See* politics: vicious cycles of failure in

"semantic treasures" (Bakhtin), 233

"semantic values" (Bakhtin), 193

Shahnameh, 264

Shakespeare, William, 22, 57, 195, 221, 233–34, 281

Shmelev, Nikolai, 173

silos, epistemological/experiential, 121–22, 128n93

Sim, Stuart, *Fundamentalist World*, 18–20

Sinyavsky, 49n91

Sivan, Emmanuel. See *Strong Religion*

"60-30-10" rule, 49

skepticism: Christian rejection of, 54; Erasmus's praise of, 53–54; experience as basis for, 88; "foxes" as example of, 22, 44; negative fundamentalism contrasted with, 36; relativism contrasted with, 37n62. *See also* doubt; radical skepticism

"skepticism of the instrument" (Wells), 45

Skinner, B. F., 24

"the slide," 82, 85–86, 96

Smith, Adam, 132–34, 177–80, 243–44, 265, 276; *The Theory of Moral Sentiments*, 178–79, 266; *The Wealth of Nations*, 132, 177–79

Smith, Barbara Herrnstein, *Contingencies of Value*, 249–51, 253

social Darwinism, 27–28, 88, 92–93

"social-Darwinization," 93

Social Democrats, 33, 104–5

Social Fascists, 33

socialism, 135–36, 259, 279

Socialist Workers' Party, 140

"social physics" (Comte), 24, 86

social science: fundamentalist strains in, 89; science as model for, 23–25, 86–88, 92–93, 257–58

Socrates, 118

sola scriptura (scripture alone), 14

Solzhenitsyn, Aleksandr, 120–21, 121n

Song of Songs, 214

Sophocles, *Antigone*, 209–10, 242

Soros, George, *The Crisis of Global Capitalism*, 130–32, 140

soul, 211

Soviet Union: absolute conformity required by, 49, 77, 79, 89, 104, 108, 195; consequences of central planning in, 135, 167–74; and dialectical materialism, 29, 32, 42; fundamental texts of, 48–49; middle ground as target of attack in, xxv, 36; moral revaluation in, 202–3; rejections of science in, 49, 93–94; reversal of fortunes in, 78–79. *See also* Lenin, V. I.; Marxism-Leninism

spectrum of certainty, 91–92

Spinoza, Baruch, 43, 46, 57

Squad, the (four female U.S. Representatives), 127

Stalin, Joseph, 3, 5, 11, 48–49, 77, 79–80, 84, 86, 121, 128, 203, 207

Stalin Constitution, 195

standards: changes in, 184–86, 236–38; clock parable about, 181–82, 200, 236; linguistic, 182–86; Marxist-Leninist (authoritarian), 32, 34; prejudicial use of, 186–88; religion as source of, 186–89; subjectivity/relativity as enemy of, 179, 181–82, 187–88, 236–37; truth as, 43

statistics, 143–45

Steinbeck, John, 235

Sterne, Laurence, *Tristram Shandy*, 118–20, 241

Stewart, Lyman and Milton, 13

Stiglitz, Joseph, 133, 144

stories: analytical and rhetorical role of, 145, 176–77, 244, 257–63; challenging nature of biblical, 189–94; role of, in economic thought, 145, 176–78, 257; role of the present in, 260–61

The Story of the Stone, 264

"strangeness of our condition" (Montaigne), 58

stream of consciousness, 267

Strong Religion (Almond, Appleby, and Sivan), 16, 21, 50

structuralism, 9

student loan debt, 162–64

Sudan, 16

superstition, 46

supplemental nutrition assistance program (SNAP), 159

Swift, Jonathan, 128

sympathy, 39, 266n52. *See also* compassion; empathy

The Tale of Genji, 264

Talmud, 17, 48

Tamar, 189

taxes, 159–60, 165

Thales of Miletus, 25

theoretical reasoning: characteristics of, 59, 62–63; critique of, 117–20; ethics not a fitting domain for, 58–60, 62–64, 69, 281–82; practical vs., 58–70; rationalism's valorization of, 60

tolerance/intolerance, 56, 85, 99, 123

Tolstoy, Leo, 10, 102, 117, 198, 283n15; *Anna Karenina*, 62, 66–67, 69–70, 102–3, 157, 159, 222–25, 230–31, 240, 242–43, 268–72; *War and Peace*, 38–39, 69, 240, 245, 256

Torah, 17, 48, 50, 50n94, 211

totalitarianism, 4, 114–15, 122, 241

Toulmin, Stephen, 57–64, 224, 281

trade-offs, 136–37, 137n, 139–40, 145–49, 160, 281

trade policy, 160–61
tradition, as source of meaning, 46, 48, 124, 187, 192–93, 200–201, 210–13, 232, 237
translation, 52, 195–97, 201, 220–21, 237
Trisagon, 2–3
Trollope, Anthony: *He Knew He Was Right*, xxiv; *Phineas Finn*, 261; *The Way We Live Now*, xxiv
Trotsky, Leon, 6, 106, 202, 278
Trump, Donald, 76, 80–81, 127, 128, 137n, 141, 153
truth: Christian fundamentalist view of, 39, 43–44, 46; criticism as means of seeking, 100–103; dialogue as means to, 56; failures and hindrances in recognizing, 33–34, 45–47; in novels, 72; perspicuity of, 39–47. *See also* certainty; knowledge/ epistemology
Tugwell, Rexford, 167–68
Turgenev, Ivan, 35, 113, 262; *Fathers and Children*, 114, 241, 262
Turkey, 16
twins, 219
"tyranny of principles" (Toulmin), 59

uncertainty. *See* complexity and uncertainty
University of Chicago Divinity School, 14
U.S. Constitution, 47–48n90, 194–95, 197, 236n
us vs. them mentality, xxiv, 77, 127–28. *See also* all-or-nothing mentality; evil
utilitarianism, 119, 187, 241

utopias, 24, 27, 110–11, 113, 120, 240–41, 274, 279

Valentinov, Nikolay, 104, 106–7
Verginaud, Pierre, 80
violence: in fundamentalists' response to others, 19, 104–5; not a necessary aspect of fundamentalism, 21–22; as outcome of fundamentalist extremism, 114–15
Virgil, *The Aeneid*, 263–64

Wall Street Journal, xxiii
Washington consensus, 133
WEIRD (Western, Educated, Industrialized, Rich, and Democratic) values, 204
Wells, H. G., 45
Wetter, Gustav, 42
Whitehouse, Sheldon, 95–96
"Who Whom?" (Lenin), 256
Wilson, Edward O., 24–26, 31
wisdom, 50, 69, 73, 113, 213, 236
Wittgenstein, Ludwig, 17–18, 20, 223–25, 228–30, 245; *Tractatus Logico-Philosophicus*, 224
Wolfe, Thomas, 235
world literature, 263–65
World War I, 14–15

Yew, Lee Kuan, 131, 205
Yezhov, Nikolai, 207

Zakaria, Fareed, 155
Zero Population Growth, 94
zero-sum games, xxiv, 105, 108
Zijderveld, Anton, 21n26, 36
Zuckerberg, Mark, xxiii

A NOTE ON THE TYPE

This book has been composed in Arno, an Old-style serif typeface in the classic Venetian tradition, designed by Robert Slimbach at Adobe.

CPSIA information can be obtained
at www.ICGtesting.com
Printed in the USA
JSHW042039111222
34693JS00001B/1